ROGER VERGÉ'S CUISINE
OF THE
SOUTH *of*
FRANCE

ROGER VERGÉ'S CUISINE OF THE SOUTH *of* FRANCE

BY ROGER VERGÉ

Translated by Roberta Wolfe Smoler

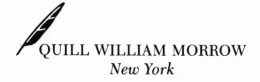

QUILL WILLIAM MORROW
New York

Color photography by Didier Blanchat

Copyright © 1978 by Editions Robert Laffont, S. A.

English translation copyright © 1980 by William Morrow and Company, Inc.

Originally published in French under the title *Ma Cuisine du Soleil,*
copyright © 1978 by Editions Robert Laffont, S.A.

Library of Congress Cataloging-in-Publication Data

Vergé, Roger, 1930–
Roger Vergé's Cuisine of the South of France.

Translation of: Ma cuisine du soleil.
Reprint. Originally published: New York :
Morrow, c1980.
Includes index.
1. Cookery, French.   I. Title.   II. Title:
Cuisine of the South of France.
TX719.V4813   1985   641.5944   85-19164
ISBN 0-688-06152-4 (pbk.)

Printed in the United States of America

First Quill Edition

1 2 3 4 5 6 7 8 9 10

BOOK DESIGN BY SALLIE BALDWIN, ANTLER & BALDWIN, INC.

To my Tante Célestine
to whom I owe my love of good food

Contents

Introduction
9

A Note to the Reader
11

Color Pictures
Following page 160

Les soupes
SOUPS
13

Les salades vertes
GREEN SALADS
30

Les petites entrées
FIRST COURSES
38

Les oeufs
EGGS
61

Les sauces
SAUCES
72

Les crustacés & les coquillages
SHELLFISH
86

Les poissons
FISH
105

Les viandes
MEATS
135

Les volailles & le gibier
POULTRY & GAME BIRDS
161

Les légumes
VEGETABLES
186

Les fromages
CHEESES
232

Les desserts
DESSERTS
239

Index
279

Introduction

For me, the happiness of good cooking is closely linked to childhood memories. I was five years old. Each Sunday and on holidays the whole family and a few friends gathered in the kitchen, which served also as dining room and living room. The soul of this kitchen was a massive dark-green enameled-iron stove with gleaming brass fixtures. The fairy godmother of the kitchen was my aunt Célestine. As long as I could remember, she had always had a little wooden bench for me to climb up on so that I could watch her cook.

How beautiful childhood recollections are! With the passage of time, they take on a radiant unreality. The smallest vignettes become vast canvases, a hobby horse is a prancing charger, the first little girl at school to capture your heart seems to have had the features of a madonna. But when it comes to the gastronomic, memories return to me with extraordinary exactness.

I can remember as if it were today the carrots so small and so tender that they were almost transparent; the peas with their white flowers still attached to the pods; the delicate leaf lettuce gathered with the dew still on it; the pearl-white onions no bigger than small radishes; succulent potatoes of a variety called *cornes de mouton*, from which the fine skins could be removed simply by rubbing them in the palms of your hands.

During the day my father was a blacksmith. But in the evening, he was an inspired kitchen gardener. The tender bouquets of vegetables he brought to my mother were so delicately flavored that they merely needed to be heated through in the big black iron casserole along with a few lean and rosy pieces of country salt pork.

That is the cuisine of happiness—the combinations of fresh produce, the search for simple harmonies, the heightened savor of a dish when it is accompanied by another that complements it.

The sweetness of onion, the freshness of tomato, the trace of bitterness in spinach, the green acidity of sorrel, the velvet of potatoes, the mellowness of leeks, the perfume of celery, celeriac, turnip, the boldness of garlic, the pepper of radishes, and so many more—and surprising—savory qualities, such as the natural ability of certain fruits to temper the bitterness of a vegetable or the heavy flavor of game . . . all these infinitely subtle nuances are part of the beauty of the art of cooking.

A joyful cuisine is the opposite of reaching for effect, of the heavy and pretentious. It is gay, healthful, and natural, gathering together the gifts of the soil like an armful of wild flowers.

To cook well, one need only be a *gourmand,* a hungry appreciator of flavors. Rather, I should probably say, one *must* be a *gourmand* to be a good cook. A recipe is like written music. One can follow it very exactly and yet achieve an unintelligent, mechanical, or mediocre result. Cooking is first of all a matter of taste, flair, and sensibility. From one day to the next, one does not make the same dish in precisely the same way. I sometimes find myself adding a pinch of sugar to a sauce that I have made a hundred times without sugar, because—heaven knows why—sugar suddenly seems to me absolutely indispensable.

The recipe is only music on the page; it is you who will make it sing. To cook is to create, to marry ingredients as poets marry words, to play chords with flavors, to invent new and subtle harmonies.

A recipe is not made to be followed to the letter. It is a canvas that you can embroider. Improvise. Improvise. Add a zest of this, a drop of that, a pinch of something else. Let yourself be guided by your palate, your nose, your eyes, and your heart.

In a word, be *gourmand,* and you will know how to cook.

ROGER VERGÉ

A Note to the Reader

I did not write this book for professionals. Nor did I write it for lovers of the sensational. My recipes are not revolutionary and I have invented nothing. In cooking, one interprets, accommodates, adapts, but one does not invent.

I have gone back to the fine old recipes of France, and elsewhere, and have tried to give them my personal touch, my taste for the sun, for the natural, a certain joy. Especially I have tried to make the recipes accessible to all who love good cooking, even if they do not know too well how to go about it.

It is particularly irritating for nonprofessionals to be forced—right in the midst of cooking—to leaf back through a book with sticky or floury fingers to find references to page such-and-such for definitions, or a sauce, or a special procedure. I have therefore written complete recipes as often as possible, simply and in detail, frequently repeating the same information in different places. Some recipes may therefore seem long, but I hope I have thereby made them clearer. I would advise you, however, to read each recipe all the way through before you start to make the dish.

Courage, my chefs! To your stoves!

✤ NOTE: Throughout this book, annotations and comments made by editor and translator are set in *italic type*.

Les soupes
SOUPS

Crème froide de coeurs d'artichauts
COLD ARTICHOKE SOUP

To serve 4:

    5 large artichokes, or 4 "globe" artichokes
    Salt
    3 cups chicken stock
    1 bunch flat-leafed parsley, young and freshly cut
    1 scant cup heavy cream
    Freshly ground white pepper

PREPARATION OF THE ARTICHOKES:

Bring 5 quarts of salted water to a boil. When the water is boiling vigorously, drop in the artichokes and cook, uncovered, for 40 minutes over high heat. At this time, pull off a leaf. If it separates from the artichoke without resistance, they are done. Take them from the heat and drain, upside down. This operation can be done in advance.

    When the artichokes are cool enough to handle, strip off the leaves and remove the fibrous choke. Save only the hearts. (*If you wish, you can also scrape the flesh from the leaves. Use a silver teaspoon. Ed.*)

13

PREPARATION OF THE SOUP:

Bring the chicken stock to a boil. Cut the artichoke hearts into cubes and add them to the stock. Simmer together about 10 minutes, then cool slightly.

Pour the artichoke hearts and broth into the container of a food processor (*see Note*) or blender, and purée them until creamy and well-blended. You can also use a food mill, proceeding in the same manner; however, you will need to refine the mixture further by pressing it through a fine sieve, or *chinois*, with the back of a cooking spoon. Chill the artichoke purée in the refrigerator.

NOTE: *A word of caution, if you are using a food processor for this operation. Because of the large quantity of liquid, I suggest that you purée the artichoke pulp first, adding only part of the broth. Then pour the purée into a bowl, and using a wire whisk, beat in the remaining liquid a little at a time. Ed.*

FINISHING THE SOUP:

Strip off the parsley leaves, discarding the stems. Chop the leaves very fine. (*There should be about ½ cup. If you wish, you can also add a tablespoon of fresh chopped chives. Ed.*)

Pour the cream into a chilled mixing bowl, and beat with a wire whisk (*or electric mixer*) until thick and voluminous—but not stiff! If you overbeat the cream, you will have butter.

Stir the cold artichoke purée and the chopped parsley into the whipped cream, adding a pinch of salt and freshly ground pepper to taste. Pour the soup into a chilled tureen and refrigerate until ½ hour before serving.

This is a small first course that is easy to make and does not take up time at the last minute. You can also serve it in individual cups.

Soupe de pois frais au curry

FRESH PEA SOUP WITH CURRY

To serve 4:

1 small head Boston or butter lettuce
1 bunch parsley (preferably flat-leafed; it has more flavor)
4 tablespoons butter, in all
1 medium-size sweet white onion (*about 5 ounces*), thinly sliced
1 level tablespoon curry powder
1½ quarts hot chicken stock
Coarse salt
10 ounces (*about 3 cups*) freshly shelled peas (or you can substitute one 10-ounce package frozen peas)
4 slices white bread, cut into small dice
5 tablespoons *crème fraîche* (*or substitute ½ cup heavy cream; Ed.*)

PREPARATION:

1. The lettuce: Wash the lettuce carefully, drain, and gently pat dry in a towel. Then cut the lettuce into coarse shreds (*chiffonade*) and set aside.

2. The parsley: Wash the parsley, drain, and dry it. Then strip off all stems and set the leaves aside.

COOKING:

Over low heat, melt 2 tablespoons of the butter in a 4- or 5-quart casserole. Add the sliced onion and cook, covered, 8 to 10 minutes. Stir frequently and do not allow the onion to brown.

When the onion is soft, add the lettuce, return the cover to the casserole, and cook 5 minutes longer or until the lettuce is completely wilted. Stir occasionally. Add the curry powder and cook, uncovered, over very low heat, 3 or 4 minutes. Stir frequently with a wooden spoon until the curry powder and lettuce have dissolved into a paste.

Pour the hot chicken stock over it and add salt to taste. Bring the broth to a boil and keep it boiling for 5 minutes. Then add the parsley leaves and peas. Above all, so that the peas will retain their bright green color, do not cover the casserole. Cook the soup at a gentle boil for 10 to 15 minutes or until the peas are tender.

THE CROUTONS:

While the soup is cooking, melt the remaining 2 tablespoons of butter in a small skillet and sauté the diced bread until crisp and golden. (*Add more butter if needed. Ed.*) Keep the croutons warm until the soup is ready to serve.

FINISHING THE SOUP:

Cool the soup slightly, then reduce it to a purée. Use either a food processor (*see Note*) or blender, or press it through a food mill, using the fine grate. If you use a food mill, complete the purée by straining it again through a fine sieve, or *chinois*. Press down hard with the back of a large cooking spoon to extract the more supple portions of the purée.

NOTE: *Because of the large quantity of liquid, I found using a food mill preferable to a food processor. Ed.*

Return the soup to a simmer and add *crème fraîche*. Bring just to a simmer, taste for seasoning, and serve the soup with the croutons passed separately.

NOTE: *If you have used a highly spiced curry powder, it would not be amiss to add a dollop of cold* crème fraîche, *sour cream, or whipped cream to each individual serving of soup. Ed.*

Soupe au pistou
PROVENÇAL VEGETABLE SOUP

To serve 6:

⅔ pound shelled fresh white beans, or ½ pound dried white beans
(*Great Northern, marrow, or other dried white beans; Ed.*)
Bouquet garni (1 large sprig thyme, 1 bay leaf, and 4 large sprigs
parsley, tied together)
Coarse salt
2 medium-size carrots, about 2 ounces each
2 young turnips, about 3 ounces each
2 young zucchini, about 4 ounces each
1 medium-size white onion, about 7 ounces
1 large handful string beans, about 5 ounces (preferably flat
green beans, or Romano beans, about 8 inches long and ½
inch wide)
1 leek, white part only
2 stalks celery, taken from the heart of the plant
8 tablespoons olive oil, in all
3 quarts chicken stock
1 medium-size potato, about 6 ounces
4 ripe tomatoes, about 6 ounces each
6 cloves garlic
30 fresh basil leaves
Freshly ground pepper, preferably white

PREPARATION (the evening before):

If you do not have fresh white beans, soak dried beans overnight in
3 quarts cold water.

PREPARATION (the next day):

1. The beans: If you are using dried beans, drain them and put
them into a pan with 2 quarts fresh cold water. Add the *bouquet
garni* and bring to a gentle simmer. After the beans have cooked 5
minutes, skim the foam from the surface and add salt. The cooking
should take about 1 hour, but test the beans for doneness from time
to time.

17

If you have fresh white beans, proceed in the same manner; however, the cooking time should be no longer than 30 minutes. Check them frequently.

When the beans have finished cooking, keep them hot.

2. The vegetables: An hour before you intend to cook the vegetables, peel and wash them, but do not let them soak for very long.

Cut the carrots, turnips, zucchini, onion, and string beans into ½-inch dice.

Cut the leek and celery into very thin slices.

COOKING:

Place all the vegetables in a large 7- to 8-quart casserole with 4 tablespoons of the olive oil and 4 tablespoons cold water. Cook the vegetables 10 to 15 minutes, covered, over medium heat. Stir frequently with a wooden spoon.

While the vegetables cook, they will release their juices and then absorb them again, lending their flavor to the soup without losing their own.

After 15 minutes, there should not be any water remaining in the casserole. However, take care not to let the vegetables scorch!

Add the chicken stock to the vegetables and bring to a vigorous boil. Let boil 5 minutes, then add salt.

Peel the potato and cut it into pieces the same size as the other vegetables. Drop the potato into the boiling chicken stock and cook 20 minutes. Watch the broth at all times to be sure that it does not reduce too much. If this should happen, add some of the cooking liquid from the white beans.

PREPARATION OF THE PISTOU SAUCE:

While the soup is cooking, drop the tomatoes into boiling water, count to 10, and plunge them into cold water. (This will make them easy to peel.) Peel the tomatoes, removing the core, then cut them in half crosswise and squeeze out the seeds and water. Chop the tomatoes into small manageable pieces.

Peel the garlic and strip the stems from the basil leaves.

THREE METHODS FOR FINISHING THE SAUCE:

1. To use a mortar and pestle: Drop the cloves of garlic and the basil leaves into the mortar, and with the pestle, crush them completely into a paste.

Add the chopped tomato and continue to crush the mixture with the pestle until you obtain a smooth purée. Slowly add the remaining 4 tablespoons of olive oil, and turning the pestle in the mortar, mix carefully. Then give the purée several good turns of the pepper mill.

2. To use a food processor or blender: Put the garlic and basil into the container of the machine with 2 tablespoons of olive oil. Grind them briefly, then add the tomatoes. Purée the tomatoes with the garlic and basil, while slowly adding the remaining 2 tablespoons of olive oil. Season with several good turns of the pepper mill.

3. To use a food mill: Press the garlic, basil, and chopped tomatoes, in that order, through the fine grate of a food mill into a bowl. Stir in the olive oil, added in a slow steady stream as for mayonnaise. Season with several good turns of the pepper mill.

TO FINISH THE SOUP:

You now have ready:

1. The hot cooked white beans
2. The vegetable soup
3. The purée of garlic, basil, tomatoes, and oil (*pistou*)

Remove the *bouquet garni* from the beans and mix them, with their broth, into the casserole of vegetable soup. Bring the soup to a simmer and taste for salt.

Over very low heat, use a wooden spoon to incorporate the *pistou* sauce into the soup. Be careful not to bring the soup to a boil again.

Carry the soup to the table. The aroma that will precede you will make it unnecessary to name the dish.

This soup can be made in advance but, above all, do not stir in the *pistou* (the purée of garlic, basil, tomatoes, and oil) until the last moment. The soup can be served equally well hot, lukewarm, or cold—but never ice-cold.

In this preparation, the vegetables are not at all indispensable and can be replaced by others. For example, peas could replace the string beans, some other squash could replace the zucchini; or perhaps omit the string beans and potatoes and make use of small pasta shells (*coquillettes*).

I have also greatly appreciated this soup without the vegetables. It was prepared by my friend Toinette, who lives in the little village of Var. Needing to improvise, she had simply sautéed a chopped onion in olive oil, added 2 quarts of salted water, brought it to a boil, and dropped in ½ pound of pasta shells. To finish it, she stirred in a superb *pistou*—composed of 4 large ripe tomatoes, a bunch of basil, 2 cloves of garlic, 5 tablespoons of olive oil, and a good turn of the pepper mill. What could be easier! But it is this simplicity that is the best way to entertain true friends—those whom one likes and who like you. Believe me, the *provençaux* know how to be the best friends in the world—but one must also know how to conquer the hearts of people who lack the *provençal* temperament.

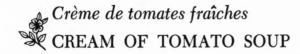

Crème de tomates fraîches
CREAM OF TOMATO SOUP

To serve 4:

    2 medium-size sweet onions (preferably new white onions), about
        ⅔ pound
    2 tablespoons butter
    2 pounds ripe tomatoes
    1 clove garlic, finely chopped
    1 sprig fresh thyme (*or substitute ¼ teaspoon dried thyme; Ed.*)
    A pinch of sugar (*optional*)
    2 cups hot chicken stock
    ⅔ cup heavy cream
    2 egg yolks
    Coarse salt
    Freshly ground white pepper

PREPARATION:

Peel the onions and cut them into thin slices. Then place them in a casserole with the butter and 4 tablespoons of water. Over low heat, cook the onion, covered, 10 to 15 minutes or until soft. Stir occasionally and take care not to allow the onion to brown.

Meanwhile, wipe the tomatoes and cut out their cores. Depending on size, cut each tomato into 4 or 6 pieces.

When the onion has softened, add the tomatoes to the casserole with the finely chopped garlic, thyme, and a pinch of sugar.

Raise the heat under the casserole, and stirring continuously with a wooden spoon, cook the tomatoes about 10 minutes. Then add the hot chicken stock to the tomato sauce and boil the soup 2 or 3 minutes.

Extract the sprig of thyme and pass the rest of the soup through a food mill held over a clean casserole, or purée it in a food processor or blender. Then return the soup to a simmer.

FINISHING THE SOUP:

In a large bowl, combine the heavy cream with the egg yolks. Mix well with a wire whisk until thoroughly combined. Then pour the hot tomato purée into the cream, stirring vigorously. Return the soup to the casserole and warm it over low heat while continuing to stir. Just before the soup shows the first sign of a simmer, remove it from the heat, but continue to stir for 2 more minutes. Add salt and freshly ground pepper and taste for seasoning.

Pour the cream of tomato soup through a fine sieve into a hot tureen and serve at once.

You can bring a touch of fantasy to the presentation of this soup by serving it in large cups, or bowls, with a *garniture* of lightly salted whipped cream. At the last moment, place a dollop of cream in the center of each serving, and sprinkle it with a pinch of freshly chopped chervil (*or substitute fresh chives or basil; Ed.*).

Crème au lait d'amandes
ALMOND SOUP

To serve 4:
1 large leek (white part only), thinly sliced
1 tablespoon butter
1 quart strong hot chicken stock
1 tablespoon short-grain rice, rinsed and drained
1 cup finely ground blanched almonds
2 egg yolks
1¼ cups heavy cream
Salt
Toasted sliced almonds (optional); Ed.

PREPARATION:

Place the leek in a 2-quart casserole with the butter and 1 tablespoon of water, and cook 5 minutes over low heat, covered. Stir occasionally.

Pour the hot chicken stock over it, bring to a boil, and then add the rice and ground almonds. Cover the casserole, reduce heat to low, and cook 30 minutes, keeping the broth at almost, but not quite, a simmer.

TO FINISH THE SOUP:

Beat the egg yolks, and using a wire whisk, mix them well with the heavy cream. Set aside.

After the soup has cooked 30 minutes, purée it in a blender or food processor, or pass it through a food mill using the fine grate.

Pour the soup into a clean 2-quart casserole and stir in the cream and egg yolk *liaison*, mixing well with a wire whisk. Place the casserole over low heat, and stirring continuously, bring the soup almost to a simmer. Add salt to taste and strain the soup through a fine sieve.

Serve the soup in hot cups.

NOTE: *If you wish, you can add a garniture of toasted sliced almonds. In warm weather, this soup is quite satisfying served cold. In this instance, you could garnish it with freshly chopped chives or chervil. Ed.*

Crème antillaise
SPINACH AND COCONUT SOUP

To serve 4:

- 14 ounces fresh spinach leaves
- 2 tablespoons butter
- 2 medium-size onions (preferably sweet white onions), thinly sliced
- 1½ quarts hot beef stock
- ⅓ cup short-grain rice, rinsed
- 3 tablespoons freshly grated coconut
- Freshly grated nutmeg
- Coarse salt
- 6 tablespoons *crème fraîche* (*or substitute ⅔ cup heavy cream; Ed.*)
- Freshly ground white pepper

PREPARATION:

Strip off the stems of the spinach and wash the leaves in several changes of water. Then drain the leaves well in a colander.

Over medium heat, melt the butter in a 4-quart casserole. Add the sliced onions and sauté about 15 minutes or until they are soft and golden. Stir frequently with a wooden spoon, and above all, do not let the onions brown.

Pour the hot beef stock over the onions and bring to a boil. Toss in the rice, followed by the grated coconut. Reduce heat to medium and simmer the soup, uncovered, for 20 minutes or until the rice is almost tender. Then add the spinach, return the soup to a boil, and cook 5 minutes longer. Add a generous grating of nutmeg, and depending on the saltiness of your stock, season to taste.

FINISHING THE SOUP:

Purée the soup in a blender or food processor (*see Note*), or pass it through a food mill using the fine grate. Then, using the back of a large cooking spoon, complete the purée by pressing it through a fine sieve, or *chinois.*

NOTE: *Because of the large quantity of liquid, I found using a food mill preferable to a food processor. Ed.*

Stir the *crème fraîche* into the soup and bring it just to a simmer. Add 5 or 6 good turns of the pepper mill and taste for salt. Then pour the soup into a warmed tureen and serve very hot. This creamy soup will have a beautiful soft green color.

In the Antilles, they serve forth a very rustic soup called *la Calalou* or *Kalalou*, which is the name of a plant resembling spinach. This soup is made of beef broth, thickened with rice, in which they cook the calalou leaves. One finishes with the juice of a freshly grated coconut that has been squeezed in order to extract the milk. This soup, copiously seasoned with pepper, is called "pepper pot" in Jamaica. *La crème antillaise* is an adaptation of this recipe, but made with ingredients that one can find easily in any supermarket.

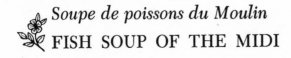

Soupe de poissons du Moulin
FISH SOUP OF THE MIDI

It is indispensable that the fish for this soup have just left the water and, for the most part, are still alive and wiggling. Besides which, the soup must be made the same morning—as soon as the fish have been caught. It can easily be reheated.

To serve 8:
> 5½ pounds freshly caught rockfish (*poissons de roche*) from the Mediterranean shores (*see Note*)
> ⅝ cup olive oil
> ¾ pound onions, thinly sliced
> 1 small unpeeled head of new garlic, cut in half crosswise
> 2 pounds red ripe tomatoes, cored and each cut into eighths
> 4 dried fennel stalks (*or 2 teaspoons fennel seeds; Ed.*)

2 large sprigs fresh thyme (*or substitute 1 teaspoon dried thyme; Ed.*)
1 bay leaf
Coarse salt
Freshly ground pepper, preferably white
½ teaspoon saffron threads

NOTE: Only if you live in the region of the Mediterranean can you prepare this recipe authentically. Here, in the homes of fishermen, you will find it often. Generally it is made from the very smallest rockfish, tiny crabs, species of crayfish, and so on. One or 2 pieces of eel would not be disdained and will give the soup an unctuous, slightly oily appearance.

Above all, do not clean, scale, or wash the fish after they have left the sea.

COOKING:

Pour the olive oil into a very large heavy casserole (*8 to 10 quarts, with a wide bottom*). Add the onions and cook over medium to high heat, stirring frequently with a wooden spoon. Allow the onions to brown slightly, then turn the heat to its maximum force and add the fish all at once.

Follow with the garlic, tomatoes, and herbs (fennel, thyme, bay leaf), while turning the fish with two wooden spoons. Press down on all the ingredients to squeeze out their juices. This should take about 10 minutes.

Then, maintaining a high heat, add 5 quarts of cold water. Bring the water to a boil and let boil vigorously for 20 to 30 minutes, without lowering the heat. At the last moment add salt, freshly ground pepper, and saffron, then remove from heat.

FINISHING THE SOUP:

Pass the soup through a food mill, a few cups at a time, into a clean casserole. Try to extract every bit of the essence of the fish, tomatoes, and garlic—but remove the branches of herbs as they appear.

Bring the soup to a boil and—only just before serving—pour it through a sieve into a heated soup tureen of substantial size. A conical sieve—a *chinois*—is very practical for this operation. Hold the sieve over the tureen with your left hand, and pour as much of this marvelous bouillon as possible through it, while rubbing the sieve back and forth with a cooking spoon.

If you are not able to serve the soup immediately, pour it into another receptacle to cool. Then, when you wish to serve it, just bring it briefly to a simmer, which will bring out all the fragrant aromas.

With this soup you should forget the *rouille* and cheeses. It should be eaten only with thin slices of *pain-baguette* rubbed with garlic. (Pain-baguette *is the long thin loaf of French bread. Ed.*)

When you serve this soup, it doesn't matter whether the sun is shining or not—because it is hotter than the sun of the Midi. . . .

I am going to give you yet another fish soup. This one is for the *Parisiens*; which is to say that in the Midi, everyone who lives north of Aix is considered to be a Parisian. There is nothing wrong with them—they are just different. So let them have their own soup.

Yes, you will find the good aromas of the Midi in their homes— but they won't be quite the same. But it is very good anyway, this soup that the *Parisiens* make. . . .

Soupe de poissons parisienne
FISH SOUP WITH CROUTONS

The success of this soup depends on the choice of fish and, most important, their freshness. Use small fish with bright eyes and rose-red gills. The scales should be translucent and the flesh firm.

To serve 8:
    Approximately 6 pounds assorted fish (*see Note*)
    ⅝ cup olive oil
    ¾ pound onions, thinly sliced
    1 small unpeeled head of new garlic, cut in half crosswise
    2 pounds red ripe tomatoes, cored and each cut into eighths

5 dried fennel stalks—yes, one more stalk than the original recipe
(*or substitute 2½ teaspoons fennel seeds; Ed.*)
2 large sprigs fresh thyme (*or substitute 1 teaspoon dried thyme;
Ed.*)
1 bay leaf
Coarse salt
Freshly ground pepper, preferably white
½ teaspoon saffron threads

NOTE: *In France one would choose rougets, grodins, vives, congre,
small lottes, black crabs, perhaps eel, and the indispensable merlan
(whiting).*

*From our own waters you can use: red mullet, small red snapper,
goatfish, sea robin, eel, blue-claw crabs, small sea bass, porgy, and
of course whiting. Whatever assortment of fish you choose, take only
the freshest possible.*

PREPARATION:

Scale the fish, clean and rinse them, and wipe dry. Be sure to leave
the heads on, but remove the gills. If you are using eel, or any large
fish, cut it into manageable pieces.

COOKING:

Pour the olive oil into a very large heavy casserole (*from 8 to 10
quarts, with a wide bottom*). Add the onions and cook over medium
to high heat, stirring frequently with a wooden spoon. Allow the
onions to brown slightly, then turn the heat to its maximum and add
the fish all at once.

Follow with the garlic, tomatoes, and herbs (fennel, thyme, bay
leaf), while turning the fish with two wooden spoons. Press down on
all the ingredients to squeeze out their juices. This should take about
10 minutes.

Then, maintaining a high heat, add 5 quarts of cold water. Bring
the water to a boil and let boil vigorously for 20 to 30 minutes, without lowering the heat. At the last moment add salt, freshly ground
pepper, and saffron, then remove from heat. Set aside ½ cup of
strained, grease-free broth for the *rouille.*

FINISHING THE SOUP:

Pass the soup through a food mill, a few cups at a time, into a clean casserole. Try to extract every bit of the essence of the fish, tomatoes, and garlic—but remove the branches of herbs as they appear.

Bring the soup to a boil and—only just before serving—pour it through a sieve into a heated soup tureen of substantial size. A conical sieve—a *chinois*—is practical. Hold the sieve over the tureen with your left hand and pour as much of the bouillon as possible through it, while rubbing the sieve back and forth with a cooking spoon.

If you do not serve the soup immediately, pour it into another receptacle to cool. Then, just before serving, bring it briefly to a simmer.

And yes, for this *soupe de Parisiens*, you should make a *rouille*. And, absolutely, do serve it over croutons rubbed with garlic! A recipe for *rouille* follows.

NOTE: *To make croutons, cut slices from a long thin loaf of French bread, preferably a* pain-baguette. *Place the slices on a baking sheet liberally greased with olive oil, and toast them in a 350°F oven, turning to toast both sides, until they are crisp and golden. Ed.*

La rouille

GARLIC AND SAFFRON MAYONNAISE

To serve 8:
    1 cup diced French bread
    7 tablespoons hot fish broth
    4 cloves garlic
    A pinch saffron threads
    1 egg yolk
    ½ cup olive oil
    Coarse salt
    Freshly ground white pepper, or cayenne pepper

PREPARATION:

Place the diced French bread in a small bowl with the fish broth. Soak the bread until it can be mashed into a paste.

Peel the garlic, and using a mortar and pestle, crush it into a paste. Then incorporate the saffron, egg yolk, and well-saturated bread, and work them with the pestle until thoroughly blended.

While turning the pestle with a circular motion, add the olive oil in a slow steady stream. When all the oil has been incorporated, the *rouille* will resemble a thick, mayonnaiselike emulsion. Add salt and pepper to taste.

NOTE: If you prefer to use a blender or food processor for this operation, rather than a mortar and pestle, follow the same procedure—but run your machine at its lowest speed.

If the *rouille* should become oily and tend to separate, add 2 tablespoons hot fish broth (or water, if necessary) and continue to stir.

Serve the *rouille* in either a sauceboat or a bowl, with toasted croutons (page 28) to soak in the soup.

Les salades vertes

GREEN SALADS

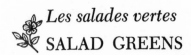

Les salades vertes
SALAD GREENS

The salad is a dish that finds its place in all meals and in all climates. Whatever greens you use or seasonings you choose, a salad always brings a touch of cheerfulness, a moment of refreshment and communion with nature.

In the *Physiology of Taste*, Brillat-Savarin declares: "The salad gladdens the heart." He could have added: "The palate, the eyes . . . the stomach." These are the salad greens of France. You have many of them in America:

Barbe de capucin (monk's whiskers)—from November to April
This salad is cultivated in sand, in dark caves, or under haystacks. Season with walnut oil.

Batavia—from May to November
This lettuce is very tender when it is young, becoming crunchy and delicately crinkled, with its tones traveling from light yellow to a dark green edged with reddish-brown. Season with olive oil.

Chicorée frisée (curly chicory)—from March to May
A very crisp green variety with a white heart.

Chicorée frisée (curly chicory)—from September to December
A white lettuce with delicately curly leaves. Season with walnut oil.

Cornette—from December to March
This lettuce resembles chicory in its slightly bitter taste. The leaves are crisp and very dark green, turning a reddish color when cold appears. Season with walnut oil.

Cresson (watercress)—from March to December
The character of this plant is derived from its peppery fragrance. Its only needs are that its roots be kept in water and that it be shaded from intense summer heat. Season with olive oil.

Endive—from October to April
This is a shade plant which is cultivated buried in sand and, more often, in caves. Most endives come from Belgium and are called "les Witloofs." Season with olive oil.

Laitue (lettuce)—from March to December
This is the most commonly found lettuce. It exists in numerous varieties, but the most well-known in our countryside is a head lettuce —which is not, in my opinion, the best. I find it insipid and lacking in texture. By contrast, the tender green leaf lettuce that does not form a head is full of delicacy. Season with olive oil, or just *crème fraîche* and lemon.

Mâche (lamb's lettuce or field salad)—end of November to April
It is also called *doucette* or *boursette*. It is cultivated, but can be found in the meadows. Its greenness becomes darker after the frost and its pungency fades, becoming more delicate. Season with olive oil.

Mesclun—all year
Mesclun is not a lettuce, but a whimsical mixture of several lettuces. Originally, it was composed of field lettuces: Rocket (arugula), dandelion, lamb's lettuce, purslane, wild chicory, and so on. I have even found it with black mustard (*senneson*)—the field plant with little yellow tufts that one usually saves to give to canaries.

31

Today, *mesclun* is more often composed of small cultivated lettuces, the mixture varying with the season.

One can find in it curly chicory, Batavia, *cornette*, lamb's lettuce, dandelion, escarole, *trévise*, sprigs of chervil, parsley, and even fennel. This salad is mostly eaten between Cannes and Menton and each village has its own version—prepared, always, with olive oil.

Pissenlit (dandelion)—end of November to March

Here is a salad that one must know well to pick it! The easiest way to identify it is to look for the pretty yellow flowers that sprout up in the open meadows. That is what I was doing when, as a small child, my mother sent me to look for lettuces for the evening. Surely, with my basket filled in the wink of an eye I could now go to play with my friends. On my return, however, the dressing-down was not for the salad, but for me!

My dandelions went for dinner in the rabbit hutch—because dandelion in flower must be shunned. One has to pick the leaves after the freeze, choosing the smallest. One can also take the ones with the flower still scarcely a bud (it makes me think of the winder on the pocket watches of our grandfathers).

In order to finish this disquisition on dandelions, I must specify one horrible thing: It is under dried cow dung that one finds the tenderest dandelions, and also under the excavation of molehills. Season with walnut oil.

Romaine—from June to September

Le chicou is its common name. This beautiful lettuce grows tall and compact. Its leaves are glossy, very crisp, and so fragile that my aunt Célestine refused to inflict on them the ordeal of washing or of drying in the salad basket. She detached the leaves, one by one, and wiped them delicately with a towel. An act of love. Season with olive oil.

Scarole (escarole)—from September to February

This is a hearty lettuce, strong, with a touch of bitterness. It is not afraid of frost—which reddens the edges of the leaves. Season with olive oil.

Trévise—from October to April

This is a superb lettuce, purplish-red in color and usually only used with other lettuces (lamb's lettuce, chicory). It is very bitter and crunchy. Cold temperatures are beneficial to it and give it a dark coloring.

Les vinaigrettes

VINAIGRETTE SAUCE FOR SALADS

The basis of these sauces is generally an oil: olive, walnut, peanut, sunflower, corn, grape-seed, soy, poppy-seed, cotton, sesame. . . .

Next come the vinegars: cider, wine, sherry, Malmsey, honey, and many fruits, such as pineapple, raspberry, cherry, and currant. One can (alas!) name as well the alcohol vinegars, neutral in taste but strong in acid. Generally, a vinegar's acidity can be compensated for by cutting it with lime juice or mustard.

Herbs also have an important place in salads. Some are: chervil, parsley, chives, tarragon, celery, garlic, onion, and hot peppers.

Finally, of course, come the salt and pepper.

All of these elements marry, more or less well, with each other, and accompany, more or less well, this or that lettuce. It is clearly a question of taste, but one can nevertheless bear in mind the fragile or robust character of a lettuce, in order best to complement its delicacy or its force.

La vinaigrette traditionnelle
TRADITIONAL VINAIGRETTE SAUCES

One does not drink wine with this kind of salad. The acidity of the *vinaigrette* sauce irreparably kills the taste of the wine.

NOTE: *Though the quantities of the ingredients given here are large enough for 2 or 3 persons, they can easily be doubled, or increased many times over, to serve a larger number of people.* (See Note) *Ed.*

To serve 2 or 3:
1. Simple *vinaigrette*:
   1 tablespoon vinegar
   4 tablespoons oil
   Salt
   Freshly ground pepper

If you wish, you can replace the vinegar with the same quantity of lemon juice.

2. Mustard *vinaigrette*:
   1 teaspoon extra-strong Dijon mustard (*moutarde forte de Dijon*)
   1 tablespoon vinegar
   5 tablespoons oil
   Salt
   Freshly ground pepper
3. Herb *vinaigrette*:

Compose either the simple *vinaigrette* or the mustard *vinaigrette*, and add to it: freshly chopped chervil, tarragon, chives, parsley, basil, shallots, onions, or garlic.

NOTE: If you make a salad every day, you can very easily prepare a large quantity of *vinaigrette* in advance. One quart of oil will roughly correspond to about 25 salads.

Prepare the *vinaigrette* in a bowl, then transfer it to a bottle—so that you will have only to reach for it when you are ready to season each salad.

However, remember that herbs must not be added to a salad until the last moment.

La vinaigrette à la crème d'ail

VINAIGRETTE SAUCE WITH
GARLIC AND CREAM

This sauce best accompanies assertive lettuces, such as romaine, curly chicory, and escarole.

To serve 2:

    1 clove garlic
    Coarse salt
    ½ teaspoon extra-strong Dijon mustard (*moutarde forte de Dijon*)
    1 teaspoon wine vinegar
    2 tablespoons *crème fraîche* (*or substitute heavy cream; Ed.*)
    1 tablespoon olive oil
    Freshly ground white pepper

PREPARATION:

Flatten the garlic with the side of a knife, then peel it. (*If there is any sign of a green sprout, be sure to remove it, or else it will impart an unpleasant hot burning taste to the sauce. Ed.*)

Place the garlic in a small bowl, add a pinch of coarse salt, and using a fork, grind the garlic to a paste. Add the remaining ingredients, one at a time, stirring with a wire whisk after each addition. Taste for seasoning.

Sauce au Roquefort
ROQUEFORT SAUCE FOR SALADS

I will give you two recipes for this sauce. One is for tender and delicate salad greens—leaf lettuces such as Bibb, butter, or Boston; lamb's lettuce (*mâche*); endive, celery, romaine.

The other is for strong assertive salad greens—curly yellow chicory, escarole, bitter dark green chicory (*cornette*).

When buying the Roquefort, ask your cheese merchant to give you the crumbs. There are always some whenever the cheese is cut. This should suit both of you, as these unsalable morsels usually come from the center of the cheese, which is the best part.

Sauce for delicate salads; to serve 4:

$1\frac{1}{2}$ ounces Roquefort cheese
1 tablespoon wine vinegar
5 tablespoons heavy cream
1 tablespoon fresh chopped chives
Salt (probably not necessary, since the Roquefort should be salty enough)
Freshly ground white pepper

PREPARATION:

Using a fork, crush the Roquefort on a plate. (*Better yet, use a soup bowl and prepare the sauce in the same bowl. Ed.*) Then scrape the cheese into a small bowl, and using a wire whisk, incorporate the vinegar and heavy cream, a little at a time. Add the chives and seasonings and refrigerate until ready to serve.

Sauce for strong assertive salads; to serve 4:

   1½ ounces Roquefort cheese
   ½ teaspoon extra-strong Dijon mustard (*moutarde forte de Dijon*)
   1 tablespoon wine vinegar
   4 tablespoons walnut oil
   Salt (with the mustard and the cheese, this should not be
      necessary)
   Freshly ground pepper

   PREPARATION:
Using a fork, crush the cheese on a plate (*or in a soup bowl*), then
scrape it into a small mixing bowl, and using a wire whisk, incorporate
the remaining ingredients, one at a time.

Les petites entrées

FIRST COURSES

Salade de râble de lapereau aux feuilles de mesclun

WARM RABBIT SALAD WITH WILD LETTUCE

(Color picture 4)

To serve 2:

Only the saddle (*le râble*) and the liver of the rabbit are needed for this recipe. If you wish, you can use the rest to make a Terrine of Rabbit in Aspic (*gâteau de lapereau en gelée du Moulin*, page 57).

1 saddle, and the liver, from a young 4½-pound rabbit, dressed
Coarse salt
Freshly ground pepper
2 tablespoons rendered goose fat, or lard
5 tablespoons butter, in all
2 handfuls mixed lettuces: curly chicory, romaine, escarole, *trévise*, lamb's lettuce (*mâche*), or—if you live in Provence—a gathering of wild lettuces (*mesclun*) from the countryside
8 asparagus spears, trimmed and tied in a bundle (optional)
1 large red ripe tomato, about 6 to 8 ounces

7 ounces fresh white mushrooms (*about 4 large mushrooms*)

2 ounces preserved duck liver (*foie gras de canard*), cut into small cubes (optional)

2 large slices black truffle (optional)

1 tablespoon coarsely chopped fresh chervil (*or substitute fresh parsley; Ed.*)

PREPARATION OF THE RABBIT:

1. The rabbit liver: Remove any filament and sprinkle the liver with salt and pepper. Melt the goose fat or lard in a small casserole over low heat. Add the liver and cook very slowly. Allow about 10 to 15 minutes for this operation, turning the liver frequently.

When the liver is cooked, remove it from the casserole and set aside on a plate, covered, to keep warm.

2. The saddle (*le râble*): The saddle is situated between the first rib and the hind legs. Remove the legs, separating them at the joint where they are attached to the saddle. Then, using a large heavy knife or meat cleaver, separate the saddle from the chest cavity.

By running your fingers over the meat, you will feel the protruding ends of the ribs. Also, notice a fine dividing line of white fat. Using this as a guide, cut off the "flaps" of meat attached to the saddle. Set them aside, with the rest of the rabbit, to be used at another time.

With the help of a very thin sharp knife, carefully remove the fine transparent skin (pellicle) covering the saddle, exposing the pale flesh. Sprinkle the meat with salt and freshly ground pepper.

Over low heat, melt 1½ tablespoons of the butter in a heavy cast-iron casserole just large enough to hold the saddle, and arrange the meat within. Cover the casserole, and cook the rabbit over very low heat for about 20 to 25 minutes. Turn the meat frequently (*every 3 to 5 minutes*), and watch the heat very carefully to be sure that neither the rabbit nor the butter browns. The rabbit must remain white and the butter pale and creamy.

To test the meat for doneness, pierce it with the point of a kitchen needle or skewer. The juice that appears should be very clear and white. When the rabbit is done, set it aside, covered, to keep warm.

PREPARATION OF THE SALAD:

1. The lettuces: Wash the lettuces, drain them, and dry in a lettuce dryer or towel.

2. The asparagus: Use if they are in season. Drop the asparagus into a 2-quart pot of boiling salted water. Depending on their size, cook the asparagus between 5 and 8 minutes. Then lift them from the pot, plunge them into cold water and, after ½ minute, set aside to drain.

3. The tomato: Drop the tomato into boiling water, count to 10, then plunge it into cold water. This will make it easy to peel. Cut the tomato in half crosswise, and gently squeeze out the seeds and water. Cut each of the tomato halves into approximately 8 pieces.

4. The mushrooms: Rinse and dry the mushrooms and cut them into thin slices.

ASSEMBLING THE SALAD:

1. Warm two deep plates by rinsing them with hot water. Dry the plates and arrange a bed of well-drained lettuce leaves on each one.

2. Compose a small fan of sliced mushrooms, slightly overlapping, toward the edge of each plate.

3. Remove the rabbit from the casserole and reserve the cooking butter and juices. Carve the saddle in long thin slices, parallel to the backbone. Divide the slices and arrange them, slightly overlapping, on one side of each plate.

4. Cut the rabbit liver, on the diagonal, into long thin slices. Place the slices, slightly overlapping, on the other side of the plate. Cube the ends of the liver that can't be conveniently sliced.

5. In the center of each plate, make a bouquet with the pieces of tomato.

6. Gather the asparagus spears together, also forming a bouquet on the plate.

7. Arrange the cubes of liver in a mound and top them with a slice of truffle.

8. Season lightly over all with coarse salt and freshly ground pepper, then set the plates in a warm place at the back of the stove.

THE SAUCE:

Add 3 tablespoons of water to the remaining butter and juices in the casserole used to cook the rabbit. Bring the liquid to a boil, and using a wire whisk, quickly stir in the remaining 3½ tablespoons cold butter cut into tiny pieces, a few pieces at a time. The butter and water will form a *liaison.*

Off heat, mix in the chopped chervil, and nap the two salads with the sauce. Serve at once.

On occasion, I have replaced the chervil in the butter sauce with 1 tablespoon of chopped fresh raw truffle. It surely doesn't do the dish any harm, but it is definitely not obligatory.

Salade de concombres à la crème de cerfeuil
CUCUMBER SALAD WITH CHERVIL AND CREAM

To serve 4:

   4 cucumbers, about 7 ounces each
   3 tablespoons coarse salt
   4 heaping tablespoons cold *crème fraîche* (*or substitute commercial sour cream; Ed.*)
   1 heaping teaspoon Dijon mustard
   Juice of 2 lemons
   ½ cup coarsely chopped fresh young chervil leaves
   Freshly ground white pepper

PREPARATION OF THE CUCUMBERS:

Use a vegetable peeler to peel the cucumbers, then cut them in half lengthwise, and with a teaspoon, scrape out the seeds. Cut the cucumber halves into slices, as thin as possible.

Gather the cucumber slices in a bowl and sprinkle them with 3 tablespoons of coarse salt (fine salt will also do). Mix well and place the bowl in the refrigerator for 2½ hours. The quantity of salt may seem enormous, but it is needed to draw the water out of the cucumbers, and most of it will disappear when you drain them.

PREPARATION OF THE SAUCE:

While you are waiting for the cucumbers, prepare the sauce. Using a wire whisk, mix the *crème fraîche* with the Dijon mustard in a 1-quart bowl. Then add the lemon juice, a little at a time. (*If you are substituting commercial sour cream, 1 lemon should be sufficient. Taste the sauce for tartness. Ed.*)

Whisk the ingredients together until thick and creamy. Then add the chopped chervil and several turns of the pepper mill. When beating *crème fraîche*, take care that you do not overbeat or you will turn it into butter. Beat the *crème fraîche* only until it catches in the whisk.

TO FINISH THE SALAD:

After 2½ hours, rinse the cucumbers and drain them in a coarse sieve or a colander. Press down on the cucumbers to squeeze out their water and salt, then pat dry with a towel.

Mix the cucumbers with the sauce, taste for seasoning, and serve very cold.

Salade de haricots verts à la crème et aux noisettes

STRING BEAN SALAD WITH HAZELNUTS AND CREAM

To serve 4:

1 pound very young string beans (*see Note*)
Salt
2 ounces (*about ½ cup*) freshly shelled hazelnuts (*sometimes called filberts*)
4 tablespoons cold *crème fraîche* (*or substitute ¼ cup commercial sour cream mixed with 2 tablespoons heavy cream. See Note; Ed.*)

1 rounded teaspoon extra-strong Dijon mustard (*moutarde forte de Dijon*)

Juice of ½ lemon

Freshly ground white pepper

2 tablespoons chopped fresh chervil (*or substitute fresh parsley or dillweed; Ed.*)

8 pale tender leaves from the heart of a lettuce

It is very important that the string beans be absolutely fresh. To make sure, break one. If it snaps, it is fresh. If not, and if it is pliable, it is old.

The ideal string beans are those no thicker than the tines of a fork and that still have their flowers attached. If you use these, watch them carefully while they cook, as they will take no longer than 4 or 5 minutes. However, if you can't find them, choose the firmest and freshest possible.

String beans should not be cooked more than 2 hours ahead of time, or they will wither.

NOTE: *Often in the fall, when hazelnuts are most available, string beans can be larger and less tender than those intended for this recipe. Encountering this problem, I performed an experiment—which was successful. Under these circumstances:*

Trim the ends of the string beans, then run them through a tiny multibladed device designed to "French cut" string beans. The French have probably never heard of such a gadget, but I imagine it is so named because this procedure results in thin strips of string bean which (in size only) resemble those delicate string beans most coveted in France. This operation also enables the moist flesh of the cut beans to absorb the sauce better. Ed.

HAVE READY:

1. The string beans: Nip off the ends and wash the beans, then drain in a colander. Bring 2 quarts of salted water to a boil, drop in the string beans, and when the water returns to a boil, cook them, uncovered, for 4 or 5 minutes. They must remain crunchy to the bite. Because the size of string beans will vary, it is impossible to give an exact cooking time. You will need to test one and judge for yourself.

Drain the beans quickly, then plunge them into a bowl of ice water. This will keep them crisp and preserve their green color. When they have chilled, drain carefully and pat dry with a towel. Keep them cold in the refrigerator.

2. The hazelnuts: Using a small sharp knife, cut the hazelnuts into paper-thin rounds. Place the hazelnuts in a small skillet and toast over high heat, stirring continuously to keep them white. Do not allow them to brown. (You can also toast the nuts in a 350°F oven for about 15 minutes, shaking the pan frequently.)

When finished, turn the hazelnuts out onto a plate and let cool.

PREPARATION OF THE SAUCE: (This sauce should not be prepared more than ½ hour before it is to be served.)

NOTE: *Because a somewhat tart cream is needed in this recipe, this is one instance where our commercial sour cream can work in place of* crème fraîche. *Stir 2 tablespoons of heavy cream into ¼ cup of commercial sour cream in order to thin it to the same consistency as* crème fraîche. *Ed.*

Pour the cold *crème fraîche* into a chilled metal bowl. (If possible, place the bowl in the refrigerator or freezer in advance.) Add the mustard, lemon juice, salt, and freshly ground pepper. Stir lightly with a wire whisk until combined.

Then add freshly chopped chervil and the string beans. Use a large wooden spoon to turn the string beans in the sauce. Taste for salt.

TO SERVE:

Arrange two pale lettuce leaves on each plate in the shape of two open hands. Place a mound of string beans on each lettuce leaf and sprinkle with crisp toasted hazelnuts. Serve at once.

Salade de pamplemousse au crabe
GRAPEFRUIT AND CRAB MEAT SALAD

To serve 2: (*By increasing the proportion of grapefruit and crab meat, this recipe will serve 4 or more persons. The ingredients for the sauce make almost enough for 4. Ed.*)

- 1 large live crab, about 1¾ pounds, or one 6½-ounce can Alaskan or other variety of Pacific crab meat (*see Note*)
- Coarse salt
- 2 grapefruit (pink grapefruit are preferable, as they are generally sweeter)
- 1 yellow heart of a Boston or butter lettuce
- 5 rounded tablespoons thick *crème fraîche* (*or substitute commercial sour cream; Ed.*)
- 2 teaspoons tomato ketchup
- 1 tablespoon cognac
- A pinch cayenne pepper, or 3 drops Tabasco

NOTE: *If you are using a whole crab, the Dungeness variety is preferable. However, even when in season, they are usually sold precooked. This is fine, as it eliminates one step of work. Out of season, these crabs can often be found frozen. They should always be defrosted in the refrigerator.*

If a whole Dungeness crab or other large crab is unavailable, rather than resort to the use of canned crab meat I would suggest that you buy either a 6-ounce package of frozen Alaskan king crab meat, or crab meat sold in bulk from your fish merchant. Ed.

PREPARATION:

1. The live crab: Plunge the crab into rapidly boiling salted water and cook 25 minutes. Drain and cool the crab, then chill in the refrigerator.

Twist off the claws and legs and crack them with the back of a meat cleaver (*or use a nutcracker; Ed.*). Take care not to crush the meat. Extract the morsels of crab meat and set them aside on a plate.

Then pull back the apron found on the underside of the body, discard the spongy fingerlike gills and intestinal matter, and break the

45

body in half. Extract the pieces of meat from within the crevices of cartilage and gather them together with the leg and claw meat. Set aside in the refrigerator.

2. Canned (*or frozen*) crab meat: Drain (*or defrost*) the crab meat, then pick through it, discarding any cartilage and tiny pieces of shell. Place the crab meat on a plate and set aside in the refrigerator.

3. The grapefruit: Peel the grapefruit close to the flesh, cutting away all the white pith. Then, using a small, very sharp knife, separate each section of fruit from the membrane. Do this over a bowl, catching all the juices. Place the sections of fruit on a plate and refrigerate them. Strain the juice through a fine sieve and keep it cold also.

4. The lettuce: Cut out the core of the lettuce and carefully detach each entire leaf. Rinse the leaves well and pat them dry with a towel.

5. The sauce: Spoon 5 tablespoons of *crème fraîche* into a 1-quart mixing bowl, and using a wire whisk, beat in the ketchup and cognac. Add 4 tablespoons of the reserved grapefruit juice, one at a time, beating after each addition. Season with salt and either cayenne pepper or Tabasco to taste.

Beat the sauce until it becomes thick and creamy, but take care not to overbeat or it will separate. (*If you are using commercial sour cream, it will become somewhat thinner with the additions of liquid, but it should remain creamy. Ed.*) Refrigerate the sauce until ready to serve.

TO SERVE:

Line the sides of two individual salad bowls with whole lettuce leaves. Distribute well-drained sections of grapefruit over the lettuce and scatter the morsels of crab meat over all.

Nap the salad with sauce and serve very cold.

Salade Mikado

TOMATO, AVOCADO AND MUSHROOM SALAD

To serve 2: *(The ingredients for this salad can easily be doubled to serve 4. Ed.)*

¾ pound firm ripe tomatoes
1 yellow heart of curly chicory
1 avocado, about 8 ounces
Juice of ½ lemon (optional); Ed.
2 very large white mushrooms
3 ounces truffles (optional)

The vinaigrette sauce:
    1 tablespoon red wine vinegar
    ½ teaspoon Dijon mustard
    Coarse salt
    Freshly ground pepper
    3 tablespoons olive oil

PREPARATION:

1. The tomatoes: Drop the tomatoes into a pot of boiling water. Count to 10, remove, and plunge them into cold water. This will make them easy to peel. Cut out the core, peel the tomatoes, then cut them in half crosswise. Gently press the tomatoes to extract the seeds and water. Dice the tomatoes and place them in a sieve or colander until ready to use.

2. The chicory: Separate the leaves and wash them well. Shake them, and dry in a basket or spin in a lettuce dryer.

3. The avocado: Cut the avocado in half lengthwise, remove the seed, and pull off the skin. It should separate easily from the flesh of the fruit. Then cut the avocado into long thin slices and divide between two plates, arranging the slices on one side of each plate, slightly overlapping. This can be done in advance, but the slices must be covered with plastic wrap to prevent their darkening. *(Another precaution would be to brush them lightly with lemon juice. Ed.)*

4. The mushrooms: Use only the mushroom caps. Wipe them with

a damp cloth or rinse briefly under running water. Dry the mushrooms thoroughly and cut them into thin slices.

TO ASSEMBLE THE SALAD:

Place a few tufts of chicory in the center of each plate. Divide the other ingredients into 2 parts—the well-drained tomato and the mushrooms—arranging the slices neatly overlapping.

If you wish, you can complete the plate by arranging fine julienne strips of truffle in the center.

THE VINAIGRETTE SAUCE:

In a small bowl, combine the vinegar with the mustard, a pinch of coarse salt, and freshly ground pepper. Then beat in the olive oil, a tablespoon at a time.

Sprinkle the salad lightly with salt and freshly ground pepper. Spoon over the *vinaigrette* sauce and serve.

There is nothing grandiose about this salad, but it brings together products of the same delicacy of taste and texture. Sometimes one doesn't need any more than that to do great things.

What is there of the Japanese in this *salade Mikado*?

In reality, next to nothing. I'll tell you why I call it that: When I thought of the salad for the first time, I assigned the making of it to one of my chefs who happened to be Japanese. As he had a name that was absolutely impossible to pronounce, I had given him the nickname of "Mikado." Don't look further for authentication.

L'anchoyade

ANCHOVY SAUCE FOR CRUDITÉS

To serve 8: (This sauce can be kept very well in a jar in the refrigerator, so you can have it on hand for several meals.)

Two 2-ounce tins anchovy fillets packed in oil, drained
1 cup olive oil (imported virgin olive oil, if possible)
2–3 large cloves garlic, chopped
2 teaspoons fresh thyme flowers, or leaves (*or substitute 1 teaspoon dried thyme; Ed.*)
3 tablespoons chopped fresh basil
1 tablespoon Dijon mustard
1 tablespoon wine vinegar
½ teaspoon freshly ground pepper

PREPARATION:

1. Using a blender or food processor: Put all of the ingredients together in the container of your machine and blend until they are reduced to a purée. Then scrape the sauce into a terrine or bowl that can be used by your guests to dip their vegetables.

2. Using a food mill: In a small casserole, barely warm the anchovies in 3 tablespoons of the olive oil, stirring with a wooden spoon until they are slightly dissolved. Then turn them out into a food mill, set over a large bowl. Add the garlic, thyme, and basil, and as you turn the mill, rinse the ingredients with olive oil. When all of the substance has passed through, scrape the underside of the grate with a rubber spatula in order to recapture every bit of the purée.

Using a wire whisk, beat in the mustard, vinegar, freshly ground pepper, and the remainder of the olive oil. Continue to beat the mixture vigorously until homogenously blended.

Serve from the bowl in which it was prepared.

NOTE: If you are using only part of this sauce, scrape the rest into an airtight jar and store it in the refrigerator. Let it stand at room temperature 30 minutes before serving.

TO SERVE:

The *anchoyade* can be served with large slices of hot grilled *pain de campagne* or *pain-baguette*, accompanied by a salad—such as Wild Lettuces (*mesclun*, see page 31), and black olives, quarters of tomato, and hard-cooked eggs. (Pain de campagne *is a round loaf of coarse-textured French country bread, and* pain-baguette *is the long thin loaf of French bread. Ed.*)

A large *anchoyade* (*La Grande Anchoyade*) is a true meal in itself. Along with slices of toasted bread, you can serve a basket of raw vegetables, such as: cherry tomatoes, mushrooms, celery, radishes, fennel, cucumber, peppers, hearts of lettuce; and tiny cooked artichokes, cooked fresh broad beans, and lemon wedges, hard-cooked eggs, black Niçoise olives, and so on.

Above all, don't forget to serve plenty of cold wine. And an *anchoyade* should be served out of doors, under the shade of a majestic tree.

Tapenade
OLIVE, ANCHOVY AND CAPER CONDIMENT

Tapenade can be used in many ways:

1. Spread on toasted slices of French bread and served with apéritifs.

2. As an hors d'oeuvre with raw vegetables and hard-cooked eggs.

3. With a salad (prepared with good olive oil, of course) to which small croutons, rubbed with garlic or not, have been added.

4. Spread on bread as part of a sandwich. The bread should be the long thin loaf of French bread (*pain-baguette*), split in half and toasted, then layered with slices of tomato, hard-cooked eggs, sweet new onions, and a few anchovy fillets.

5. Or *gourmandise*—on slices of toasted bread, covered with rounds of cheese, such as Goat Cheese Marinated in Olive Oil with Dried Herbs (*Picodons marinés à l'huile d'herbes sèches*, page 232).

To make about 2 cups:

    1 pound large plump black olives (*see Note*)
    One 2-ounce tin anchovies preserved in oil
    1 large clove garlic, peeled and slightly crushed
    3 tablespoons capers preserved in vinegar, well drained
    3 tablespoons olive oil
    Freshly ground pepper

NOTE: *The olives you select are crucial to this recipe. Buy the plump variety (slightly wrinkled) that are cured in oil, rather than in brine. They can be found, sold in bulk, in stores specializing in Middle Eastern foods. Ed.*

PREPARATION:

Pit the olives. This is more easily accomplished with an olive pitter, but if you don't have one, crush the olive meat (but not the pit) with the flat side of a large knife or cleaver, and extract the seed. Put the olive meat into a food processor or blender, or if you have the strength, use a mortar and pestle.

Add the tin of anchovies—with their oil—and the garlic, capers, olive oil, and a few good turns of the pepper mill. Blend the ingredients together all at once. Keep this preparation brief, so that the purée retains a coarse texture.

If you are using a mortar and pestle, grip the pestle with one hand over the other and work vigorously. The result is worth the effort.

To store the *tapenade*, it is preferable to pack it in small jars. Level off the mixture by tamping it down and float a thin film of olive oil over the surface. Cover the jars tightly and keep them in the refrigerator.

Tapenade makes for one of those little indulgences that you are always happy to find when you open the door of the refrigerator to calm a small hunger or to satisfy a sudden attack of greediness.

Nougat de boeuf de ma tante Célestine
TERRINE OF BEEF AND
VEGETABLES IN ASPIC

This dish should be prepared at least the evening before you plan to
serve it. It can be kept for several days in the refrigerator.

To serve 8:

3½ pounds lean beef (round, shoulder, chuck, etc.)
3 tablespoons chopped onion
2 large carrots, cut into 2-inch segments and quartered lengthwise
Bouquet garni (sprigs of parsley and thyme, 1 stalk celery, 1 bay
   leaf, and 1 orange zest, tied together)
5 whole cloves garlic, flattened and peeled
1 teaspoon crushed peppercorns
2 bottles (*6 cups*) dry red wine, such as Côtes de Provence
2 calves' feet, split in half
7 ounces lean salt pork (*unsmoked bacon*), in one piece
24 very small new white onions
8 small new carrots
1½ tablespoons butter
Coarse salt
¾ pound tomatoes
Beef stock (*about 5 cups*)
Flour (*about 1 cup*)
4 tablespoons capers, drained
4 tablespoons freshly chopped parsley

HAVE READY:

1. The beef: Make sure that the meat is trimmed of all fat, then
cut it into small cubes weighing about 2 ounces each. Place them in
an 8- or 9-quart casserole (preferably enameled cast iron), and add
the chopped onion, 2-inch sticks of carrot, *bouquet garni*, whole cloves
of garlic, crushed peppercorns, and the 2 bottles of red wine.

Mix well with a wooden spoon and let the meat marinate 4 hours in a cool place—but not in the refrigerator. Turn the meat from time to time.

2. The calves' feet: While the beef is marinating, bring the calves' feet to a boil, uncovered, in 2 quarts of unsalted water. Lift off the scum with a large cooking spoon, then simmer 15 minutes. Drain and set aside.

3. The salt pork: Cut the salt pork into *lardons* or sticks the size of your thumb. Put them in a saucepan with 2 quarts of cold water and bring to a boil. Simmer 2 minutes, uncovered, then drain in a sieve and rinse under cold water.

4. The vegetables: Peel the new onions and carrots and place them in a small heavy saucepan with the butter, 4 tablespoons of water, and a pinch of salt. Cover and cook 20 to 25 minutes over medium heat. Stir occasionally. Then turn the vegetables out onto a plate and keep them in a cool place until ready to use.

5. The tomatoes: Remove the core from the tomatoes and cut them in half crosswise. Press out the seeds and water and cut the tomatoes into large dice.

COOKING THE BEEF:

After the meat has marinated 3½ hours, preheat oven to 300°F.

After 4 hours, add the calves' feet, *lardons*, and tomatoes to the beef with enough cold beef stock to cover the meat completely by 1½ inches.

Mix flour (*about 1 cup*) in a bowl with enough cold water (*about ½ cup*) to make a paste. Cover the casserole and use this paste to hermetically seal the edges where they meet. Place the casserole in the oven and bake 5 hours, undisturbed.

PREPARATION OF THE BROTH:

After 5 hours, remove the casserole from the oven and break the seal. Lift the cover and inhale the perfume!

With the help of a slotted spoon or skimmer, carefully remove the morsels of beef and the lardons, and place them in a deep plate. (Be forewarned, the well-cooked meat will be very fragile.) Also remove the calves' feet, and extract all their bones. Cut the meat into cubes and add it to the beef and *lardons*. Set the meats aside.

Carefully skim off all visible fat from the broth, then set the casserole aside to give any remaining fat a chance to rise to the surface. The last of the grease should be easy to remove with a spoon. *(It is very important to do a thorough job. Ed.)*

Pass the broth through a fine sieve into a clean casserole, but do not press down on the residue of the *bouquet garni* and vegetables or you will cloud the sauce. Return the broth just to the boiling point, taste for seasoning, and add a pinch of salt. Then let the broth cool, allowing any sediment to settle at the bottom of the casserole.

Meanwhile, chill a 3-quart terrine, about 4 inches wide by 14 inches long and 3½ inches deep.

ASSEMBLING THE NOUGAT:

Pour 1 cup of broth into the chilled terrine, then return this to the refrigerator until it is nearly jelled.

When the broth has set, sprinkle half of the capers and parsley over it. Then make a bed of half the meats, mixed loosely together and spread evenly over the herbs.

Scatter the cooked onions over the meats and add the carrots, arranged lengthwise, symmetrically.

Fill the terrine with broth to the level of the vegetables (*about 3 or 4 cups*) and chill again until the gelatinous broth is firm.

Distribute the rest of the capers and parsley over the vegetables, then add the remaining half of the meats. Pour enough broth over the meats to cover them completely in an even layer, and place the terrine in the refrigerator overnight. It needs at least 8 hours to jell properly.

If there is any broth left over, pour it into a shallow receptacle and refrigerate to use later, chopped, as a *garniture. (Be sure not to include any cloudy sediment that has settled at the bottom of the casserole. Ed.)*

TO SERVE:

When you are ready to serve the *nougat,* dip the terrine briefly into a basin of hot water, then slide a knife around the sides to help release them. Carefully invert the terrine, unmolding the jellied meats and vegetables onto a chilled serving platter. If you have saved some broth, chop it into fine dice and scatter it around the *nougat*.

Serve the *nougat* with *cornichons* and a good green salad.

I think that I have been faithful to the memory of Tante Célestine and haven't forgotten any of the ingredients that she used. I saw her make this so many times that, when I do it, it is almost as if I were still watching her.

Pâté fin de foies de volaille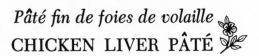
CHICKEN LIVER PÂTÉ

To serve 6:

    12 whole chicken livers, about 1½ pounds
    Milk (*about 1½ cups, in all*)
    Coarse salt
    Freshly ground pepper, preferably white
    2 tablespoons olive oil
    3 tablespoons minced onion, preferably a sweet white onion
    7 ounces fresh bread crumbs (*about 2 cups*)
    1 tablespoon finely chopped parsley
    A pinch of thyme, fresh or dried
    1 egg yolk

PREPARATION OF THE LIVERS:

Two or 3 hours before preparing the pâté, clean the livers and remove any blood, filament, and traces of green—which would give the livers a disagreeable bitter taste.

Place the livers in a bowl with enough cold milk to cover them (*about 1 cup*) and let soak 2 or 3 hours. Then drain the livers well, dry with paper towels, and sprinkle with salt and pepper. Discard the milk.

COOKING:

Heat the olive oil in a 12-inch skillet, and when the oil begins to smoke, add the livers. Take care that they do not overlap. Using a wooden spoon or spatula, turn the livers rapidly in the hot oil until they are seared on all sides. Then place them in a sieve or colander to drain.

Over very low heat, add the chopped onion to the oil remaining in the skillet. Stir the onion until soft, but do not allow it to brown. This should take no longer than 10 minutes.

While the onion is cooking, soak the bread crumbs in 4 tablespoons of cold milk.

When the bread crumbs have absorbed most, if not all, of the milk, squeeze out the excess with your hands. Then pass the bread crumbs with the drained chicken livers through a meat grinder, using the fine grate. Gather the purée in a lightly oiled 2- or 3-quart casserole.

Stir in the cooked onion, chopped parsley, thyme, and egg yolk, and place the casserole over low heat. Cook the *pâté* 5 minutes, uncovered, while stirring continuously with a wooden spoon. Do not allow the *pâté* to "bubble" more than 2 or 3 times.

It is possible that the *pâté* will be a little dry. If so, add 2 or 3 tablespoons of milk. Taste for seasoning and add a good pinch of salt and freshly ground pepper.

Spoon the mixture into a small 4- or 5-cup terrine, press it down lightly, and smooth the surface with a spatula. Cut a piece of wax paper to fit the shape of the terrine, brush one side lightly with olive oil, and lay it, oiled side down, over the *pâté*. Refrigerate until ready to serve.

NOTE: *This* pâté *is a very good cold first course which will bring you pleasure when accompanied by a mixed green salad seasoned with olive oil and wine vinegar. Generously spread the* pâté *on large thick slices of toasted* pain de campagne. *You will see that there are good things in life.* (Pain de campagne *is a round loaf of coarse-textured French country bread. Ed.*)

Gâteau de lapereau en gelée du Moulin
TERRINE OF RABBIT IN ASPIC
(Color picture 3)

To serve 6:

If you use the whole rabbit, this recipe will serve 6 persons, but if you reserve the back (*le râble*), which is the meatiest part of the body, for another recipe—such as Warm Rabbit Salad with Wild Lettuces (*salade de râble de lapereau aux feuilles de mesclun*, page 38—it will only serve 4. (In either case, do *not* change the proportions of any of the other ingredients.)

> 1 young rabbit, about 4½ pounds dressed
> 1 cup dry white wine
> 2 tablespoons chopped parsley
> 2 tablespoons chopped shallots
> 1 clove garlic, chopped
> 1 large sprig fresh thyme (*or substitute ½ teaspoon dried thyme; Ed.*)
> 1 sprig fresh rosemary (*or substitute ¼ teaspoon dried rosemary; Ed.*)
> Freshly ground pepper
> ½ pound very lean salt pork from the belly (*Have your butcher remove the skin and slice the pork very thin, exactly like bacon. Ed.*)
> 2 cups clear golden aspic (*see Note*)

NOTE: *Plan to marinate the rabbit 2 days before you wish to serve it.*
To serve, use a large spoon instead of cutting into slices, allowing a sizable morsel for each person. Ed.

PREPARATION OF THE RABBIT:

If possible, choose a domestic rabbit with an abundance of good white fat. Pull off the fat and extract the heart, kidneys, lungs, and liver. Save only the liver. Cut off and discard the head and feet. Then cut up the rabbit in the following manner:

1. Using a sharp medium-size knife, detach the shoulders—making a clean incision behind each one—freeing the front legs.

2. Separate the back (*le râble*), which lies between the first rib and the joint attaching the hind legs. If you are saving the back for another recipe, keep it whole. If you are using it here, cut it in half.

3. Cut off the flaps of meat attached to the ribs of the chest cavity. These and the neck and the part at the top of the abdomen are of no interest to you (though they may be to your dog or cat). Cut the rib section in half.

4. Detach the 2 hindquarters, and cut each piece of meat in half.

In addition to the back, you should have 8 pieces of meat—2 front legs, 2 rib sections, and 4 hindquarter pieces—plus the liver.

PREPARATION OF THE MARINADE:

Pour the white wine into a large mixing bowl and add the parsley, shallots, garlic, thyme, and rosemary. Add a generous amount of freshly ground pepper, but do not add salt. (The salt in the aspic and in the salt pork should be sufficient.)

Arrange the rabbit pieces and the liver in the bowl, making sure that there is enough liquid to cover the meat. Add more wine if necessary. Marinate the rabbit in the refrigerator 12 hours, or overnight.

NOTE: *In France, one can buy aspic ready-made, at the neighborhood delicatessen* (charcuterie). *Alas, in the United States we are not so fortunate, and must prepare our own. I suggest that you make 4 cups of aspic rather than 2, so as to be sure not only of having enough, but also to have a little extra to chop later for use as a* garniture. *Ed.*

To make 4 cups of aspic:
  4 cups strong chicken or veal stock
  3 packages (3 tablespoons) unflavored powdered gelatin
  ¼ cup dry white wine
  3 egg whites, and their shells
  ¼ lemon
  1 or 2 tablespoons Madeira

Preparation of the aspic: Set aside ¾ cup cold stock and sprinkle the gelatin over it to soften. Pour the remaining stock into a 4-quart cas-serole and add the white wine.

Using a wire whisk, beat the egg whites to a froth. Then add them, with their crushed shells and a squeeze of lemon juice, to the stock. Gently heat the stock, and when the gelatin has softened, stir it into the hot (but not boiling) liquid.

Stirring continuously with a wire whisk, bring the stock to a boil. When a foam begins to rise up and threatens to boil over, give the stock a final stir, and remove the casserole from heat. Let stand, un-disturbed, 10 minutes.

Saturate a dish towel with cold water, then wring it out thor-oughly. Place a fine sieve over a large deep bowl and line the sieve with the damp cloth. Then slowly and carefully pour the stock through the sieve into the bowl. Do not disturb the towel or the sieve until all the liquid has drained through. Then remove them, and add Madeira to taste.

COOKING THE RABBIT:

Preheat the oven to 300°F.

Line the bottom and sides of a rectangular (4½ inches by 8½ inches) 1½-quart terrine for *pâté* completely with strips of salt pork. Place them neatly, one next to the other without overlapping. In this instance, do not leave any excess to fold over the top of the terrine.

Reserving the marinade, arrange the pieces of marinated rabbit, with the liver, in the terrine. Press them down. Pour in about ½ cup of the reserved marinade, or enough to cover ¾ of the rabbit. (If the aspic has become firm, liquefy it slightly over low heat, but do not let it become hot.) Then add enough aspic to the terrine to cover the rabbit completely.

Wrap the mold tightly in aluminum foil, bright side down, place it in a larger pan (*bain-marie*), and add enough boiling water to reach ⅔ of the way up the sides of the terrine. Place it in the preheated oven and bake 2 hours.

FINISHING THE TERRINE:

Take the terrine from the oven and let cool in the *bain-marie*. Then unwrap it and pour more aspic over to fill the terrine completely.

Cover with foil or plastic wrap, and refrigerate until the aspic is firmly set.

Pour any remaining aspic into a shallow pan and refrigerate until set. Then chop it to use as a *garniture* for the rabbit.

TO SERVE:

Just before serving, dip the terrine into hot water, then slide a knife around the sides to help release them. Reverse the terrine, unmolding the jellied rabbit onto a chilled platter. Return it to the refrigerator briefly, to compensate for the unmolding.

Serve the rabbit with a green salad and black olives.

It is preferable to cook this dish the day before you wish to serve it, so that the aspic has enough time to set properly. It may be kept 2 or 3 days in the refrigerator.

This is an easy dish to make, and very pleasing tasted under the shade of an olive tree. However, if you don't have an olive tree nearby, any tree will do. And if you have no tree at all, close your eyes and imagine cicadas singing and the sun of the Midi. And finally, if you have neither tree nor imagination, but the taste of a *gourmand*, then just enjoy the rabbit . . . it should be sufficient for your happiness.

Les oeufs
EGGS

Trucca cannoise ou Trouchia
SWISS CHARD AND ONION OMELETTE

To serve 2:

    1¾ pounds Swiss chard (choose young branches with the smallest
        stalks you can find)
    5 tablespoons olive oil, in all
    1 large onion (*about 6 ounces*), thinly sliced
    Coarse salt
    Freshly ground white pepper
    1 small clove garlic, flattened and peeled
    4 eggs
    A pinch of thyme flowers (*or substitute fresh or dried thyme
        leaves; Ed.*)
    1 tablespoon chopped fresh parsley
    6 large fresh basil leaves, chopped
    1 tablespoon fine fresh bread crumbs
    2 tablespoons freshly grated Parmesan cheese

PREPARATION:

1. The Swiss chard: Strip the green leaves of the chard from the stalks (the stalks will not be used in this recipe). Wash the leaves in 3 changes of cold water, then drain well in a colander. Pat the leaves dry with a towel and chop them into coarse shreds.

Heat 2 tablespoons of the olive oil in a 2-quart casserole and sauté the sliced onion 5 to 10 minutes over medium heat. Stir the onion frequently and do not allow it to brown.

When the onion is soft, add the Swiss chard and continue to cook, uncovered, about 15 minutes. Stir frequently. When every bit of moisture remaining in the leaves has totally evaporated, season with salt and freshly ground pepper. Set aside to cool slightly.

2. The eggs: Put the garlic in the bottom of a 1-quart bowl, add a pinch of coarse salt, and using the tines of a fork, grind it to a paste. Then break the eggs into the bowl and add thyme, parsley, basil, and freshly ground pepper. Beat the eggs with a fork until well blended. *(Let the eggs stand for 15 minutes so that they become permeated with the herbs. Ed.)*

Add the cooled onion and Swiss chard (without a trace of liquid) to the eggs. Stir carefully until thoroughly combined.

COOKING THE OMELETTE:

Over medium heat, warm the remaining 3 tablespoons of olive oil in a well-seasoned 9-inch skillet or omelette pan. When the oil begins to smoke, pour in the onion-chard-egg mixture and stir briefly with a fork. Turn the heat to very low (*see Note*) and continue to cook without further stirring.

When the eggs begin to hold together as a mass, sprinkle the bread crumbs over the surface. Cover the pan with an inverted serving plate of equal size and quickly reverse the omelette onto it. Then carefully slide the omelette, bread-crumb side down, back into the pan. Cook the omelette 2 or 3 minutes more, or long enough to brown the bread crumbs. Then, using the same serving plate as before, cover the pan and turn the omelette out onto it so that the golden bread-crumbed side is presented upright.

Sprinkle the warm surface with freshly grated Parmesan cheese, and serve from its plate.

This omelette can also be served cold, brushed with olive oil and accompanied by little black Niçoise olives.

NOTE: It is quite important to this recipe that the omelette be cooked over very low heat. You could also cook it just as well in a low oven.

Omelette arlequin
LAYERED OMELETTE WITH TOMATO, CHEESE AND SPINACH

To serve 4 or 6:
    1 pound fresh young spinach leaves
    7 tablespoons olive oil, in all
    2 cloves garlic, peeled
    Coarse salt
    1 pound ripe tomatoes
    A pinch of fresh thyme flowers, or leaves (*or substitute 2 large fresh basil leaves, finely chopped; Ed.*)
    9 eggs
    8 tablespoons heavy cream, in all
    Freshly ground white pepper
    3 ounces freshly grated *comté* or *Gruyère* cheese
    Freshly grated nutmeg

PREPARATION:

If you wish, the preparation and cooking of the spinach and tomatoes can be done in advance. Ed.

1. The spinach: Strip off the stems of the spinach and wash the leaves in 3 changes of water. Drain well, and carefully pat the leaves dry with a towel.

Heat 3 tablespoons of the olive oil in a 4-quart casserole. When the oil begins to smoke, add the spinach with the garlic and a pinch of salt. Toss the spinach continuously with a pair of wooden spoons

63

until all the water has evaporated. Discard the garlic and set the spinach aside on a plate to cool.

2. The tomatoes: Drop the tomatoes into boiling water, count to 10, then plunge them into cold water. This will make them easy to peel. Cut out the core and peel the tomatoes, then cut each tomato in half crosswise and squeeze out the water and seeds. Lay the tomatoes on a cutting board and chop them coarsely.

Heat 2 tablespoons of olive oil in a 2-quart casserole. When the oil begins to smoke, add the chopped tomatoes with a pinch of thyme and a pinch of salt. Cook the tomatoes over high heat until all the water has evaporated, then set them aside on a plate to cool.

HAVE READY:

Oven preheated to 350°F.

1. The eggs: Break 3 whole eggs into each of three 1-quart bowls.

2. Bowl 1: Mix the 3 eggs with 2 tablespoons of the heavy cream. Add the cooked tomato (*without catching any residue of water*), a pinch of salt, and freshly ground pepper. Beat the mixture with a fork until thoroughly combined.

3. Bowl 2: Mix the 3 eggs with 3 tablespoons of the heavy cream, the grated cheese, a pinch of salt, and freshly ground pepper. Beat the mixture with a fork until well blended.

4. Bowl 3: Mix the 3 eggs with the remaining 3 tablespoons of heavy cream. Add the cooked spinach (*squeeze the spinach gently to extract any remaining moisture; Ed.*), freshly grated nutmeg, a pinch of salt, and freshly ground pepper. Beat the mixture with a fork until thoroughly combined.

ASSEMBLING AND COOKING THE OMELETTE:

NOTE: *The volume of this omelette is about 6 cups. I have prepared it several times, each time in a 7-cup mold of a different shape. I found that the cooking time varied in every case, depending on whether the mold was rectangular, cylindrical, deep, or shallow. Usually a longer cooking time was needed than estimated—a deep cylindrical mold needing the longest.*

Since the omelette must have time to settle before serving, and is more savory warm than hot, I suggest that you compensate for this variable by planning to finish the omelette ½ hour before you intend to serve it. During the resting period, keep the oven hot in case the omelette might need to be returned for another 15 minutes.

The eggs should unmold as a smooth, colorful custard. Slip a knife around the inside of the mold to insure their release. Then, holding an inverted serving plate over the top of the omelette, very carefully begin to reverse the mold. You will soon know if the eggs are done. Ed.

Liberally grease a 7- to 8-cup terrine, or a soufflé mold, with the remaining 2 tablespoons of olive oil.

Pour in the tomato-egg mixture (bowl #1) and set the mold within a larger pan (a *bain-marie*), adding enough hot water to reach halfway up the sides of the mold.

Carefully slide the pan into the preheated oven and bake the tomato-egg mixture 15 minutes. (*At the end of this time, the eggs should be barely set and very "loose," but if it seems that they have not set at all, bake 5 minutes longer. Ed.*)

After 15 minutes, gently slide the egg-cheese mixture (bowl #2) over the layer of egg and tomato. Return the mold to the oven for 20 minutes.

After the layer of egg and cheese has cooked 20 minutes (*if you are using a rectangular mold, check it after 15 minutes; Ed.*), carefully add the final layer of spinach and egg (bowl #3), spooning it evenly over all. Return the mold to the oven for about 25 minutes.

TO FINISH AND SERVE THE OMELETTE:

After the last 25 minutes, the omelette should be perfectly cooked. (*If you are using a rectangular mold, check it after 20 minutes. Ed.*) Remove it from the oven, but let the mold remain in its water bath for 10 to 15 minutes before unmolding it onto a platter.

Serve the omelette hot, cut into either wedges or thick slices, depending on the shape of your mold.

This omelette can also be served cold (*but not refrigerated*) as an hors d'oeuvre, accompanied by a cruet of good olive oil.

Omelette à la tomate fraîche et aux feuilles de basilic
TOMATO AND FRESH BASIL OMELETTE

To serve 2 or 3:

> 4 large ripe tomatoes (the size of tennis balls), about 7 ounces each
> 4 tablespoons olive oil, in all
> 1 bay leaf
> 1 small clove garlic
> 1 large sprig thyme
> 10 large fresh basil leaves, coarsely chopped
> 4 sprigs parsley, coarsely chopped
> 6 eggs
> Coarse salt
> Freshly ground white pepper

PREPARATION:

1. The tomatoes: Drop the tomatoes into boiling water, count to 10, then plunge them into cold water. This will make them easy to peel. Remove the core and peel the tomatoes, then cut them in half crosswise and press firmly to release the seeds and water. Chop the tomatoes into large dice (*about 16 to 20 pieces per tomato*) and set them aside on a paper towel.

Heat 2 tablespoons of the olive oil in a 9-inch casserole or skillet, until almost smoking. Then add the tomatoes, with the bay leaf, and cook over high heat until all of the water has evaporated. This will take about 15 to 20 minutes. Stir the tomatoes frequently with a wooden spoon, then discard the bay leaf, and set aside to cool.

2. The eggs: Flatten the clove of garlic and peel it. Place the garlic in the bottom of a mixing bowl, and using the tines of a fork, mash it to a paste. Rub the leaves from the sprig of thyme, and add them to the garlic with the freshly chopped basil and parsley.

Break the eggs into the bowl of garlic and herbs, and add salt and freshly ground pepper. Beat the eggs with a fork, then add the cooled cooked tomato and mix well.

COOKING THE OMELETTE:

In a well-seasoned 10-inch omelette pan or skillet, heat the remaining 2 tablespoons of olive oil until almost smoking. Then pour in the beaten eggs, and using a fork, stir them with a circular motion.

When the eggs begin to hold together, yet are still creamy, stop stirring and let them continue to cook 1 minute or longer, so that the bottom of the omelette has an opportunity to brown slightly.

Then slide a spatula around the edge of the omelette—to make sure that it doesn't stick—and place an inverted serving plate over the pan. Quickly reverse the eggs onto the plate. The surface of a golden omelette will appear.

This omelette can be served hot, warm, or cold, with tiny black Niçoise olives.

Omelette aux rouelles de courgettes
ZUCCHINI OMELETTE

To serve 2:

>   10 ounces small, firm, unblemished zucchini (*about 3 ounces each*)
>   6 tablespoons olive oil, in all
>   5 eggs
>   Coarse salt
>   Freshly ground white pepper
>   1 teaspoon finely chopped fresh basil
>   1 tablespoon finely chopped fresh parsley

PREPARATION:

1. The zucchini: Scrub the zucchini and dry them with a towel. Then trim off each end. Do not peel them. Using a *mandoline* or other slicing device, cut the zucchini into rounds as thin as possible.

Heat 4 tablespoons of the olive oil in a 9-inch omelette pan or skillet, and when it begins to smoke, drop in the slices of zucchini, all at once. Sauté them over high heat, tossing continuously, until they are wilted but still crunchy to the bite. Then drain the zucchini in a colander or coarse sieve.

2. The eggs: Break the eggs into a bowl and season with salt and freshly ground pepper. Then add the freshly chopped basil and parsley, and beat the eggs well with a fork.

COOKING THE OMELETTE:

Using a paper towel, wipe clean the skillet used to sauté the zucchini, and add the remaining 2 tablespoons of fresh olive oil. Heat the oil gently, then return the drained slices of zucchini to the pan. Sprinkle lightly with salt, and when the zucchini is sufficiently hot, pour the beaten eggs over the zucchini.

Using a fork, stir the eggs into the zucchini with a circular motion. As the eggs begin to hold, lower the heat and stir carefully—but less frequently, to avoid disturbing the crust which will begin to form underneath the eggs.

When you are ready to serve the omelette, slide a spatula around the edge of the eggs to make sure that they do not stick. Then place an inverted serving plate over the pan and quickly reverse the omelette onto it. The golden brown side will appear on top.

Serve the omelette hot, warm, or cold, with a *garniture* of small black Niçoise olives, and brushed lightly with olive oil.

This is Provence on your plate.

Oeufs brouillés aux filets d'anchois
SCRAMBLED EGGS WITH ANCHOVIES

To serve 2 or 3:
    6 eggs
    12 green olives, pitted
    10 anchovy fillets (*one 2-ounce tin, drained*)
    4 tablespoons butter

Coarse salt (*optional*)
Freshly ground white pepper
2 thick slices white bread (*Cut your slices from a round loaf of French bread; do not use sandwich bread. Ed.*)

PREPARATION:

1. The eggs: Break the eggs into a bowl. Beat them well, but do not add salt.
2. The olives: In a small saucepan, bring ½ quart of water to a boil. Drop in the olives, and as soon as the water returns to a boil, remove the saucepan from heat.
3. The anchovies: Cut 6 of the anchovies in half lengthwise. Carefully set them aside on a plate without breaking them.

COOKING:

Over low heat, melt 2 tablespoons of the butter in a 2-quart casserole. Add the 4 remaining anchovies and stir them with a wooden spoon until dissolved.

Pour the beaten eggs into the casserole and cook, stirring continuously, until they hold together but are still light and creamy.

During the last moments of cooking the eggs, toast the 2 slices of bread.

Off heat, add a pinch of salt to the eggs (*depending on the saltiness of the anchovies, this may not be necessary; Ed.*), and a few good turns of the pepper mill. Then, using a wooden spoon, incorporate the remaining 2 tablespoons of butter, cut into tiny pieces.

Working quickly, divide the eggs between two warm plates and make a crosshatch over them with the long thin halves of anchovies. Scatter the olives, well-drained, over all.

Cut each slice of toasted bread into 4 long fingers (*mouillettes*) and compose them to frame the eggs. Serve at once.

Oeufs au plat avec la giclée de vinaigre de vin
FRIED EGGS WITH WINE VINEGAR

To serve 1: (*This recipe can serve any number of persons; however, each portion must be prepared individually. Ed.*)

    4 teaspoons fine salt
    2 extra-large fresh eggs, preferably with brown shells (or 3 eggs, if you like them as much as I do)
    1 tablespoon butter
    Coarse salt
    Freshly ground pepper
    2 tablespoons red-wine vinegar

PREPARATION:

Clean a 7-inch skillet by scrubbing it with 4 teaspoons fine salt. Then wipe the skillet thoroughly, to make sure that no trace of salt remains.

Depending upon your appetite, break 2 or 3 eggs into a small bowl.

Heat the butter in the skillet, and as soon as it begins to color, carefully slide in the eggs. Be sure that the yolks stay well separated from the whites. As the eggs cook, pierce with the point of a knife any blisters that chance to form. Do not worry if the edges of the whites crisp and curl. Season with a pinch of coarse salt and a good turn of the pepper mill.

When the eggs are cooked to your taste, slide them out of the pan onto a hot plate. Immediately add 2 tablespoons of wine vinegar to the pan, and as soon as the vinegar is reduced to 1 tablespoon, pour it over the eggs. Clean the pan with a towel and you are ready to begin again.

Here is a recipe of great controversy! For some, the butter must stay white; for others, the whites of the eggs must cook separately, then be joined by the yolks to finish cooking on top of them (salt the whites first, so as not to mar the egg yolks).

Surely all these notions have a reason to be, but I am giving you the recipe as I prepare it for myself and my friends. And do you know that among the *gourmandises*, fried eggs are the most tempting? How many times after midnight I have had a longing to fix myself three fried eggs! At this moment, I find myself with friends and customers who have dined but continue the evening with a glass of brandy. The simple mention of my desire for fried eggs makes them all rally 100 percent. I know of few dishes which are able to do that.

Les sauces

SAUCES

Yes, it is true, one can judge a chef by his sauces. Because it is in a sauce that he reveals himself as a man, a poet, an artist—in brief, a chef. In addition, on any given day his sauce is an expression of a moment, a mood, a state of mind. A mere nothing is sufficient to change the strictest recipe—a thought that occurs, a remembrance of a flower, or of a woman, the bouquet of a wine, the fragrance of a fruit, or of a truffle, or an herb. . . . In the long run, only a happy chef makes a good sauce.

Here are some sauces. Great sauces? Unimportant. Essentially, isn't it rather that they should add a stroke of character, a note of cheer, a touch of personality—to a steak, a scallop, a chicken, or a fish?

Sauce grelette à la tomate fraîche
COLD FRESH TOMATO SAUCE

To serve 4:

> 4 ripe tomatoes, about 4 ounces each
> Coarse salt
> 3 heaping tablespoons *crème fraîche (or in this instance, you can substitute commercial sour cream; Ed.)*
> 1 rounded teaspoon extra-strong Dijon mustard (*moutarde forte de Dijon*)
> 2 tablespoons wine vinegar
> 1 teaspoon cognac
> A good pinch (*about ⅛ teaspoon*) cayenne pepper, or a few drops Tabasco
> 1 tablespoon finely chopped chervil
> 1 tablespoon finely chopped parsley
> 10 fresh tarragon leaves, chopped (or if necessary, substitute 15 leaves of tarragon preserved in white wine or vinegar)

PREPARATION OF THE TOMATOES:

Drop the tomatoes into 2 or 3 quarts rapidly boiling water, count to 10, then plunge them into cold water. This will make the tomatoes easy to peel. Peel the tomatoes, removing the core, then cut them in half crosswise and squeeze out the seeds and water.

Cut 3 of the 8 tomato halves into ½-inch pieces and drop them into a coarse sieve placed over a bowl. Salt the tomatoes lightly, toss briefly, and let them stand about 30 minutes to give off the maximum of water possible.

Chop the remaining 5 tomato halves until reduced to a purée, and sprinkle lightly with salt. Transfer the tomatoes to a fine sieve placed over a bowl, to drain.

PREPARATION OF THE SAUCE:

Put the *crème fraîche* into a bowl. Then, using a wire whisk, blend in the mustard, vinegar, and cognac. Add salt, and a pinch of cayenne or 2 or 3 drops of Tabasco, and mix together until the texture is smooth and creamy. Do not let it separate.

73

Using a wooden spoon, stir in the finely chopped tomato and the chopped chervil, parsley, and tarragon. When they are completely incorporated, add the small, well-drained pieces of tomato. Taste for seasoning.

Chill the sauce until cold and serve in a sauceboat. For fish, shellfish, salads, or vegetables.

About 20 years ago, I was looking for a sauce to accompany a *pâté de sole en croûte*. It had been easy enough to arrive at this combination of ingredients, in order to obtain a sauce that was not too assertive but that had a freshness of taste. However, it remained to name the sauce, which tended to be tart. *Aigrelette* . . . ? Well, why not? But the word (*meaning sour or tart*) seemed not to have sufficient gracefulness for the delicacy of the sauce. So it remained for me to cut off the aggressive part of the word. Thus it was baptized *la sauce grelette*.

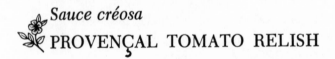

Sauce créosa
PROVENÇAL TOMATO RELISH

This is an excellent sauce, which one eats a little like a salad with grilled or roasted meats, and with all kinds of barbecue—even fish.

To serve 8 to 10: (It is difficult to make this sauce for fewer than 8 persons, but it has the advantage that it can be kept for several days and improves with age.)

   1 pound tomatoes
   1 cucumber, about 7 ounces
   1 sweet red pepper, about 5 ounces
   1 sweet white onion, about 7 ounces
   4 ounces (*⅔ cup, chopped*) small tart *cornichons* preserved in vinegar

4 ounces (*6 tablespoons, drained*) capers
1 teaspoon chopped fresh tarragon
1 large bunch parsley, chopped
4 tablespoons Dijon mustard
⅞ cup olive oil
3 tablespoons wine vinegar
Coarse salt
Freshly ground pepper

PREPARATION:

Have a stoneware or porcelain tureen ready to receive the ingredients.

1. The tomatoes: Remove the core, then cut them in half crosswise and press them gently to squeeze out the seeds. Cut the tomatoes into fine dice and place them in the tureen.

2. The cucumber: Peel the cucumber, cut it in half lengthwise, and using a teaspoon, scrape out the seeds. Then cut the cucumber into small dice and add it to the tomatoes.

3. The sweet pepper: Cut the pepper in half and remove the core, seeds, and any white membrane. Chop it into tiny pieces, like the cucumber dice, and add it to the tureen.

4. The onion: Peel the onion, chop it coarsely, and add to the rest of the vegetables.

5. The *cornichons*: Drain the *cornichons* and cut them into the same small dice as the other vegetables.

Add the *cornichons* to the tureen with the drained capers and chopped tarragon and parsley.

Using a wooden spoon, stir in the mustard, olive oil, and wine vinegar. Season liberally with coarse salt and freshly ground pepper.

Cover the tureen and keep it in a cool place, but not the refrigerator.

Do not serve this sauce any sooner than 24 hours after you have prepared it, as the ingredients must have time to steep together.

NOTE: *If the weather makes it absolutely necessary to use the refrigerator (it can happen in summer), take the sauce out of the refrigerator at least 1 hour before serving. Ed.*

I discovered this preparation in South America, where it is served communally on every table. However, their way of preparing it is simpler. It is generally composed of tomato, onion, and pepper, bathed in distilled vinegar, and often given a strong boost of hot pepper.

Sauce cressonnette
WATERCRESS SAUCE

This sauce may be served as an accompaniment to cold white meats, fish, shellfish, and hot or cold poached vegetables.

To serve 6:

> 2 bunches watercress, about 12 ounces each
> Salt
> 1 egg yolk
> 1 teaspoon extra-strong Dijon mustard (*moutarde forte de Dijon*)
> 1 small juicy lemon
> 7/8 cup olive oil
> 1/2 cup heavy cream
> Cayenne pepper

PREPARATION OF THE WATERCRESS:

Bring 2 quarts of salted water to a boil. Drop in the watercress, count to 10, drain, and quickly plunge it into cold water. When the watercress has chilled, drain again in a sieve or colander.

Detach 50 leaves and set them aside in a bowl of cold water. Press the rest of the watercress between your hands to extract as much moisture as possible. Then reduce it to a fine purée in a food processor or blender. The paste may be a little dry. If this is the case, add 3 or 4 tablespoons of olive oil. If the purée contains any fibers, pass it through a fine sieve.

Keep the purée in the refrigerator until ready to use.

PREPARATION OF THE MAYONNAISE:

To begin with, some simple advice:

1. For truly successful mayonnaise, none of the ingredients should be cold—not even the bowl you make it in.

2. If you add the oil too fast, then accelerate the movement of the whisk and add a scant teaspoon of warm water.

So, in order to prepare mayonnaise, it is sufficient to place in a bowl: 1 egg yolk, 1 teaspoon strong mustard, a pinch of salt, and the juice of ½ lemon.

Mix the ingredients, then forget about them for 5 minutes.

In a slow steady stream, add about 13 tablespoons of olive oil, stirring continuously until each addition of oil is well incorporated. Then add the juice from the other half of the lemon, and that's it!

TO FINISH THE SAUCE:

Add the watercress purée to the mayonnaise.

In a small bowl, beat ½ cup heavy cream until thick. Add a pinch of salt.

Whisk the mayonnaise and cream together, then drain the watercress leaves and dry them with a towel. Using a wooden spoon, fold them into the mayonnaise cream. Taste for salt and add a pinch of cayenne.

Refrigerate the sauce and serve cold from a sauceboat.

This lightly aromatic sauce is a perfect accompaniment to summer dishes such as cold roasted or poached chicken, string beans, small new potatoes, zucchini, and other vegetables.

It is equally delicious with cold or hot fish.

Apropos of mayonnaise, I could write a whole chapter on the foolishnesses and superstitions that I have heard on this subject—along the likes of: "For a successful mayonnaise, one must only use a wooden spoon . . . One must not breathe anywhere near the bowl (this can't be easy!) . . . One must never change the direction of stirring . . . In summer, one must make mayonnaise in the cellar, or in a cold

place (if one lives in an apartment, can one shut himself in the refrigerator?) . . ." and even that "certain phases of the moon are disas-
trous to mayonnaise!"

Is this sauce so capricious? Nonsense! Nothing is more simple to
make than mayonnaise if you bear in mind my little bits of advice.

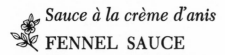

Sauce à la crème d'anis
FENNEL SAUCE

This sauce is to be served with hot or cold fish or shellfish.

To serve 6:

    1 small fennel bulb, about 4 ounces
    Salt
    2 hard-cooked eggs
    1 rounded teaspoon Dijon mustard
    Freshly ground white pepper
    1 small juicy lemon
    ⅓ cup olive oil
    ¼ cup heavy cream
    1 teaspoon *Pastis (or you can substitute another anise-flavored*
        apéritif, such as Ricard or Pernod; Ed.)

PREPARATION:

1. The fennel: Clean the fennel bulb and cut it into quarters. (*If it
is large, pull away outer stalks until only a 4-ounce heart remains. Ed.*)

Bring 1 quart of salted water to a boil, add the fennel, and cook
until tender. (This will take about 20 minutes.) When the fennel is
done, drain, and press it dry with a towel to extract all the moisture
possible.

2. The sauce: Pass the 2 hard-cooked eggs, with the fennel,
through a food mill placed over a 2-quart bowl. Be sure to scrape off
the purée adhering to the underside of the food mill.

To this purée add the mustard, a pinch of salt, 2 or 3 turns of the pepper mill, and the juice of ½ lemon. Mix well with a wire whisk and beat the sauce continuously, as for mayonnaise, while slowly incorporating the oil in a fine steady stream.

Pour the heavy cream into a small bowl with the *Pastis*. Whisk vigorously until the cream is very thick. (*NOTE: I found it more satisfactory to add the* Pastis *after the cream had begun to thicken. Added earlier, it delays this operation. Ed.*)

Then scrape the sauce into a large bowl, and fold in the whipped cream. Taste for seasoning. Add a pinch of salt and pepper and perhaps, depending on your taste, a little more lemon juice.

There you have a very pleasing sauce with an aroma of the Midi.

Beurre fondu BUTTER SAUCE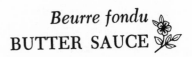

This sauce is served with fish, poached shellfish, and roasted or grilled meats. It also goes very well with vegetables, such as artichokes, asparagus, the whites of leeks, broccoli, and so on.

To serve 2 or 4 (*depending on how the sauce is to be used; Ed.*):

5 tablespoons water
Coarse salt
8 tablespoons (*1 stick*) cold butter, cut into tiny pieces
½ lemon (optional)

PREPARATION:

In a small saucepan, heat the water with a pinch of salt. When the liquid reaches a rapid boil, add half the butter, and stir with a wire whisk until it is thoroughly incorporated. Then, off heat, whisk the remaining pieces of butter into the sauce, one at a time.

If you wish, you can stir the juice of ½ lemon (or less, depending on your own taste) into the thickened butter sauce.

Serve immediately in a hot sauceboat.

Beurre blanc
FOAMY WHITE BUTTER SAUCE

Here is one of the great subjects of controversy and discussion. For a long time, persons have depicted this unfortunate sauce as domain reserved for the great specialists—so that many cookbooks don't dare to mention it, for fear they will be attacked by indignant critics.

Probably one hundred recipes exist, all culminating in practically the same result. Each of these recipes boasts that it is the true one. It is not so much the most authentic that I offer you (it risks being proclaimed a heresy by many). Nonetheless, it has the advantage of being simple and, for my part, I find it very good. Judge for yourself!

To serve 2 or 4 (*depending on how the sauce is to be used; Ed.*):

This is a delicate sauce to accompany poached fish and shellfish, asparagus, artichokes, leeks, lambs' or calves' brains . . . in fact, most foods cooked in water or a *court-bouillon*.

3 tablespoons white-wine vinegar
5 tablespoons dry white wine
1 teaspoon chopped shallot
1 tablespoon *crème fraîche* (*or substitute heavy cream; Ed.*)
5 tablespoons cold butter, cut into tiny pieces
Coarse salt
Freshly ground white pepper

PREPARATION:

Place the vinegar, white wine, and chopped shallot in a small heavy saucepan. Over medium heat, reduce the liquid to 2 tablespoons.

Add the *crème fraîche*, and as soon as it comes to a boil, reduce the heat to as low as possible.

Then whisk in the butter, a little at a time. When the butter is incorporated, add a dash of salt and freshly ground pepper, and pour the sauce through a fine sieve into a hot sauceboat.

Tell me, therefore, where do you see the problem—perhaps it is from the unnecessary complications that someone has inflicted upon you from time to time? And which were of no help at all!

In principle, *beurre blanc* should be used as soon as it has been prepared. However, if you are obliged to prepare the sauce in advance, you can reheat it very gently while beating continuously with a wire whisk.

Coulis frais de tomate
COOKED FRESH TOMATO SAUCE

This sauce can be served as an accompaniment to baked fish, pasta, rice, poached vegetables (such as cauliflower, zucchini, fennel, white beans), poached lambs' or calves' brains, or sautéed veal scallops or chops.

To serve 4:

- 2 pounds ripe tomatoes (about 8 tomatoes, weighing 4 ounces each)
- 1 sweet white onion, about 7 ounces
- 4 tablespoons butter
- 1 *bouquet garni* (1 sprig fresh thyme, 1 bay leaf, 1 small stalk celery with leaves, and 4 sprigs parsley, tied together)
- 1 large clove garlic, flattened and peeled
- ¼ teaspoon sugar
- Coarse salt
- Freshly ground white pepper

PREPARATION:

Wipe the tomatoes and cut out the core. Then cut them in half crosswise and squeeze out the seeds and water. Cut each tomato into quarters and set them aside on a paper towel to drain.

Peel the onion, cut it into thin slices, and place in a casserole with 2 tablespoons water and 3 tablespoons of the butter. Cook the onion over low heat, covered, about 5 minutes or until soft. Stir occasionally with a wooden spoon and do not allow the onion to brown.

Off heat, stir in the tomatoes and let stand 5 minutes.

During this time, assemble the *bouquet garni* and add it to the casserole with the garlic, sugar, and a pinch of coarse salt.

Stirring continuously, cook the tomatoes, uncovered, 10 to 15 minutes. (At certain times of the year, tomatoes can be slightly dry. If this should be the case, add a few tablespoons of water.)

When the sauce has finished cooking, discard the *bouquet garni* and pass the sauce through a food mill, or better yet, purée it in a food processor or blender. Add a pinch of salt and freshly ground pepper. Reheat and serve.

If you like the perfume of Provence, add several fresh basil leaves, finely shredded, and 2 tablespoons olive oil. A genuine treat!

NOTE: *This is not a thick sauce. If you wish, you can reduce it further over medium to low heat. Ed.*

I give three sauces to accompany panfried meats, such as a single rib of beef, sirloin steak, flank steak, skirt steak, or rump steak.

These sauces must be prepared in the pan used to cook the meat.

Sauce marchand de vin
WINE SAUCE FOR BEEF

To serve 4: (*The ingredients for this sauce may be halved to serve 2 persons. Ed.*)

- 8 tablespoons butter
- 4 tablespoons finely chopped onion
- 1 cup red wine
- 1 large clove garlic, peeled and crushed
- 1 large sprig fresh thyme (*or substitute ½ teaspoon dried thyme; Ed.*)
- 1 teaspoon Dijon mustard
- Freshly ground pepper
- Salt (optional)

PREPARATION:

After cooking the meat, remove it from the pan and keep warm. Pour off the fat, but do not wash the pan. The particles of caramelized meat juices adhering to the pan will contribute to the success of your sauce.

Add 1 tablespoon of the butter and the chopped onion to the hot pan. Sauté the onion over low heat for about 2 or 3 minutes, then pour in the red wine. Add the garlic and thyme, raise the heat, and cook until the wine is reduced by half. Remove the pan from heat and stir in the remaining butter, cut into tiny pieces, followed by the mustard. Add freshly ground pepper and taste for seasoning. The sauce should already be salty enough.

TO SERVE:

Arrange the meat on hot plates. Stir into the sauce any juices that have accumulated during the meat's repose. Strain the sauce through a fine sieve, pressing down on the onion.

Nap the meat with the sauce and serve at once.

You will have a great sauce with very little effort.

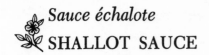

Sauce échalote
SHALLOT SAUCE

I prefer this sauce with a skirt steak or flank steak. These are not the cuts of meat that are especially esteemed, as are the *filet*, sirloin, or rump steak, which are held to be the choice of connoisseurs of meat. But often enough they are the most desirable juicy pieces of meat that the butchers and cooks save for their staffs. I counsel you to try them.

To serve 2 or 4:

NOTE: *The number of persons this sauce will serve depends on the size of your piece of meat. If you use larger but thinner cuts of beef— such as flank steak or skirt steak, the sauce will serve only 2. However, if you use a thick piece of beef of smaller dimension, the sauce will be sufficient for 4 persons. Ed.*

    4 tablespoons butter
    3 ounces finely chopped shallots (*about ½ cup*)
    4 tablespoons wine vinegar
    Coarse salt
    Freshly ground pepper
    1 small bouquet of parsley, chopped (*about 4 tablespoons*)

PREPARATION:

Remove the hot cooked meat from the skillet and add the butter. When it foams, add the chopped shallots, and over medium to low heat, cook 2 minutes.

Pour in the vinegar, and stirring continuously with a wooden spoon, cook until reduced by half. Add salt and a generous turn of the pepper mill. Then stir in the chopped parsley and any juices that have accumulated from the cooked meat.

TO SERVE:

Arrange the meat on hot plates and cover it with the shallot sauce.

Sauce fondue d'anchois
ANCHOVY SAUCE

To serve 2 or 4:

    4 tablespoons butter
    4 anchovy fillets
    ½ lemon
    2 tablespoons freshly chopped parsley
    Freshly ground pepper

PREPARATION:

Over low heat, melt the butter in a small saucepan or skillet. Add the anchovies, crushing them with a fork, and when they are dissolved, add the juice of ½ lemon. Stir in the parsley and add a generous turn of the pepper mill.

The moment the sauce is blended, spoon it over each piece of meat and serve.

You can accompany this dish with a mixed salad, but for myself, I most appreciate it with a flank steak, cooked very rare, and sandwiched between two pieces of a long thin loaf of French bread (*pain-baguette*).

In this instance, the bread is cut in half lengthwise, lightly toasted under the broiler grill, and then brushed with the anchovy sauce.

The bread or the meat—I don't know which one tastes better!

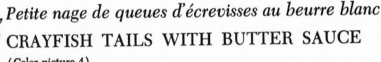

Les crustacés & les coquillages

SHELLFISH

Petite nage de queues d'écrevisses au beurre blanc
CRAYFISH TAILS WITH BUTTER SAUCE
(Color picture 4)

To serve 2:
    2¼ pounds live crayfish (*see Note*)
    Coarse salt

Vegetable *court-bouillon*:
    1 carrot, thinly sliced
    1 leek (white part only), thinly sliced
    1 stalk celery, thinly sliced
    2 shallots, thinly sliced
    1 sweet white onion, thinly sliced
    1 teaspoon butter
    Coarse salt
    ½ bottle (about 1⅝ cups) dry white wine

Bouquet garni and spices, tied together in a cheesecloth bag:
    1 bay leaf
    1 stalk fennel

86

10 peppercorns
1 large sprig fresh thyme (*or substitute ½ teaspoon dried thyme; Ed.*)

The butter sauce (*le beurre blanc*):
2 shallots, coarsely chopped
6 tablespoons dry white wine
3 tablespoons white wine vinegar
8 tablespoons (*1 stick*) cold butter, cut into 8 pieces
Coarse salt
Freshly ground white pepper

Herb *garniture* (strip the leaves from the stems of the herbs):
2 large branches of fresh young flat-leafed parsley
1 small bouquet fresh young chervil
8 large fresh tarragon leaves

PREPARATION OF THE CRAYFISH:

NOTE: *In areas of the United States where crayfish are unobtainable, substitute ¾ pound large uncooked shrimp. Ed.*

It is indispensable that the crayfish be live. A dead crayfish voids itself very quickly and becomes inedible. You will generally find that crayfish raised commercially have been disgorged.

However, if you have the good luck to have wild crayfish, it is necessary, just before cooking, to "*châtrer.*" That is to say, remove the intestinal vein. In order to do this, hold the crayfish by the head with one hand, and with the other, grasp the center flipper of the tail between your thumb and index finger. Pull it quickly backward, while giving it a quarter of a turn. This procedure must be done immediately before cooking; otherwise the crayfish will expire rapidly.

For domesticated crayfish this operation is done as soon as possible after cooking.

TO COOK THE CRAYFISH:

Over high heat, bring 4 quarts of water to a boil with 2 tablespoons of coarse salt. When the water is boiling rapidly, plunge in the crayfish. Let the water return to a boil and cook the crayfish 4 minutes. (*If you are substituting shrimp, cook them 3 minutes without waiting for the water to return to a boil. Ed.)*

Drain the crayfish in a colander and rinse lightly with cold water. Clean them, if this has not already been done.

Remove the shells of the crayfish by crushing them between your thumb and index finger. Set the meat aside and reserve 2 of the heads.

PREPARATION OF THE VEGETABLE COURT-BOUILLON:

Place the slices of carrot, leek, celery, shallots, and onion together in a 4-quart casserole. Add the butter and 4 tablespoons of water. Sprinkle with coarse salt. Cover the casserole, and over low heat, stew the vegetables about 20 minutes to release their juices. (*Stir occasionally to make sure that they do not scorch. Ed.*)

Then pour the white wine over the vegetables and tuck the aromatic spice bag into the center of the casserole. Simmer the vegetables 15 to 20 minutes. Bear in mind that they must remain faintly crisp. Stir and check them frequently.

PREPARATION OF THE BUTTER SAUCE (*le beurre blanc*):

Place the 2 chopped shallots in a small heavy saucepan with the 6 tablespoons of dry white wine and the white wine vinegar.

Over high heat, reduce the wine and vinegar until no more than 2 tablespoons of liquid remain. If you have made the reduction too great, you can add a little of the *court-bouillon* from the vegetables.

Then remove the casserole from heat, and stirring continuously with a wire whisk, incorporate the pieces of butter, one at a time. The consistency must be that of a lightly thickened sauce. Season with a little coarse salt and freshly ground white pepper.

If for some reason the heat was too high or you have added the butter too quickly and the sauce shows signs of separating, it will suffice to pour 2 tablespoons of the vegetable *court-bouillon* into another small saucepan, and pouring the butter in a slow steady stream, whisk it into the broth until a creamy *liaison* is achieved.

If you wish to keep the *beurre blanc* hot, it is sufficient to arrange a newspaper on the bottom of a very large casserole and place the small saucepan containing the butter sauce within. Keep the 2 pans together over the lowest heat possible. This way the sauce will stay at a lukewarm temperature. It absolutely must avoid high heat!

TO FINISH THE CRAYFISH:

Bring the vegetable *court-bouillon* to a boil, then quickly stir in the crayfish, *beurre blanc,* and fresh herbs. Return the vegetables and crayfish to not-quite-a-simmer and taste for seasoning.

Divide the preparation between two warmed wide-rimmed soup bowls or deep plates, and decorate each with a crayfish head thrust spiritedly upright in their midst.

Gratin de belons au champagne
OYSTERS WITH CHAMPAGNE SAUCE

To serve 2: (*If you wish, the ingredients for this recipe can be doubled to serve 4 persons. Ed.*)

    12 oysters, heavy with their own seawater
    3 tablespoons champagne (*brut*)
    Freshly ground white pepper
    12 ounces fresh spinach
    Fine salt
    Coarse sea salt (*gros sel de mer*)
    ½ cup heavy cream
    1 egg yolk
    1 teaspoon butter
    Seaweed, kelp, or other marine algae, to make a bed for the oysters

PREPARATION:

1. The oysters: Open the oysters in the manner to which you are accustomed, then detach the delicate meat by slipping the point of a knife under the muscle securing it to the shell. Catch the oysters and their seawater in a bowl. Reserve the deeper portion of each shell.

Place the oysters in a small casserole with their juices, first strained through a fine sieve lined with cheesecloth. Add the champagne and a pinch of pepper (the oysters should be salty enough). Bring the liquid just to a simmer, then immediately remove the casserole from heat. Using a slotted spoon or skimmer, lift out the oysters and plunge them directly into a bowl of ice water to firm them. After 15 to 20 seconds, drain the oysters and set them aside on a plate.

Over medium heat, reduce the liquid remaining in the casserole to no more than 2 tablespoons.

2. The spinach: Strip off the stems and wash the leaves well in several changes of water. Drain, and place the spinach in a casserole containing a very small amount of boiling salted water. Cook the spinach about 3 minutes, uncovered. Then drain in a sieve, and refresh under cold running water. Drain again, pressing the leaves to extract all moisture possible.

Chop the spinach coarsely with a knife.

3. The reserved shells: Spread coarse sea salt over a shallow baking pan and arrange the shells white side up. (*The reason for the salt is to keep the shells balanced and safe from tipping. Ed.*) Place them in a low oven (about 325°F) for 5 minutes or until dry.

4. The sauce: Beat the cream with a wire whisk until thick and voluminous, but not completely stiff. Then add the egg yolk and mix until thoroughly combined.

Incorporate the cream-and-egg-yolk mixture into the champagne reduction and return the casserole to very low heat. Stirring constantly, warm the sauce until slightly thickened. (Take great care to be sure that the sauce does not even approach a boil, or it will separate.) At the moment the sauce has thickened, remove it from heat and taste for seasoning.

FINISHING THE OYSTERS:

Preheat the broiler to its maximum temperature.

During this time, reheat the spinach separately. Add a pinch of salt and freshly ground pepper, and stir in a teaspoon of butter.

Divide the spinach among the warm shells and top each with an oyster, followed by a dollop of sauce.

Pass the shells with their *garniture* under the preheated broiler grill just long enough for a golden skin to form.

Arrange the seaweed over two serving plates and divide the oysters between them. Serve very hot.

Coques ou bucardes au vin nature de Champagne
SHELLFISH IN CHAMPAGNE SAUCE

In this dish, cockles may be replaced by mussels or hard-shell clams. Both lend themselves well to this preparation. But whichever shellfish you choose, take care not to overcook it.

To serve 2:

2 quarts cockles, about 2 pounds
1 cup *vin nature de Champagne* (*use a dry white wine—such as* blanc de blancs, *made from Champagne grapes; Ed.*)
1 tablespoon finely chopped shallot
⅜ cup heavy cream
1 egg yolk
1½ tablespoons butter
1 heaping tablespoon chopped fresh chervil
1 heaping tablespoon chopped fresh parsley
Freshly ground white pepper
Coarse salt (*optional*)

PREPARATION:

Scrub the cockles thoroughly and pull off any little crabs or other undesirable squatters, which one often finds on these shellfish. Soak them in cold water, changing the water at least 4 times or until it remains clear. Then drain the shellfish in a colander.

91

COOKING:

Pour the wine into a large casserole. (Choose a size big enough to hold twice the actual volume of the shellfish.) Add the chopped shallot and bring the wine to a boil. Then cover the casserole and steam the shellfish only until they open. Stir occasionally, bringing those from the bottom of the casserole to the top, so that they do not stew in the cooking broth. This operation should take no more than 10 minutes.

When the shells have all opened, hold the cover of the casserole slightly ajar and pour off the cooking liquid. Pour the broth through a fine sieve lined with several thicknesses of cheesecloth, into a 1-quart measuring cup. Let the broth stand for a few minutes, so that any residue of sand will sink to the bottom of the cup, then transfer it to a saucepan. Take care to leave the residue in the bottom of the cup.

Place the saucepan over high heat and rapidly reduce the cooking broth until only about 3 tablespoons remain. Add 5 tablespoons of the cream and bring to a simmer.

Pour the rest of the cream into a small bowl, and using a wire whisk, mix it with the egg yolk until well combined. Off heat, add the cream-and-egg-yolk mixture to the saucepan with the broth and cream. Then return the saucepan to very low heat and stir continuously until the sauce is slightly thickened. Do not let it reach a simmer.

Mixing with the whisk, add the butter, cut into tiny pieces, a little at a time. Then add the chopped chervil and parsley and freshly ground pepper. Taste for seasoning. (*The reduced shellfish broth should have made the sauce sufficiently salty. Ed.*)

TO SERVE:

With the help of a skimmer or slotted spoon, lift the shellfish out of the casserole and divide them among two warmed deep plates or soup bowls. Do not scoop up any sand from the bottom of the casserole.

Pour the sauce over the shellfish and serve at once.

I recommend that you eat this dish with a spoon. And without fail, you must have a good half of a thin loaf of French bread to enjoy all the sauce. It is so good that you do not want to leave a drop on your plate. Do not forget, either, to have a bowl on the table to collect the empty shells.

Fricassée de homard à la crème de Sauternes
LOBSTER WITH SAUTERNES AND CREAM

To serve 2: (*If you wish, the ingredients for this recipe can be doubled to serve 4 persons. Ed.*)

2 small lively lobsters, about 1¼ pounds each
Coarse salt
2 tablespoons butter
2 tablespoons finely chopped carrot
1 tablespoon finely chopped shallot
2 tablespoons finely chopped celery
1 rounded teaspoon tomato paste
1 tablespoon cognac
⅓ cup Sauternes
1 small sprig (8 to 10 leaves) fresh tarragon (*or if necessary, substitute 10 tarragon leaves preserved in wine or vinegar, rinsed, or ½ teaspoon dried tarragon; Ed.*)
¾ cup heavy cream
Freshly ground white pepper
1 small bouquet fresh young chervil leaves, stems removed (*or substitute young parsley leaves; Ed.*)

PREPARATION OF THE LOBSTER:

1. Cooking: In a large casserole, bring 6 quarts of water to a boil with 2 tablespoons of coarse salt. When the water is boiling rapidly, plunge in the 2 live lobsters. Maintain the water at a vigorous boil for 15 minutes, then take the casserole from heat, and let the lobsters remain in their cooking water 5 minutes.

Then remove the lobsters and let cool 5 to 10 minutes.

2. Extracting the meat from the shell: Here, this becomes a little more complicated. Read the directions before beginning this task, then proceed with the work.

First, detach the large claws, twisting them off where the smaller joint is attached to the body. You can pull out the bonelike piece of cartilage at the same time. Break the shell of the large part of each claw by hitting it with the dull edge of a meat cleaver. Take care not to crush the lobster meat. Crack the shell only as much as is necessary to extract the meat in one piece. Do the same thing with the other parts of the claws. (*Very often, a poultry shears, or even small pruning shears, can simplify this task. Use them to cut directly through the shell, without damaging the meat. Ed.*)

Set the meat aside on one plate and reserve the pieces of empty shell on another.

Separate the tail from the body by giving it a good turn and a pull. Take care not to break it.

Using a kitchen scissors, extract the tail meat in one piece, first carefully cutting through the underside of the tail shell from top to bottom. You should be able to lift out the entire piece of tail meat without difficulty. Set it aside with the meat from the claws. Reserve the empty shell.

Detach all the small legs where they join the body. Set 8 of the legs aside on a separate plate with 1 of the 2 empty body shells.

Put the remaining 8 legs together with the rest of the empty shells and the other body shell.

You now have 3 plates:

1. A plate with the meat from the claws and tails.
2. A plate with 8 legs and 1 undamaged body shell.
3. A plate with the empty pieces of shell, body cartilage, joints, remaining legs, and the other body shell.

TO PREPARE THE SAUCE:

Using a meat cleaver, coarsely chop all the shells, legs, body shell, etc. that were on the third plate into smaller, more manageable pieces.

Melt the butter in a 3-quart casserole with the finely chopped carrot, shallot, and celery. Over medium heat, cook this *mirepoix* until soft and lightly colored.

Then, using a wooden spoon, blend in the tomato paste. Add all the broken pieces of shell, turning them in the casserole for 3 or 4 minutes.

Sprinkle the shells with warmed cognac and ignite. When the flames subside, pour the Sauternes over the shells and simmer the liquid until reduced by half. Add the tarragon and cream. Over medium heat, simmer the sauce about 5 minutes, uncovered, stirring frequently. Then cover and simmer 10 minutes longer.

Season the sauce lightly with salt, then pass it through a fine sieve into a clean casserole. Press down hard on the shells in order to extract all the cream and the essence of the lobster and *mirepoix*.

Taste for seasoning, adding a good pinch of freshly ground pepper and, if necessary, salt.

TO SERVE:

At the moment you are ready to serve, return the morsels of lobster to the sauce, and bring briefly to a simmer. Then sprinkle with delicate young chervil leaves, and divide the lobster and sauce between two warmed deep plates.

With a scissors, cut the reserved body shell in half lengthwise, and decorate each plate with half a shell and 4 small legs, arranged amusingly.

Why the marriage of lobster to Sauternes and cream? Simply because the 3 ingredients are of the same intensity in taste. The meat of the lobster is so sweet to the tongue that it is a pity to overwhelm it under too strong a sauce. The essential culinary matter is, above all, to respect the personality of the product that one is cooking.

Homard en civet de vieux Bourgogne
LOBSTER SIMMERED IN RED WINE

To serve 2: (*If you wish, the ingredients for this recipe can be increased to serve 4 persons. Ed.*)

    1 live lobster, about 2½ pounds, or 2 smaller lobsters
    Coarse salt
    Freshly ground pepper
    2 tablespoons olive oil
    8 tablespoons butter, in all

2 shallots, finely chopped (preferably gray shallots, *échalotes grises*)

1 small carrot, finely chopped

¼ cup cognac, warmed

¾ bottle (2¼ cups) Burgundy, at least 4 years old (preferably a Pommard)

Bouquet garni (2 sprigs parsley, 1 small stalk celery, 1 small bay leaf, 1 sprig fresh thyme, tied together)

8 small white onions

¼ teaspoon powdered sugar

10 small white mushrooms

1 tablespoon flour

1 teaspoon freshly chopped parsley

PREPARATION OF THE LOBSTER:

Use a large heavy chopping knife or meat cleaver (*aided by a mallet if necessary; Ed.*) to sever the lobster tail from the body or head. Then split the body in half lengthwise, and remove the tomalley and—if the lobster is female—the roe (coral). Set them aside. Discard the small dark sac found in the front end of the head. Twist off the claws and cut the tail in half crosswise.

Sprinkle the pieces of lobster with salt and pepper.

TO COOK THE LOBSTER:

NOTE: *The cooking time will vary, depending on the size of the lobster you have chosen. But when planning your meal, be sure to allow enough time for the job of extracting the lobster meat from the shell. Ed.*

Heat the olive oil in a large heavy casserole. When the oil begins to smoke, add the pieces of lobster and cook, turning them often, until the shells are bright red on all sides. Then remove the lobster from the casserole and set aside. (*If necessary, sauté the pieces in several batches, adding more oil as needed. Ed.*)

Without washing the casserole, add 2 tablespoons of the butter, and over low heat, cook the *mirepoix* of shallots and carrot, covered, until soft but not browned. Stir frequently.

Return the lobster to the casserole, pour the warmed cognac over it, and ignite. Cook, stirring constantly, until the flames extinguish themselves. Then add the red wine and *bouquet garni*.

Sprinkle lightly with salt and freshly ground pepper, cover the casserole, and simmer over low heat for 15 to 20 minutes, depending on the size of the lobster. Turn and baste the pieces from time to time.

PREPARE THE VEGETABLE GARNITURE:

1. The onions: Place the onions in a small casserole just large enough to hold them in 1 layer, with 3 tablespoons of water, 1 tablespoon of the butter, and the powdered sugar. Over medium heat, cook the onions, turning them frequently, until they are slightly caramelized. Take care not to let them burn. (*Allow about 10 minutes for this. Ed.*) When the onions have finished cooking, cover the casserole and set aside.

2. The mushrooms: Sauté the mushrooms in 1 tablespoon of the butter until lightly browned. Cover and set aside.

TO FINISH THE LOBSTER AND PREPARE THE SAUCE:

1. Place the remaining 4 tablespoons of butter, softened, in a small bowl with the flour, tomalley, and if any, the coral. Use a knife and fork to cream them together until well blended. This will serve as a *liaison* for the sauce.

2. Carefully extract the meat from the tail and claws of the lobster. Remove the intestinal vein from the tail. Then cut the tail meat into medallions and the claw meat into pieces of uniform size. Cover the meat to keep warm.

3. While you are preparing the lobster meat, boil down the wine-broth remaining in the casserole until reduced by half.

4. Using a wire whisk, incorporate the butter-tomalley *liaison* into the wine reduction. Taste for salt and add a few good turns of the pepper mill.

With the help of a wooden spoon, press the sauce through a fine sieve into a clean saucepan. Then reheat the sauce gently without allowing it to reach a simmer.

TO SERVE:

Arrange the lobster meat on warmed deep plates and strew the hot vegetable *garniture* over all. Pour the sauce over the lobster, sprinkle with a little chopped parsley, and serve very hot.

This is a delicate dish, but it has a rustic aspect and should be accompanied by plain, perfectly cooked noodles, prepared at the last moment, drained, and seasoned with fresh butter.

 Langouste au poivre rose

SPINY LOBSTER WITH PAPRIKA CREAM SAUCE

To serve 2:

   2 live spiny lobsters, about 1¼ pounds each, or one 2¼-pound
      spiny lobster (*see Notes*)
   2½ tablespoons butter
   1 tablespoon chopped shallot
   1 teaspoon sweet Hungarian paprika
   1 rounded teaspoon tomato paste
   3 tablespoons cognac, warmed
   ⅓ cup dry white wine
   1 sprig fresh tarragon (*or substitute 1 teaspoon dried tarragon
      leaves; Ed.*)
   ¾ cup heavy cream
   Freshly ground white pepper
   Coarse salt (optional)
   2 tablespoons coarsely chopped fresh young chervil leaves (*or
      substitute fresh parsley; Ed.*)

The small spiny lobsters are more tender than large ones. If possible, it is better to buy 2 lobsters of smaller size. Choose the red variety called *royales*, or red Atlantic lobsters are also very good.

   In any case, pick the most lively—because if a lobster is dead, it gives up all its vital juices and the meat loses its substance.

98

If you must buy your lobster in advance, fold the tail of the crustacean under the body, then roll it compactly in newspaper. Keep it in the vegetable drawer of your refrigerator. Be careful—too cold a temperature will kill it.

NOTE: *Spiny lobsters* (langouste)—*also called rock lobsters commercially—are found live only in certain parts of the United States, especially the West Coast, although they are sold frozen (the tail section) almost everywhere.*

If you live on the East Coast of the United States—where live North Atlantic lobsters are readily available—do not hesitate to use live East Coast lobster rather than frozen spiny lobster tails. Ed.

PREPARATION OF THE LOBSTER:

Lay the lobster on your chopping board, holding it flat. Thrust the point of a large heavy knife or cleaver between the two horns at the top of the head. Then press down hard on the rest of the blade, splitting the lobster in half lengthwise down the back. (*I find it helpful, after positioning the blade, to tap it firmly with a mallet. Ed.*)

If this operation is too painful for you, bring 4 or 5 quarts of salted water to a rapid boil, plunge in the lobster, and let boil vigorously for 5 minutes. Then remove the lobster and proceed to split it as directed. In either case, do not kill the lobster until you are ready to cook it. (*Note: If you are using East Coast lobsters, you may prefer to detach the claws, making the lobster more manageable. Ed.*)

COOKING:

Over very low heat, melt the butter in a large 12- to 14-inch skillet and add the chopped shallot. When the shallot has softened slightly, add the sweet paprika and mix well with a wooden spoon, dissolving any lumps. Then stir in the tomato paste.

Place the split lobsters, flesh side down, in the sauce and sear them briefly over medium heat. Add the warmed cognac and ignite. This will seal their juices. When the flames subside, pour on the white wine, add a sprig of tarragon, and turn the lobsters so that the exposed flesh is up. Baste with the cooking juices.

Cover the casserole and cook the lobsters over low heat. Allow 20 minutes cooking time for 1¼-pound lobsters and 30 minutes for a 2¼-pound lobster.

Watch that the lobsters and sauce do not cook too rapidly. Baste occasionally, and if the cooking liquid should reduce too fast, add 1 or 2 tablespoons of water.

TO FINISH THE LOBSTER AND THE SAUCE:

When the lobsters are cooked, remove them from the skillet, separate the tail sections from the bodies, and arrange them in two deep plates. Cover the tails to keep warm.

NOTE: *If you are using East Coast lobsters, discard the bodies, but save the small legs to arrange attractively with the claws in a composition around the tails. Ed.*

Return the skillet to medium heat and reduce the cooking liquid until no more than 1 or 2 tablespoons remain. Then add the heavy cream, and boil about 5 minutes or until the cream thickens. Stir continuously with a wooden spoon.

Add a generous turn of the pepper mill and taste for seasoning. Depending on the lobster, add a pinch of salt if necessary.

Then pass the sauce through a fine sieve into a small casserole or saucepan. Stir in the freshly chopped chervil and nap the lobsters with sauce.

Serve at once with plain rice.

Langouste grillée au beurre de basilic
SPINY LOBSTER GRILLED WITH BASIL BUTTER

To serve 2:

2 live spiny lobsters, about 1 pound each, or one 2¼-pound spiny
   lobster
20 fresh basil leaves, chopped
8 tablespoons (*1 stick*) butter, softened
Coarse salt
Freshly ground pepper, preferably white
2 tablespoons olive oil

See the preceding recipe for choosing and storing your lobsters.

PREPARATION:

Preheat the broiler.

1. The butter: In a saucepan, combine 20 freshly chopped basil
leaves with the softened butter. Then, over very low heat, melt the
butter without letting it reach a simmer. Stir constantly to keep the
butter thick and creamy. Set aside.

2. The lobster: Lay the lobster on your cutting board. Holding it
flat, force the point of a large heavy knife or cleaver between the two
horns at the top of the head. Then press down hard on the rest of the
blade, dividing the lobster in half lengthwise down the back. (*I find it
helpful, after positioning the blade, to tap it firmly with a mallet. Ed.*)

If this operation is too painful for you, bring 4 or 5 quarts of salted
water to a boil, plunge in the lobster, and let boil rapidly for 5 minutes. Then remove the lobster and proceed to split it as I have just
described.

In either case, do not kill the lobster until you are ready to grill it.

GRILLING THE LOBSTER:

Arrange the lobster halves in a shallow roasting pan and sprinkle
lightly with coarse salt and freshly ground pepper. Brush them with

olive oil and pass them under the broiler unit with the flesh side up for 5 minutes. Then turn the halves and grill the shell side for another 5 minutes.

If you are barbecuing the lobsters, arrange them shell side down for the first 5 minutes, then turn them and grill flesh side down for 5 minutes.

Using either method, now turn the lobster halves flesh side up and brush the meat generously with the basil butter. Continue to baste the lobsters frequently with the butter until they are done. Small lobsters will take about 10 minutes longer to finish cooking and larger lobsters will need about 20 minutes.

TO SERVE:

Serve the lobster unaccompanied. The butter, with its basil fragrance, will enrich the lobster sufficiently.

Noix de Saint-Jacques aux poireaux
SEA SCALLOPS AND LEEKS IN CREAM

To serve 4:

16 sea scallops in their shells, or 1½ pounds shucked
1 pound young leeks, about 8
4 tablespoons butter, in all
Coarse salt
2 tablespoons freshly chopped shallot
¼ cup dry white vermouth
⅜ cup dry white wine (this should be the same wine that you plan to serve with the meal)
⅜ cup *crème fraîche* (*or substitute ½ cup heavy cream; Ed.*)
Freshly ground white pepper
1 bouquet fresh young chervil

PREPARATION:

1. The scallops: Slip a small sharp knife between the two shells, severing the muscle that holds them together. Then use a tablespoon to release the morsel of scallop attached to the deeper shell, and remove the gelatinous beard enveloping it so that you have only the white kernel.

If the scallops have a roe (a small fat orange crescent), detach and reserve it, but remove the black sac connected to it. Discard the remains.

Wash the scallops in several changes of cold water to remove any traces of sand, then drain them on a towel.

2. The leeks: Cut off the root end of each leek and discard the first layer of leaves, which have had contact with the earth. Then split the leeks in half lengthwise and cut off the dark green leaves, saving only the white part. Wash the leeks thoroughly under lukewarm running water. This will help to dissolve any earth and sand more easily. Then shake the leeks so that they are well drained, and cut them into matchsticks about 1½ to 2 inches long.

3. The chervil: Strip the leaves from the stems and set aside.

COOKING:

Place the leeks in a small casserole with 2 tablespoons of the butter and ½ cup of cold water. Sprinkle lightly with salt, and cook, covered, about 20 minutes over low heat. Stir occasionally with a wooden spoon. When the leeks are done, set them aside, covered, to keep warm.

Cut each whole scallop in half through the thickest part. Leave the roe intact.

Heat the remaining 2 tablespoons of butter in a casserole with the freshly chopped shallot. Add the scallops and their roe, followed by the vermouth and white wine. Do not add salt. Bring the liquid to a boil, then immediately reduce heat and simmer about 2 minutes.

Lift out the scallops, using a skimmer or slotted spoon, and transfer them to the casserole with the leeks to keep warm.

THE SAUCE:

Return the casserole to high heat and reduce the cooking broth. Also add any juices that have accumulated from the cooked leeks. Boil down the liquid until only about ⅓ cup remains. Then add the *crème fraîche*.

Return the sauce to a simmer and let bubble gently for 1 minute or until slightly thickened. Add a pinch of salt and freshly ground white pepper. Taste for seasoning.

TO SERVE:

Pour the hot sauce over the scallops and leeks, and sprinkle with delicate young chervil leaves. Stir gently to coat the scallops with the sauce, but do not cook further.

Divide the scallops and their sauce among four warmed deep plates and serve at once.

Les poissons
FISH

Turbotin braisé à l'oseille
TURBOT WITH SORREL SAUCE

To serve 2 or 4: (*This recipe will serve 2 as a main dish or, with smaller portions, 4 as a first course. Or if you prefer, you can purchase a larger fish and lengthen the cooking time accordingly. Ed.*)

1 turbot, about 2¼ pounds (*see Note*)
Coarse salt
Freshly ground white pepper
3 ounces fresh sorrel (*about 3 cups, tightly packed*)
2 tablespoons butter
2 shallots, finely chopped
½ cup dry white wine
½ cup *crème fraîche* (*or substitute ¾ cup heavy cream; Ed.*)

NOTE: *Turbot, a European fish, is not found in our waters. Because this recipe calls for a whole fish, you could substitute either a whole 2½-pound flounder, which in testing corresponded to the cooking time given for turbot; or a 2½-pound striped bass, which, being of firmer flesh, needs a slightly longer cooking time. Ed.*

HAVE READY:

1. The turbot: Clean the fish, leaving the head and tail intact. Remove the gills, and using a kitchen scissors, cut off all of the fins.

Cleanse the fish by soaking it in ice water for 5 to 6 hours, changing the water once. (*This procedure applies only to turbot. Ed.*) Dry well with a towel, then sprinkle both sides of the fish with salt and pepper.

2. The sorrel: Pick over the sorrel and strip off the stems, working from the bottom to the top of each leaf. Wash the leaves and drain them well.

Then bunch portions of leaves together and roll them in the shape of a cigar. Lay these "cigars" on your work surface and cut the rolls into very thin shreds. This is a *chiffonnade*.

COOKING THE TURBOT:

Preheat oven to 400°F.

Grease the bottom of a shallow roasting pan (*not aluminum*) with 2 teaspoons of the butter and distribute the chopped shallots evenly over all. Lay the turbot in the pan, white-skin side down, pour the white wine over it, and bake the fish 20 to 25 minutes.

To test that the fish is done, press the central bone near the head with your finger. If you meet resistance, the fish is done. You can press the fish before you bake it to be certain of the difference.

PREPARATION OF THE SAUCE:

Leave the fish in the pan in which it was cooked, but carefully pour off all the cooking broth into a heavy casserole. Boil the broth until it is reduced to 2 or 3 tablespoons of syrupy juices. Add the *crème fraîche* and return the sauce to a boil. Then, off heat, drop in the sorrel, and mix carefully with a wooden spoon.

Return the sauce to a simmer and taste for seasoning. Add a pinch of salt and freshly ground pepper. Remove the casserole from heat, and beat in the remaining butter, cut into tiny pieces. Cover the sauce and set aside in a warm place.

TO FINISH THE FISH:

Carefully peel off all the black skin on the top side of the fish. It should pull away easily. Also extract all the small bones around the fish where the fins were cut off. This is easily accomplished by tucking a plate under the sides of the fish and, using a small knife, scraping out the bones onto the plate. Leave the head intact.

Transfer the fish to a lightly buttered serving platter and keep it in the turned-off oven with the door open (*but not for very long; Ed.*).

Just as you are ready to serve, nap the fish, except for the head, with a little of the sauce. Serve the rest of the sauce separately in a hot sauceboat.

The fresh green of the sorrel sauce will not fail to captivate you.

Blanc de Saint-Pierre à la crème de petits légumes
FISH COOKED IN CREAM WITH VEGETABLES
(Color picture 6)

To serve 4:

1 *Saint-Pierre*, about 4 pounds (*to yield 1¾ to 2 pounds fish fillets; see Note*)
1 large carrot
1 leek, white part only
1 celery heart
¾ pound medium-size asparagus (optional, depending on the season) and/or
40 very thin young string beans
Coarse salt
1 small bunch chives
1 large Idaho potato, about 8 ounces
2 tablespoons butter, in all
1 cup heavy cream
Freshly ground white pepper

NOTE: Saint-Pierre—*also called John Dory—is not easily available in the United States. However, almost any firm-fleshed white fish can be used in this recipe. Sea bass and striped bass are excellent prepared in this manner; or you could use monkfish (also called goosefish, anglerfish, belly fish), red snapper, or hake. Ed.*

PREPARATION OF THE SAINT-PIERRE:

(Depending on the fish you have selected, these directions may not apply. Ed.)

Have your fish merchant fillet and skin the *Saint-Pierre* (if he is agreeable). Otherwise, clean and rinse the fish, lay it on your cutting board, and proceed in the following manner:

Insert the point of a knife through the skin to one side of the skeleton of the fish; then go around it—as if you were tracing the fish exactly—but within ½ inch inside its contour. Next, insert the knife from head to tail, even with the central bone. Slide the knife underneath the flesh, scraping against the bones, and detach each fillet. You should have 4 beautiful fillets.

Now, it only remains to remove the skin from each fillet (undoubtedly, at this point you have decided to change fish merchants). Lay one of the fillets on your cutting board, skin side down. While holding the tail section firmly against the board, slide your knife between the flesh and the skin, making small back-and-forth movements and keeping the knife close to, and parallel to, the skin at all times.

When the fillet is released, cut it into strips the thickness of your index finger.

PREPARATION OF THE VEGETABLES:

1. The carrot, leek, and celery heart: Cut the 3 vegetables into large julienne strips the length and width of the tines of a carving fork.

2. The asparagus (optional): Use only the first 4 inches of each tip. Peel them if necessary, and cut each tip diagonally into two 2-inch pieces.

Drop the asparagus into 2 quarts of boiling salted water. Cook about 7 minutes, keeping them firm. Drain, and plunge the asparagus into ice water. When chilled, drain again and set aside.

3. The string beans: Nip off the ends of the string beans and drop them into 2 quarts of boiling salted water. When they are done, they should remain somewhat crisp. (*If the beans are truly young, 5 minutes cooking time should be sufficient. Ed.*) Drain, and plunge the string beans into ice water. Drain again and set aside.

4. The chives: Finely chop the chives and set them aside in a small bowl covered with a sheet of plastic.

5. The potato: Peel and rinse the potato and cut it into large cubes. Place them in a saucepan with salted water to cover, and cook until done. Drain and set aside.

COOKING:

1. The vegetable julienne: While the potato is cooking, place the julienne strips of carrot, leek, and celery heart in a casserole with a pinch of coarse salt, ½ cup of water, and 2 teaspoons of the butter. Cover the casserole and cook the vegetables over medium to high heat, letting the liquid evaporate.

Base the cooking time on the carrot. Here also, the vegetables must remain slightly crisp. This operation should take no more than 10 minutes. (*Stir occasionally to make sure that the vegetables do not scorch. Ed.*)

When the vegetables are done, keep them warm, covered, off heat. (*There should not be any trace of liquid remaining in the casserole. If there is, add it to the cream. Ed.*)

2. The fish: Pour the cream into a 2-quart casserole. Add a pinch of salt and the strips of fish. Bring the cream to a simmer, and cook the fish, uncovered, for 2 minutes—but no more! (*The fish will finish cooking later. Ed.*)

THE SAUCE:

Place a sieve over a deep bowl and drain the fish. Then add the fish to the casserole with the vegetables, and pour the fish-flavored cream into the container of a blender.

Add half of the cubes of cooked, drained potato to the cream. Run the machine briefly, then add the remainder. You should have a lightly thickened sauce. Add the rest of the butter, a generous amount of freshly ground white pepper, and if needed, salt.

TO FINISH THE FISH:

Add the well-drained asparagus and/or string beans to the casserole with the fish.

Pour the potato-thickened cream sauce over the fish and vegetables, and bring it to a full boil. Add the chopped chives and stir once or twice. Then divide the mélange among four warmed deep plates.

In this recipe, you will find a delicate harmony of flavors in a velvety sauce—all natural.

Saint-Pierre des pêcheurs du Suquet

FISH BAKED WITH POTATOES, ONIONS AND TOMATOES

To serve 4:

1. *Saint-Pierre*, about 4 pounds (*to yield 1¾ to 2 pounds fish fillets; see Note*)—ask your fish merchant to fillet the fish
6 tablespoons butter, in all
2 medium-size onions (about 7 ounces each), thinly sliced
¾ cup strong chicken stock
¼ teaspoon saffron threads
4 large Idaho potatoes, about 7 ounces each
Coarse salt
Freshly ground pepper, preferably white
4 ripe tomatoes, about 3 ounces each
4 cloves unpeeled garlic, flattened slightly
1 large branch fresh thyme (*or substitute ½ teaspoon dried thyme; Ed.*)
2 bay leaves, broken

NOTE: Saint-Pierre—*also called John Dory—is not easily available in the United States. Excellent substitutes for this fish would be: striped bass, sea bass, red snapper, grouper, monkfish, or other thick, firm-fleshed white fish fillets. Ed.*

PREPARATION:

Preheat oven to 425°F.

1. Melt 2 tablespoons of the butter in a skillet, add the sliced onions, and cook over low heat until soft and golden. Allow about 10 minutes for this.

2. In a small saucepan, bring the chicken stock to a boil. Then add the saffron, stir until dissolved, and set aside.

3. Peel the potatoes and wipe dry with a towel. Do not rinse them. Then slice the potatoes into rounds about 1/16-inch thick. Spread them out on a towel and sprinkle with salt and freshly ground pepper.

TO ASSEMBLE THE FISH:

1. Grease the bottom and sides of a shallow oval roasting pan or *à gratin* dish liberally with butter (*use about 1 tablespoon*). Make a bed of potatoes, consisting of 1 layer spread over the bottom of the pan.

2. Cover the layer of potatoes with the sautéed onions.

3. Sprinkle both sides of the fish fillets with salt and freshly ground pepper, and arrange them over the onions.

4. After removing the core, cut the tomatoes into thick slices and lay them on top of the fish.

5. Stick the flattened unpeeled cloves of garlic around the sides of the pan, and scatter the thyme leaves and broken bay leaves over the tomatoes.

6. Cover the tomatoes and fish with the rest of the potatoes. Then dot the potatoes with the remaining 3 tablespoons of butter, cut into tiny pieces.

Slowly pour the saffron-flavored chicken stock evenly over the potatoes, taking care not to disturb the butter.

COOKING:

Bake the fish in the preheated oven 1 hour, basting frequently. At the end of this time, the liquid should have completely evaporated and the top layer of potatoes should have a beautiful golden crust.

Serve this dish from the pan in which it was cooked.

The first time that I ate this was with the fishermen from the Saint-Pierre wharf in Cannes. It had been prepared with two beautiful *Saint-Pierre*, sporting monstrous heads, each lying in an oval earthenware *tian* or terrine. (This is a shallow casserole made of glazed terra cotta that is used locally for all roasting, gratinéeing, or oven-braising.)

With the gold of the saffron-dyed potatoes, brilliant red tomatoes, yellow onions, blue-green thyme leaves, bright green bay leaf, the steel gray of the fish—all that together with the terra cotta terrine formed a magnificent picture bathed in the light of a May morning.

The fishermen had taken these large terrines to the bakery. Then one and a half hours later they had returned, the terrines now topped with a golden crust emanating an extraordinary sweet scent, an aroma, so powerful and yet so subtle that you cannot imagine how unbelievably good it was.

We were a dozen friends in all and we ate standing up—an honor the dish merited.

Daurade royale rôtie au laurier avec sa fondue d'orange et de citron à l'huile d'olive

 BAKED FISH WITH BAY LEAVES AND CITRUS SAUCE

To serve 4:
  1 *daurade royale*, or other whole fish, about 3½ to 3¾ pounds
    (*see Note*)
  5 bay leaves (fresh, if possible)
  Coarse salt
  Freshly ground white pepper
  5 tablespoons olive oil, in all
  3 navel oranges (or other seedless oranges)
  2 lemons

NOTE: The *daurade royale* is a noble fish from our Mediterranean waters. It is recognized by its steel-gray color and, particularly, by its snub-nosed head and homely features crowned with a slight, golden-colored bump. (It is almost a Bourbon nose!)

Other fish, lower on the culinary scale but suitable to be prepared in the same manner, are: striped bass, sea bass, and red snapper.

PREPARATION:

(*This should be done at least 1 hour before you plan to cook the fish. Ed.*)

If you can, have your fish merchant clean and scale the fish. Leave the head and tail intact.

Cut 3 of the bay leaves into 8 small triangles each. (There should be 24 triangles in all.)

Liberally season the fish, inside and out, with salt and pepper. Then, using the point of a sharp knife, make 12 tiny incisions horizontally on each side of the fish. Cut only through the skin—guiding the knife parallel to the flesh without damaging it. With the help of the knife, lift up the skin at each incision and insert a small triangle of bay leaf.

When you have finished, massage the fish from head to tail with the tips of your fingers, so that the flavoring of the bay leaf will penetrate the flesh.

Then place the remaining 2 bay leaves in the ventral cavity, and using either your fingers or a brush, baste each side of the fish with 1 tablespoon of the olive oil.

Let the fish stand 1 hour before cooking.

COOKING:

Preheat oven to 475°F for 20 minutes.

Lay the fish on a grill (*almost any kind of large wire rack will do; Ed.*) and place it over a shallow roasting pan. Fill the pan half full of boiling water and place it in the hot oven.

Bake the fish 15 minutes, then carefully turn it to the other side. Bake the fish about 25 minutes longer, but check it for doneness after 15 or 20 minutes. The cooking time will vary slightly, depending on the kind of fish, and the size, you have chosen. To check that the fish is perfectly cooked, slip the point of a knife into the area of the dorsal bone, right behind the top of the head. If the flesh breaks easily, all the way through to the bone, the fish is done.

PREPARATION OF THE SAUCE:

While the fish is cooking, prepare the oranges and lemons.

Using a small sharp knife, peel the fruit close to the flesh, leaving no trace of white pith. Then cut through each segment, detaching the sections of fruit from the membrane. Do this over a bowl, catching all the juices.

Place the orange and lemon segments, and their juice, in a small casserole with the remaining 3 tablespoons of olive oil, a little salt, and freshly ground white pepper. Just before serving, gently warm the fruits over low heat. Be careful! If you get them too hot, they will disintegrate.

TO SERVE:

Carefully transfer the fish to a hot platter. Serve the fruits in a separate sauceboat.

In this recipe, the sharpness of the lemon is tempered by the sweetness of the oranges and the olive oil. This is a summer dish—a recipe of the sun. The preparation of citrus fruits can also be served with grilled fish.

NOTE: *Though M. Vergé presents this recipe as a summer dish, it brought sunshine to my table in the dead of winter—when citrus in the United States is at its best! Ed.*

Suprême de loup au vert de laitue
STRIPED BASS WRAPPED IN GREEN LETTUCE LEAVES

To serve 4:

2 or 3 heads lettuce (*preferably Boston or butter lettuce*), very green and not too sandy

Coarse salt

1 striped bass, or sea bass, about 3¾ pounds (*to yield about 1¾ pounds fish fillets; Ed.*)

Freshly ground white pepper

2 tablespoons flour

5½ tablespoons butter

1 tablespoon olive oil

1 tablespoon finely chopped shallot

3 tablespoons dry white wine

3 tablespoons dry vermouth

3 tablespoons heavy cream

1 egg yolk

PREPARATION:

1. The lettuce: (*If the heads of lettuce are very large, and the outer leaves are undamaged, 2 heads will be sufficient. Ed.*)

Bring 4 quarts of lightly salted water to a boil. During this time, detach the outer lettuce leaves and rinse them well; then rinse the hearts. When the water reaches a boil, drop in the leaves and hearts, and as soon as they are well submerged, immediately use a skimmer to lift them out. Plunge the lettuce into a large basin of ice water, then drain in a colander. (*This operation is not intended to cook the lettuce, but to set the green color. Ed.*)

Split the hearts of lettuce in half vertically, and flatten each portion slightly with your hand. Carefully spread out the hearts and the leaves between two towels and sponge them lightly until dry.

2. The fish: Clean and scale the bass, detach the 2 fillets from the central bone, and remove the skin. (If your fish merchant is in a good mood, ask him to do this for you.)

Divide each fillet into 4 pieces, giving you 8 pieces in all. Sprinkle each piece with salt and freshly ground pepper, then dip lightly in flour, shaking off the excess.

Over medium to high heat, melt 1 tablespoon of the butter with the olive oil in a large skillet. Sear the pieces of fish, about 1 minute on each side, and set them aside on a plate.

ASSEMBLING AND FINISHING THE COOKING OF THE FISH:

Preheat oven to 350°F.

Grease a shallow casserole or *à gratin* dish lightly with 1½ teaspoons of the butter. Sprinkle the chopped shallot over all. Then arrange the halves of lettuce hearts, spread out slightly, over the bottom of the casserole.

Carefully wrap the partially cooked fish fillets in large green lettuce leaves, forming neat packages. Allow 2 leaves of lettuce for each piece of fillet. Distribute the green parcels over the bed of lettuce hearts and sprinkle the wine and vermouth over all.

Bake the fish in the preheated oven for 12 minutes.

After 12 minutes, drain the parcels of lettuce and the hearts, catching all the juices. Spread the hearts out over a warm serving platter and arrange the parcels of fish over them. Cover them tightly with aluminum foil to keep warm.

PREPARATION OF THE SAUCE:

Pour all the cooking broth into a small casserole. Bring it to a boil, then reduce until only 2 tablespoons of liquid remain.

In a small bowl, mix the cream with the egg yolk, and using a wire whisk, stir it into the casserole. Stir continuously over medium heat until the sauce almost reaches a simmer.

Remove from heat immediately, and beat in the remaining 4 tablespoons of butter, cut into tiny pieces. Add a pinch of salt and freshly ground pepper and nap the lettuce parcels with the sauce.

Serve at once.

This recipe is hardly difficult and is composed of ingredients that are easy to come by. Nevertheless, it constitutes a good example of the quest for delicate harmonies and fine details:

1. The lettuce guards the soft texture of the fish, but brings with it a very subtle touch of bitterness that one also finds in the vermouth.

2. The dry white wine marries its perfume with that of the shallots.

3. Searing the fish before wrapping it in lettuce leaves allows it to retain all its juices. Otherwise, it would lose its flavor—trailing away in whitish streaks of liquid. (This would be a pity and a shame.)

4. The striped bass is a fish whose flesh is among the finest and most delicate. Nevertheless, it can be replaced in this recipe by fillets of red snapper, hake, haddock, pollock, or even such freshwater fish as pike.

The main points lie in the freshness of the fish and, certainly, in the quality of the sauce.

Les petits rougets de mon ami Pierrot
PANFRIED RED MULLET WITH ORANGE SAUCE

To serve 4:

2½ to 3 pounds small whole *rougets de roche* (red mullet; *see Note*)
13 tablespoons imported virgin olive oil, in all
½ teaspoon whole white peppercorns, crushed
2 large juicy oranges
2 small fennel bulbs
1 lemon
Salt
Freshly ground white pepper
12 thin slices day-old *pain-baguette* (*the long thin loaf of French bread; Ed.*)
3 cloves garlic, flattened and peeled
Flour
5 anchovy fillets

The *rouget de roche* should not be any larger than the length of a small hand. If you have the good luck to live on the shores of the Mediterranean, choose in preference the first catch of the morning. This fish is a beautiful bright pink color with a shimmering wavelike pattern of yellow or gold.

You can also use the red mullet of the Atlantic, which is of excellent quality and adapts perfectly to this preparation.

NOTE: *Very small red snapper, and also goatfish, will work well prepared this way. It is important that the fish be as small as possible. This is because they must be cooked quickly in order to keep their colorful skin intact and to prevent the flesh from becoming mushy. Try to keep the weight of the individual fish from 4 to 6 ounces, with 8 ounces as an absolute maximum. Ed.*

PREPARATION OF THE ROUGETS (at least 8 hours in advance):

Scale and clean the fish, and if you are using genuine *rougets de roche*, save their livers. Then, using a needle, prick both sides of the fish all over, peppering them with tiny holes.

Arrange the fish on a deep platter and coat them on both sides with 9 tablespoons of the olive oil. Sprinkle the crushed white peppercorns over all.

Cut one of the oranges into thin slices and lay them over the fish. Marinate the fish at room temperature at least 8 hours, covered with a cloth. The fish will become impregnated with the delicate perfume of the olive oil and aroma of orange. (*Turn the fish once or twice during this time, but keep the orange slices on top. Ed.*)

COOKING:

1. The fennel: Chop off and discard the celerylike stalks of the fennel and rinse the bulbs. Cut the bulbs in half crosswise, then into small quarters (*about 16 pieces to each bulb; Ed.*).

Place the fennel in a saucepan with 1 quart of cold water, the juice of 1 lemon, and a good pinch of salt. Cover the saucepan, bring the water to a boil, and cook the fennel until tender (*about 30 minutes*).

Drain well in a sieve, then purée the fennel in a food processor or blender, or press it through a food mill into a clean saucepan. Stir 1 tablespoon of olive oil into the purée, taste for seasoning, and add a pinch of salt and freshly ground white pepper. Cover and keep warm. (*If you wish to make this in advance, the fennel can be warmed gently, over very low heat, just before you are ready to serve. Ed.*)

2. The *tartines*: Cut the bread into 12 thin slices and let them dry slightly, at room temperature, 1 hour. Then rub the bread well on each side with crushed whole garlic cloves. Heat the 3 remaining tablespoons of olive oil in a large skillet and fry the bread on both sides. Add more oil if necessary. Set the *tartines* aside in a warm place.

3. The *rougets*: About 30 to 45 minutes before you are ready to cook the fish, take it from the marinade and drain on a wire rack placed over the deep platter with the remainder of the marinade.

Discard the orange slices, but save every bit of orange-scented oil that you accumulate. It will be used to cook the fish.

NOTE: *If, between the marinade remaining in the platter and that drained from the fish, you have not collected 8 tablespoons of orange-scented oil, supplement the oil for frying the fish with fresh virgin olive oil. But, be certain to set aside 4 tablespoons of orange-scented oil for the sauce. Ed.*

Dry the fish with paper towels, season them with salt, and sprinkle lightly with flour.

Heat 4 tablespoons of the orange oil in a large skillet, and when it is hot, fry the fish. Two minutes cooking time for each side should be sufficient, as you want the flesh to retain its delicate texture. When the fish are cooked, arrange them side by side, without crowding, on a hot serving platter.

TO PREPARE THE SAUCE AND SERVE THE FISH:

Discard the oil used to cook the fish, and off heat, add the 4 tablespoons of reserved oil to the hot pan. Then add the anchovy fillets and crush them with a fork. Over very low heat, stir in the juice of ½ the second orange. (*There should be about ⅓ cup of juice; if you wish, the remaining ½ orange can be sliced as a garniture. Ed.*)

Season the sauce with freshly ground pepper, and when the ingredients are well blended, pour it over the fish.

Serve the fish at once, with the *tartines* and the fennel purée passed separately.

This dish can be eaten cold, but should never be refrigerated. In this instance, also serve the fennel cold, in a separate bowl.

I ate this for the first time prepared by my friend Pierrot the fisherman. We drank a white Saint-Tropez, cold from the well, and we grilled large *tartines* of coarse country bread, held on the point of a knife over the wood embers which were also to serve for cooking a *bouillabaisse*. It is, perhaps, all too simple, but other, greater feasts cannot make me forget moments such as these.

Escalopes de saumon frais, mariné à l'huile de basilic

MARINATED RAW SALMON WITH OIL AND BASIL

To serve 2 or 4: (*The quantities of salmon and mushrooms make servings for 2 that are quite generous. Depending on the rest of your meal, the portions could be divided to serve 4 as a first course. Ed.*)

¾ to 1 pound very fresh boneless salmon (from the tail)
1½ lemons
Salt (preferably sea salt, *sel de mer*)
Freshly ground white pepper
10 large fresh basil leaves, or substitute 1 teaspoon chopped fresh
    dillweed, or serve simply, without herbs (*see Note*)
5 tablespoons olive oil, in all
7 ounces fresh unblemished white mushrooms
1 tablespoon chopped fresh parsley

NOTE: *Fresh dill is usually available year-round in most parts of the United States, but fresh basil, when in season, is preferable. Ed.*

Fish

PREPARATION OF THE SALMON:

Ask your fish merchant to give you an absolutely fresh salmon fillet weighing ¾ to 1 pound. If he is unable to provide this service, proceed to bone the fish yourself in the following manner:

Scale the fish, then insert a boning knife along the dorsal spine near the stomach cavity. Cut out the fillets and remove the small bones that are the source of the ventral and dorsal fins.

Using a very long thin knife, cut the fillet on a diagonal into wide thin slices, without breaking through the skin. (*The slices should have the same delicate thinness as professionally sliced smoked salmon. Ed.*) Spread the slices out on chilled plates, without overlapping. Sprinkle with the juice of 1 lemon, salt, and several good turns of the pepper mill.

Cut the basil leaves into fine julienne strips and scatter them over the salmon. Then let 1½ tablespoons of the olive oil run over the surface of each portion. Tilt the plate from side to side until the entire surface of the salmon is coated. (*If you have divided the salmon among four plates, allow ¾ tablespoon of oil for each serving. Ed.*)

This must not be done any earlier than 30 minutes before the salmon is to be served.

PREPARATION OF THE MUSHROOMS:

Trim the mushrooms and wipe with a damp cloth, or rinse briefly without letting them soak. Dry the mushrooms and cut them into thin slices. Then mix with salt, freshly ground pepper, the remaining 2 tablespoons of olive oil, the freshly chopped parsley, and the juice of ½ lemon.

TO SERVE:

When ready to serve, arrange a fan-shaped *garniture* of sliced mushrooms on each plate next to the slices of salmon, or if you wish, serve them separately on a small plate.

This dish has a delicacy that makes it a pleasant cold *entrée* and it is very easy to prepare.

121

Don't throw away the skin of the salmon. Cut it into strips the size of your little finger, sprinkle with salt, and fry without any fat. Then give the crisp strips a generous grinding of pepper and serve with apéritifs or, separately, with the cold slices of salmon.

Escalopes de saumon frais en marinière

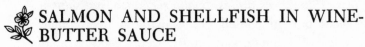
SALMON AND SHELLFISH IN WINE-BUTTER SAUCE

To serve 2: (*This lovely dish for 2 can easily serve 4 if you increase the quantity of shellfish and salmon. You do not need to change the proportions of any of the other ingredients, as there will be sufficient sauce. Ed.*)

8 large plump mussels (*see Note*)
2 large sea scallops with their roes (*see Note*)
2 *langoustines* (*see Note*)
2 salmon fillets, about 4 ounces each (*see Note*)
⅝ cup dry white wine, preferably a Burgundy or Pouilly-Fumé
1 shallot, chopped
1 tablespoon dry vermouth
Freshly ground white pepper
2 medium to large leeks, white parts only
8 tablespoons cold butter, in all
Coarse salt
1 bunch young chervil; take only the most delicate leaves (*or substitute young fresh parsley or chives; Ed.*)

PREPARATION:

1. The mussels: (*Since it is sometimes difficult to be certain just how many mussels will be plump and beautiful before they have opened, I suggest that you buy more than you need. If they are heavy with seawater, you should have about ½ cup of broth. Ed.*)

Scrub the mussels and wash them well in several changes of water.

Then place them in a casserole, cover tightly, and shake the casserole over high heat until the mussels open. This operation must be done quickly.

Snap off and discard the top shell of each mussel, reserving the half with the morsel of meat. Save all the juices and set the mussels aside in a warm place, covered. (*Let the broth settle, then strain it through several layers of fine cheescloth, discarding any sand. Ed.*)

2. The scallops: Wash the scallops and their coral and divide each one, through the thickest part, into 3 pieces. (*In the United States the scallop roe is not esteemed and it is usually discarded at the time the scallops are shucked. There is little choice but to do without this delicacy. Ed.*)

3. The *langoustines*: Shell them raw and set aside. (*This is the smallest member of the lobster family. As with shrimp, only the tail section is edible. Ed.*)

NOTE: *If* langoustines *are not available, substitute the largest shrimp you can find. They are marketed under a variety of names, such as* scampi, *prawns, green shrimp, and red Spanish shrimp. One way to choose them is that you want 10 to 13 shrimp to a pound. They are so delicious prepared this way that you may wish to include a few extra. Ed.*

4. The salmon: *I suggest that you purchase a boneless fillet from the tail section of a small salmon. Remove the skin, and following the center line, cut the fish in half lengthwise.*

Place the salmon fillets between 2 sheets of wax paper and flatten them slightly, to an even thickness, by tapping lightly with the broad side of a meat cleaver or the bottom of a small skillet. Set aside. Ed.

COOKING:

1. The fish stock: Pour the white wine into a wide-rimmed casserole or large sauté pan (*preferably enameled cast iron, or tin-lined copper—not aluminum!*). Add the shallot, vermouth, reserved mussel broth, and a few good turns of the pepper mill.

Cook the stock 10 minutes over low heat, then cover to keep warm.

2. The vegetable *garniture*: Wash the leeks and cut them into segments 1½ inches long. Then cut each piece into fine julienne strips. Soak the leeks in ice water about 15 minutes, then drain well in a sieve.

Place the drained leeks in a small casserole with 1 tablespoon of the butter and 2 tablespoons of water. Season with salt and freshly ground pepper, cover the casserole, and over low heat, stew the leeks 15 minutes. Stir once or twice. Then set the casserole aside, covered, to keep warm.

FINISHING THE SALMON AND SHELLFISH:

Return the casserole with the fish stock to the stove. Arrange the salmon fillets in it, surrounded by the scallops, their roes, the *langoustines*, and the mussels removed from their half shells. (*If you have room in the casserole, you can leave the mussels in their shells, but if it is crowded, the sharp edges of the shells will tear the other fish. Ed.*)

Cover the casserole, bring the stock to a simmer—bubbling faintly around the edges—and cook very briefly, about 1 minute or until the *langoustines* become opaque. (*In substituting giant scampi, I found the cooking time to be about 2 minutes. If they are not cooked after 1 minute, turn them, and baste the other seafood. The salmon should be ready in 1 minute, but can remain in the hot stock for 2 minutes without harm. Ed.*)

While the salmon and shellfish are cooking, spread the julienne of leeks over the bottoms of two hot plates. Then, working quickly, use a skimmer or slotted spoon to lift the salmon and shellfish from the casserole, and arrange them over the leeks. Keep the seafood warm by covering each serving with an inverted plate.

THE SAUCE:

Return the casserole to high heat and rapidly boil down the fish stock until reduced to about 6 tablespoons. Cut the remaining 7 tablespoons of cold butter into small pieces, and using a wire whisk, beat them into the boiling stock, one at a time, until a thickened *liaison* has formed.

Remove the casserole from heat and taste for seasoning. Add a pinch of salt and freshly ground pepper, then pour the sauce over the fish. Sprinkle each serving with delicate young chervil leaves and accompany with slices of toasted French bread.

This dish has a freshness that makes one's mouth water even before it reaches the table.

Fricassée de sole aux moules à la crème de safran
SOLE WITH MUSSELS IN SAFFRON CREAM SAUCE

To serve 2 or 3: (*If you wish to serve 4 to 6 persons, double all the ingredients. Ed.*)

> 1 sole, to yield about 1 pound fish fillets (Have your fish merchant prepare the fillets for you. *See Note*)
> 1¼ pounds small mussels
> 1 tablespoon chopped shallot
> ⅓ cup dry white wine (this should be the same wine that you plan to serve with the meal)
> 1 medium-size Idaho potato, about 6 ounces
> Coarse salt
> 1½ tablespoons butter
> 1 medium-size leek, about 2½ ounces
> 1 large carrot, about 2½ ounces
> 1 tender stalk of celery
> ¼ pound thin young string beans, or ¼ pound peas to yield 2½ ounces (*about 1 cup*) shelled peas
> ¾ cup heavy cream
> A pinch saffron threads
> Freshly ground white pepper
> 2 tablespoons freshly chopped parsley

NOTE: *In France, the Dover sole that would be used in this dish is not the same fish that we know as sole in the United States. It would be best to substitute a 1-pound fillet of a firm-fleshed white fish such as striped bass, sea bass, red snapper, or hake. Ed.*

PREPARATION:

While the mussels are soaking, prepare the vegetables. Ed.

1. The mussels: Scrub the mussels and soak them in 3 or 4 changes of cold water. Then drain and place them in a 3-quart casserole. Add the shallot and white wine, cover the casserole, and cook the mussels over high heat just until they open, no longer. Between 5 and 10 minutes will be sufficient for this operation. Stir the mussels from time to time, bringing those on the bottom of the casserole to the top.

When the mussels have opened, use a skimmer to lift them out. Do not discard the cooking broth.

When they are cool enough to handle, remove them from their shells and set them aside.

2. The potato: Peel the potato and cut it into 6 pieces. Place them in a saucepan with enough lightly salted water to cover them by several inches, and cook as you would for mashed potatoes (page 225), about 20 minutes.

When the potato is done, drain it thoroughly in a food mill held over the kitchen sink. Then press the potato through the food mill into a warm bowl. Using a wooden spoon, work the butter into the potatoes until you obtain a smooth and glossy paste. Set aside, covered.

3. The leek, carrot, and celery: Split the leek in half and wash it well. Discard the dark green leaves and cut the white and yellow-green part into 2-inch segments.

Peel the carrot and cut it also into 2-inch segments.

Strip any strings from the stalk of celery and cut it into 2-inch segments.

Then cut all the vegetables into large julienne strips, approximately the size of matchsticks.

Drop the vegetables, all together, into a quart of rapidly boiling salted water. Cook, uncovered, about 2 minutes. The vegetables should remain firm. When they are done, drain them well in a colander, then set aside on a plate.

4. The string beans, or peas: Nip off the ends of the string beans, and if they are large, cut them into small sticks about 1½ inches long. Or if you are using peas, shell them at the last moment.

Drop either string beans or peas into 1 quart of boiling salted water. Cook peas about 2 minutes, uncovered, and string beans about 4 or 5 minutes, or according to their size. (One must never cover green vegetables.)

5. The sole: Cut the fish into strips the length and thickness of your little finger.

Strain the broth from the mussels through a fine sieve lined with cheesecloth into a clean 4-quart casserole. Watch the liquid carefully to be sure that you do not take any of the residue of sand from the bottom.

Then reduce the broth until only 3 tablespoons of liquid remain. Add the cream to the casserole and the strips of fish. (Do not add salt.)

Bring the cream to a simmer and cook the fish 2 minutes. Then, using a skimmer, lift out the strips of fish and place them in a colander to drain.

THE SAUCE:

Add a pinch of saffron to the fish-flavored cream and let simmer 2 or 3 minutes. Then, using a wire whisk, blend in the warm potato purée.

Beat the sauce vigorously until the potato is completely incorporated. (This can also be done in a blender, but it will give you a thinner sauce.)

TO SERVE:

When you are ready to serve, return the vegetables, mussels, and fish to the casserole, and turn them very carefully in the sauce. Add a generous amount of freshly ground white pepper and, if necessary, salt. (However, the mussels will probably have added a sufficient amount of salt to the sauce.) Add freshly chopped parsley and bring the sauce just to a simmer.

Serve the *fricassée* in deep plates that have been previously warmed.

Le brochet de mon ami Paul
PIKE WITH GARLIC AND VINEGAR SAUCE

To serve 2:

> 1 pike, about 2¾ pounds including head and tail (*see Note*)
> Coarse salt
> Freshly ground pepper, preferably white
> 1 sprig fresh thyme (*or substitute ¼ teaspoon dried thyme; Ed.*)
> 4 tablespoons butter, softened
> 16 large cloves garlic, unpeeled (If you truly like garlic, you can use up to 24 cloves.)
> 9 tablespoons wine vinegar (use the best quality available)

NOTE: The pike can be replaced by a saltwater fish, such as red snapper, striped bass, or monkfish.

To make sure that your fish is absolutely fresh, check that it is firm and rigid: Hold the fish horizontally by the tail. It should not bend. The eyes and scales must be bright and clear.

PREPARATION:

If you can, have your fish merchant clean and scale the pike.

Cut off all the fins, wash the fish under cold running water, and sponge it dry with paper towels.

Sprinkle the pike, inside and out, with salt and freshly ground pepper; then slip a sprig of thyme into the cavity.

COOKING:

Preheat oven to 425°F.

Select an oval roasting pan or *à gratin* dish just large enough to hold the fish. Rub the bottom and sides of the pan liberally with some of the butter, and scatter the unpeeled cloves of garlic over all.

Lay the pike on its belly over the garlic, spreading open the ventral area to stabilize the fish in an upright position. Press the remaining butter lavishly over the top and sides of the fish.

Bake the pike about 30 minutes, basting it every 5 minutes with the cooking butter and pan juices. (*Allow a little extra time for the time you spend basting the fish. Ed.*) Make sure that the butter does not burn. If you should hear the butter sizzle, place your roasting pan within another, slightly larger, roasting pan. The cold metal will take away some of the heat from the pan holding the fish.

After the pike has baked 15 minutes, add 3 tablespoons of the wine vinegar, sprinkling it over the fish. Every 5 minutes thereafter, baste the fish, adding another 3 tablespoons of vinegar, until you have added 9 tablespoons of vinegar in all. At this time, the cooking should be finished.

NOTE: *Check the fish for doneness by breaking the flesh behind the top of the head with a spoon. If the flesh breaks through easily to the central bone, the fish is done. Ed.*

The butter and vinegar will glaze the fish, giving it a beautiful golden brilliance. The cloves of garlic will be cooked, and thanks to the emulsion of the butter and the vinegar reduction, the juices should be the consistency of thick syrup.

Serve the fish as it is, from the roasting pan.

NOTE: *If you wish, you can use a spoon to press out the soft paste inside a few of the garlic cloves. It will act as a* liaison, *further binding the sauce. Discard any empty skins. Ed.*

It is my friend Paul Bocuse who caused me to discover this recipe. We had dined at his place, not just as chefs but as friends, because our concepts of cooking and friendship are the same. The two must always stay simple and real.

Petite bourride agathoise
FISH AND SPINY LOBSTER CASSEROLE

To serve 4:

> 2 live spiny lobsters (*langoustes*), about 1¼ to 1½ pounds (*see Note*)
> 1 pound boneless monkfish (*lotte*) (*See Note*)
> 1½ pounds fillets of sole, or other firm-fleshed white fish fillets (*see Note*)
> 12 tablespoons (¾ cup) olive oil, in all
> 4 tablespoons finely chopped onion
> 1 teaspoon tomato paste
> 2 cloves garlic, flattened and peeled
> 1 large branch fresh thyme (*or substitute ½ teaspoon dried thyme; Ed.*)
> 1 bay leaf
> 1 large branch dried fennel, or about ½ teaspoon fennel seeds
> ¼ cup cognac or Armagnac
> ½ cup dry white vermouth
> ¾ cup dry white wine
> *About ⅔ cup mild fish stock (optional); Ed.*
> 2 egg yolks
> 3 tablespoons butter
> 16 slices, about ¼-inch thick, cut from a long thin loaf of French bread (*pain-baguette*)
> 4 tablespoons freshly chopped parsley
> Coarse salt
> Freshly ground pepper, preferably white

It is absolutely indispensable when buying a crustacean—whether it be North Atlantic lobster, spiny lobster, crab, or crayfish—that it be live and wiggling about! Because if it is dead, it discharges all of its vital substance. Therefore, if someone wants to give you a better price for a dead creature—don't take it. It will be much too expensive, because you can do nothing with it.

If you must buy your lobster ahead of time—as in the morning to cook at noon or in the evening or, at worst, the next morning—take a newspaper and spread it out on the table; then bend the tail of the lobster under its body and roll the lobster tightly in the newspaper. Store it in the vegetable drawer of your refrigerator. Too much cold will kill it, however.

You can use a wide variety of other white-fleshed fish fillets as a substitute for sole and, if necessary, for the monkfish. The only requirement is that they be of firm flesh—like striped bass, sea bass, red snapper, halibut, sea robin, or hake.

NOTE: *Actually, you do not want to use an American sole in this recipe. The species of flounders that we call sole are not the Dover sole of Europe. Our fish are too fragile for this preparation.*

If you cannot find monkfish (lotte—also called goosefish or belly fish), sea robin (grodin), although smaller, has the same firm texture. Also, whiting (merlan) would be an acceptable addition to this dish.

Spiny lobsters (langouste), also called rock lobsters commercially, are found live only in certain parts of the United States, especially on the West Coast, although they are sold frozen (the tail section only) almost everywhere.

If you live on the East Coast of the United States—where live North Atlantic lobsters are readily available—do not hesitate to use live East Coast lobster rather than frozen spiny lobster tails. Ed.

PREPARATION OF THE FISH AND LOBSTERS:

1. The monkfish (*lotte*): Remove the skin from the fish and divide the fillet into 4 pieces.

2. The fish fillets: Leave the skin intact and divide each fillet in half.

3. The spiny lobsters (*langoustes*): Here is an operation that will surely give you a problem.

Holding them flat, lay the live lobsters, one at a time, on a chopping board. Insert the point of a large heavy knife, or cleaver, between the two pointed horns situated at the top of the head. Thrust down on the point, driving it into the head, then lower the rest of the blade, so that you split the lobster in two lengthwise down the back. (*I found it easiest to position the blade, then tap it firmly with a mallet. Ed.*)

Remember that it is important not to split the lobster (thereby killing it) until the last moment before you are ready to cook it—no more than 10 minutes in advance.

Using a kitchen scissors or your hands, cut or twist off the small legs of the lobster and set them aside.

NOTE: *If you are using East Coast lobsters, also twist off the large claws and crack them. Reserve the tomalley. If you have a female lobster, also reserve the roe (coral). Ed.*

If this operation is too painful for you, bring 6 quarts of salted water to a vigorous boil and plunge in the lobsters. Keep the water boiling rapidly for 5 minutes, then remove the lobsters and split them in half, as I have just described. (*This method is less satisfactory because it toughens the meat slightly and reduces the quantity of natural juices for the sauce. Ed.*)

COOKING:

Heat 4 tablespoons of the olive oil in a large casserole (preferably enameled cast-iron) with a bottom at least 12 to 14 inches in diameter.

Add the chopped onion and cook, over medium heat, until soft and golden. Stir frequently with a wooden spoon. Then mix the tomato paste with the onion and, when well blended, add the crushed whole cloves of garlic, herbs (thyme, bay leaf, and fennel), and the small legs from the lobsters.

Arrange the 4 lobster halves, shell side down, in the casserole. Then add the monkfish, and lay the other fish fillets on top.

NOTE: *If using East Coast lobster, I found it preferable to sauté the large claws, small legs, body, and tail briefly (until the shell turns red) before adding the other fish. Ed.*

Warm the cognac or Armagnac, and pour it over the lobster and fish. Ignite, and tilt the casserole so that you can spoon the burning alcohol over the seafood.

Then pour in the dry vermouth and white wine. Do not add salt.

Cover the casserole and bring the liquid to a boil, then reduce heat and simmer 5 minutes. Add ⅓ cup hot water to the casserole (*or, if you wish, mild fish stock; Ed.*) and cook 10 minutes longer. Remove the casserole from heat, but do not disturb the cover until the sauce is ready for completion. (*However, at this time, be sure that the fish and lobster are sufficiently cooked. If you are not satisfied, simmer the seafood a few minutes longer—but take care that the fish does not fall apart. Ed.*)

THE SAUCE:

While the seafood is cooking, drop 2 egg yolks into a round-bottomed bowl and mix with 4 tablespoons of warm water (*or warm fish stock, if available; Ed.*). Then, using a wire whisk, incorporate the remaining ½ cup of olive oil in a slow steady stream—the same way you would for mayonnaise. This *liaison* will be the consistency of a sauce—not too thick. Set aside. (*If you wish, you can also use a food processor or blender for this operation. Ed.*)

THE CROUTONS:

Melt the butter in a skillet and fry the slices of bread until crisp and golden (*add more butter, or oil, if necessary; Ed.*). Arrange the croutons on a plate and keep warm.

TO FINISH AND SERVE THE BOURRIDE:

Have four deep plates warmed and ready to receive the lobster and fish. Arrange half a lobster on each plate with the assorted pieces of fish and a *garniture* of the small lobster legs. Keep warm. (*I suggest that you cover the plates tightly with aluminum foil. Ed.*)

NOTE: *If you are using East Coast lobsters, add the tomalley and roe to the broth at this time. Heat for only a minute, stirring constantly. Ed.*

Pass all the cooking broth through a fine sieve. Then, using a wire whisk, stir continuously while pouring the broth slowly into the mayonnaise. When combined, pour the sauce into a clean casserole and heat gently. Stir without stopping until the sauce is hot—but remove it from the heat before the first sign of a simmer, or the egg yolks will curdle. The result that you want is a slightly thickened broth.

Mix the parsley into the sauce and add salt and freshly ground pepper to taste.

Divide the sauce among the four warm plates of seafood and serve at once with the fried croutons, passed separately.

I am very fond of this recipe, given to me by Raymond Vidal. It dates from the great days at his wonderful *Club de Cavalière* where I was chef. He told me that he cherished this recipe of his mother's and kept it as a remembrance so marvelous that no other chef in the world could be able to bring it to life again as he had known it.

The problem was that her recipe was not in writing, but was uniquely passed on from memory. Also, she changed it a little, from one week to the next. Raymond Vidal and I delved into it occasionally in passionate discussions on the subject of such and such an ingredient, which I judged absolutely incongruous and he insisted was indispensable—"Then my mother added . . ."

From time to time he'd taste it, then put his hands behind his back and groan, "Not enough salt," and I would make a semblance of salting it in order to please him.

One day a facetious cook's helper noticed the wet spoon that Raymond Vidal held behind his back, and tossed a large pinch of salt into it. Raymond Vidal, not suspecting that I had only pretended to add salt, tasted again. He made a choking sound and heroically declared, "That's better."

Then he left the kitchen and allowed me thereafter to have my own way with his mother's *petite bourride*.

Les viandes
MEATS

Fricassée de grouet jamaïquain
JAMAICAN BAKED PORK CHOPS

To serve 4:

    4 ripe tomatoes, about 1 pound
    4 pork chops, taken from the first ribs (about 8 ounces each with
        the bone in)
    3 tablespoons olive oil
    Coarse salt
    Freshly ground pepper
    Flour
    2 medium-size onions, thinly sliced
    2 cloves garlic, chopped
    Bouquet garni (1 large sprig fresh thyme, 2 sprigs parsley, 1 small
        stalk celery with leaves, and 3 small bay leaves, tied together)
    1 cinnamon stick, broken in half
    Freshly grated nutmeg
    $3/8$ cup dry white wine
    2 bananas
    3 tablespoons butter

PREPARATION:

Preheat oven to 300°F.

1. The tomatoes: Drop the tomatoes into a casserole of boiling water, count to 10, then plunge them into cold water. Peel the tomatoes and remove the core, then cut them in half crosswise and squeeze out the seeds and water. Chop the tomatoes into large dice and set aside.

2. The pork chops: Heat the olive oil in a 4-quart casserole. Sprinkle the chops with salt and freshly ground pepper, and dust them lightly with flour.

When the oil is hot, arrange the chops in the casserole and sear them on both sides. When the meat is well whitened, remove the chops and set aside on a plate.

Lower the heat slightly, and add the sliced onions to the casserole. Cook, stirring frequently, until they are soft and golden. Then add the garlic and *bouquet garni*.

Lay the pork chops on top of the bed of onions and scatter the chopped tomatoes over them. Add the broken cinnamon stick and a small grating of nutmeg. Pour the white wine over all.

Bring the wine to a simmer, cover the casserole tightly, and place it in the preheated oven. Bake the pork chops 1 hour and 15 minutes. Check the casserole from time to time to make sure that the cooking liquid has not evaporated (this can happen if the cover is not airtight). If necessary, add 2 tablespoons water.

3. The bananas: A few minutes before the pork chops are ready, peel the bananas and cut them in half lengthwise. Then divide each half into 2 pieces. Dust the pieces of banana lightly with flour.

Heat the butter in a 10-inch skillet and brown the pieces on both sides. Take care to keep them somewhat firm. Transfer the bananas to a hot plate and keep them warm.

FINISHING THE PORK CHOPS:

After 1 hour and 15 minutes, check that the pork chops are done. The tomatoes and onions should be reduced to a well-thickened purée. If not, reduce them further on top of the stove.

Remove the *bouquet garni* and cinnamon stick, and arrange each pork chop on a hot plate. Taste the purée for seasoning and spoon it over the chops. Then cross each chop with 2 pieces of banana.

Serve with the simple accompaniment of steamed rice.

This dish posed some problems for me when I first announced it under the name of *fricassée de porc jamaïquain* (Jamaican-style pork chops). Pork is often frowned on by customers (wrongly so, for it is a delicious meat). Disappointed by the small success of the dish, I decided to replace the word *porc* with *grouet*—which is the translation of pork in Swahili, the language spoken in East Africa where I once spent several years. Thus embellished with African folklore and the exoticism of the Antilles, orders for this dish increased.

Unhappily, at that time I then had a *maître d'hôtel* who refused to tell a lie (there are such). So, when a customer would ask him, "But, whatever is this *grouet*?" the poor man, not willing either to confess or to lie outright, would respond hastily, before fleeing to escape further questions, "Oh! I believe it is veal."

His honor more or less intact, he did allow the happy client to discover the enchantment and flavor of this French West Indian dish.

Côte de boeuf aux échalotes et au vinaigre
RIB OF BEEF WITH SHALLOT AND VINEGAR SAUCE

To serve 2:
    1 whole rib of beef, about 1¾ to 2¼ pounds (*Ask your butcher for the first rib. Ed.*)
    Coarse salt
    Freshly ground pepper
    4½ tablespoons butter, in all

3 shallots, finely chopped (preferably gray shallots—*échalotes grises*)

2 tablespoons wine vinegar

2 tablespoons freshly chopped parsley

A COMMENT ON COOKING MEAT:

Professionally, we control the cooking of meat by touch—that is to say, by pressing the index and third fingers on the center of the meat.

If the meat is soft to the touch, it is still very rare (*bleue* or *très saignante*); if it is firm on the surface but supple in the interior, it is rare (*saignante*); and when the pressure produces a bead or trickle of red blood, the meat is medium rare (*à point*). My advice is to keep a piece of meat rare, as this leaves it with more flavor.

It is preferable after cooking red meats (grilled, panfried, or roasted) to let them rest at least 10 minutes before serving, because if one cuts a red meat as soon as it has finished cooking, all the blood will run from it. But when the meat has had an opportunity to rest, the blood is permitted to settle within the flesh.

PREPARATION AND COOKING OF THE MEAT:

Sprinkle both sides of the rib with salt and freshly ground pepper. Then massage the meat lightly with the tips of your fingers in order to help the seasonings penetrate.

Heat 1½ tablespoons of the butter in a heavy skillet. When it foams, add the meat. It is important to keep the degree of heat at a medium temperature so that the meat does not form a dry crust that would impede the cooking. Sauté the meat about 10 minutes on each side, taking care that the butter does not burn.

Then remove the rib from the pan and put it on a small plate that you have placed upside down in the center of a larger plate. Cover with a mixing bowl (*or aluminum foil*) to keep warm. This way the juices will run off and the meat will not stew in them, which would spoil its quality.

PREPARATION OF THE SAUCE:

Discard the cooking fat and add the remaining 3 tablespoons of fresh butter to the skillet, followed by the chopped shallots. Stirring continuously with a wooden spoon, cook the shallots over medium to low heat for about 5 minutes. Take care not to let them brown.

Add the vinegar to the pan and cook 5 minutes longer, continuing to stir. Season the sauce with 3 or 4 turns of the pepper mill and add salt, if it is needed. Stir in the chopped parsley and any meat juices that have accumulated. Then transfer the sauce to a hot sauceboat.

TO SERVE:

Remove the rib bone, and slicing downward with the grain, carve the beef. First divide the heart of the meat (*noix*), then the fattier portions.

Serve the meat very hot, accompanied by the shallot sauce.

What can one add to this simple dish that gladdens the hearts of connoisseurs of meat? Why not a salad of curly yellow chicory—seasoned with olive oil, a bit of mustard, and a little wine vinegar. And if the wine that accompanies the meat is served as cool as you would serve fruit, I promise you an excellent meal.

Filet de boeuf aux raisins à la mathurini

FILET OF BEEF WITH RAISIN AND PEPPER SAUCE

To serve 4:

    1½ pounds beef *filet*, completely trimmed of fat, and cut into 4 thick slices. If you wish, you can use boneless rib (club) steaks in place of the *filet*.

    ½ cup yellow seedless raisins

    ¼ cup cognac or Armagnac

    2 tablespoons coarsely crushed black peppercorns (see below)

    Coarse salt

    4 tablespoons butter, in all

    ⅓ cup strong beef stock

PREPARATION IN ADVANCE:

1. The raisins: Bring 2 cups of water to a boil. Drop in the raisins, reduce heat, and barely simmer 5 minutes. Drain the raisins in a sieve and refresh under cold running water. Drain again.

When the raisins are well drained, put them in a small bowl, pour over them the cognac or Armagnac, and set aside.

2. The black peppercorns: To crush the peppercorns, spread them out on a towel and pound them with a rolling pin or the bottom of a small cast-iron skillet or casserole.

COOKING:

Sprinkle the slices of meat on both sides with coarse salt, and roll them in the crushed peppercorns. Press the pepper into the meat so that it adheres.

Heat 2 tablespoons of the butter in a skillet just large enough to hold the meat, and as soon as the butter begins to color, add the slices of *filet*. Over medium heat, cook them 2 or 3 minutes on each side, or about 5 minutes in all. The cooking time indicated is intended just to "hold" the meat, because it can vary, depending on the thickness as well as the texture, and certainly depending on your own taste.

When the *filets* are cooked, put them on a small plate that you have placed upside down in the center of a larger plate, so that the meat will not stew in its own juices. Cover with a large mixing bowl (*or aluminum foil*) to keep warm.

PREPARATION OF THE SAUCE:

Discard the cooking fat, but do not clean the pan. Pour the cognac, or Armagnac, and raisins into the skillet, all at once. As you do this, hold the pan far enough away from direct heat so that you do not create a fireworks display. The purpose of the alcohol is to help release the juices that adhere to the pan. Reduce the liquid, then add the beef stock. Simmer gently for 2 minutes without letting it reduce too much. Then stir in the remaining 2 tablespoons butter, cut into tiny pieces, a few at a time (about 4 or 5 additions). Stir continuously until you obtain a thickened *liaison* and take care that the sauce does not become oily from overheating. Taste for salt.

TO SERVE:

Arrange the four pieces of meat on four hot plates and nap them with the sauce. (*Or if you wish, you can return them to the skillet for a moment and baste them with sauce before serving; Ed.*)

Why the name *mathurini?*

When I served this recipe for the first time, I gave it an accompaniment of a corn cake and buttered spinach leaves. And I must confess that the spinach made me think of Popeye. Finding, however, that the name didn't seem very serious, I remembered that (in France) Popeye had a friend called Mathurin. From Mathurin to *mathurini* was no more than a step, which I cheerfully took.

Incidentally, I note that spinach does go very well with this dish.

Les filets mignons de veau au citron
FILET OF VEAL WITH LEMON
(Color picture 4)

To serve 4:
  2 *filets* of veal, about ¾ pound each; or you may use 4 loin chops, about 8 ounces each, well trimmed of fat
  2 ripe lemons
  1 teaspoon sugar
  Coarse salt
  Freshly ground pepper, preferably white
  8 tablespoons butter, in all
  ½ cup dry white wine
  1 heaping tablespoon freshly chopped parsley

PREPARATION OF THE LEMON GARNITURE:

Using a vegetable peeler, remove all of the lemon zest in long thin strips. Do not include any white pith. Then stack the zests in bands of 4 or more, and cut them into fine julienne strips about the size of toothpicks. Place the zests in a small heavy saucepan with ⅔ cup of cold water and bring to a boil. Then drain in a sieve and rinse under cold running water.

Return the drained lemon zests to the saucepan with the sugar and 2 tablespoons of water. Cook over medium to low heat, stirring continuously, until all the water has evaporated and the julienne strips are glossy bright yellow. Take the pan from heat and set aside. (*As the zests stand, they will dry and become glazed in appearance. Ed.*)

Peel the rest of each lemon close to the flesh, removing all traces of white. Then cut them into thin slices and extract any seeds. Set aside.

COOKING THE VEAL:

If you are using the boned *filets* for this recipe, cut each one into 4 thick medallions. If you are using chops, make sure they are well trimmed of fat. Sprinkle the veal on both sides with salt and freshly ground pepper.

Over medium heat, melt 3 tablespoons of the butter in a heavy skillet. When the butter sizzles, arrange the veal in the pan and brown it on both sides. Allow about 5 or 6 minutes to a side, but you can start to turn the veal in 3 minutes or as soon as it begins to brown. Adjust the heat to be sure that the meat does not burn. When the veal is cooked, remove it from the skillet and set aside on a hot platter, covered, to keep warm.

PREPARATION OF THE SAUCE:

Pour off all the cooking butter, but do not wash the skillet. Add the white wine and let it reduce over medium heat, while scraping away the particles of cooking juices attached to the bottom and sides of the pan. When the wine has reduced to 2 or 3 tablespoons, stir in the remaining butter, cut into tiny pieces. A dark rich *liaison* should form.

As soon as this happens, immediately remove the pan from heat and stir in a pinch of salt, freshly ground pepper, and the chopped parsley.

TO SERVE:

Arrange the cooked veal on hot plates, and stir back into the sauce the juices that have accumulated. Then nap the veal with sauce and top each medallion, or chop, with a slice or two of lemon.

Decorate the meat with several pinches of the fine julienne strips of lemon zest and serve at once.

Rognons de veau du Moulin
VEAL KIDNEYS IN MUSTARD SAUCE

To serve 2:

    2 veal kidneys
    Coarse salt
    Freshly ground pepper
    2 tablespoons butter, in all
    2 tablespoons chopped shallot
    3 tablespoons Calvados
    ⅓ cup heavy cream
    1 level tablespoon Dijon mustard
    2 tablespoons coarsely chopped fresh chervil (*or substitute fresh parsley; Ed.*)

PREPARATION OF THE KIDNEYS:

The kidneys must be absolutely fresh and of the best quality. The flesh should be very pink and well wrapped in dry white fat (suet).

Pull away the fat and the fine transparent skin covering the nodules of the kidney. The flesh will brighten as you do this. Split the kidneys in half lengthwise, making the cut on the side where the gristle and fat are attached. Pull out all the fat, including the sinews found on the interior. Take care to avoid damaging the rest of the kidney.

Then cut the lengths of kidney crosswise into slices ¼-inch thick and about the size of a half-dollar. Lay the slices on a plate and season with salt and freshly ground pepper.

COOKING THE KIDNEYS (*see Note*):

Over medium to high heat, melt 1 tablespoon of the butter in a heavy casserole or skillet about 10 inches in diameter. When the butter sizzles, add half the slices of kidney. Brown them well on one side, then, using a spatula, turn them and brown the other side. This will take about 4 or 5 minutes.

Drain the cooked kidney in a sieve, placed over a bowl to catch the pink juices that will be released.

Cook the remainder of the kidney slices the same way, using the remaining tablespoon of butter. Then drain them in the sieve with the first batch. (*Do not save the juices. Ed.*)

NOTE: *The reason for cooking the kidneys in two batches is because it is important that they be uncrowded and do not overlap. However, I found that using a large skillet, and 2 tablespoons of butter, I was able to cook them all at once. Ed.*)

PREPARATION OF THE SAUCE:

Do not clean the casserole. Over very low heat, add the shallot with the Calvados. Stir with a wooden spoon, detaching all particles sticking to the bottom and sides of the casserole. Be careful to keep the casserole from direct contact with the heat, so that the alcohol does not ignite. In this instance, that is not your goal.

When all the residue from the kidneys has dissolved, pour in the heavy cream and simmer 2 minutes, while stirring with a wire whisk.

Then pass the sauce through a fine sieve into a clean casserole. Press down hard so that all the sauce passes through the sieve.

Whisk in the mustard, and when well-blended, stir the drained kidneys into the sauce. Bring the sauce just to a simmer. (It is important that the sauce does not boil after the kidneys are added, or they will become rubbery.) Taste for salt, and add a pinch of freshly ground pepper and the chopped chervil.

Serve at once on hot plates.

Fricassée de rognons et de ris de veau aux feuilles d'épinards

VEAL KIDNEY AND SWEETBREAD IN CREAM WITH SPINACH

To serve 3 or 4:

1¼ pounds young leaf spinach
Coarse salt
1 whole sweetbread, about 1¼ pounds
1 veal kidney, about 8 ounces
5 tablespoons butter, in all
Freshly ground white pepper
1 tablespoon olive oil
⅜ cup dry white wine
1 shallot, finely chopped (preferably a gray shallot—*échalote grise*)
¾ cup strong chicken or veal stock
⅛ teaspoon paprika
⅞ cup heavy cream

PREPARATION IN ADVANCE:

1. The spinach: Strip off the stems and wash the leaves in several changes of water. Drain the spinach and plunge it into a large casserole of boiling salted water. As soon as the water returns to a boil, quickly drain the leaves and plunge them into a basin of cold water. When cool, drain again.

It is necessary to cook spinach—like all green vegetables—uncovered, and quickly refreshed to keep their chlorophyll.

2. The sweetbread: (*The sweetbread must be absolutely fresh and white in color, and prepared as soon as possible. Before cooking, place the sweetbread in a bowl of ice water and let it stand for 1 hour or longer, changing the water several times. Then remove as much of the fat and gelatinous membrane as possible. Ed.*)

Place the sweetbread in a casserole with 2 quarts of cold unsalted water, and over medium heat, bring just to a simmer. Maintain the water at a simmer for 5 minutes, then drain, and drop the sweetbread into a bowl of ice water. When thoroughly chilled, remove any remaining fat or membrane. (*This can be done the evening before. Place the sweetbread on a plate, weighted down slightly by another plate, and reserve in the refrigerator. Ed.*)

Cut the sweetbread into pieces about the size and thickness of a walnut, and set aside.

3. The veal kidney: (*The veal kidney should be absolutely fresh, pale, and glossy, with a milklike translucency. Ed.*)

Pull off all fat and the fine transparent skin, then cut the kidney into walnut-size pieces, about the same as those of the sweetbread.

COOKING:

1. The spinach: Squeeze the spinach with your hands to extract all water possible, then sauté it in a medium-size skillet or casserole with 2 tablespoons of butter. Turn the leaves in the butter with a fork.

Season the spinach with salt and freshly ground pepper, then cover to keep warm and set aside.

2. The veal kidney: Melt 1 tablespoon of butter with the olive oil in a 10-inch skillet or casserole over high heat. Season the morsels of kidney with salt and freshly ground pepper, and when the fat sizzles and begins to color slightly, drop them into the pan. Keep the heat high, but watch carefully to make sure that the fat does not burn. Allow about 3 minutes to sauté the pieces of kidney on all sides. Then drain them in a colander or coarse sieve placed over a bowl, and cover to keep warm. Do not wash the skillet.

3. The sweetbread: While the kidney drains, melt 2 tablespoons of butter in another 10-inch skillet or casserole over medium heat. Season the morsels of sweetbread with salt and freshly ground pepper, and as soon as the butter foams, arrange them side by side in the pan. Cook the sweetbread about 5 minutes, turning the pieces on all sides until lightly browned. When you are finished, remove the sweetbread from the skillet and place it in the receptacle with the kidney, covered, to keep warm.

PREPARATION OF THE SAUCE:

Pour the white wine into the skillet used to cook the kidney, and add the chopped shallot. Bring the wine to a boil and reduce until only about 2 tablespoons remain. Then add the chicken or veal stock and reduce again, until there is only just enough liquid to coat the bottom of the pan (*about ¼ cup*).

Add a good pinch of paprika and the heavy cream, and stirring frequently, boil the sauce about 5 minutes or until thick enough to coat the back of a spoon. Taste for seasoning.

TO SERVE:

Divide the spinach among three or four hot plates, placing a mound in the center of each one. Surround the spinach with alternating pieces of sweetbread and kidney.

NOTE: *If you suspect there is a chance that the sweetbread and kidney may have cooled slightly, stir them into the hot sauce for a moment before arranging them around the spinach. But do not cook further, or the kidney will become rubbery. Ed.*

Strain the hot sauce through a fine sieve, then coat each morsel lightly. Serve the dish very hot, and pass any remaining sauce separately in a hot sauceboat.

This dish is not very difficult to prepare. Have the spinach and sweetbread prepared in advance, and all that remains is the final cooking—just before serving. This requires no more than about 15 minutes time to sauté the spinach, kidney, and sweetbread and then to finish the sauce.

Aiguillettes de foie de veau aux radis et aux navets
CALF'S LIVER WITH RADISHES AND TURNIPS

To serve 2:

>2 thick slices calf's liver, about 7 ounces each
>1 cup milk
>5 ounces small young turnips
>9 tablespoons butter, in all
>Coarse salt
>16 small radishes, of uniform size
>1 tablespoon finely chopped onion
>3 tablespoons wine vinegar
>4 tablespoons beef stock
>Freshly ground pepper
>Flour (*about ½ cup*)
>1 level teaspoon Dijon mustard
>1 tablespoon chopped fresh parsley

PREPARATION:

1. The calf's liver: Lay the 2 slices of liver on a chopping board and cut them into strips as large as your little finger. Then drop them into a bowl of cold milk. Turn the strips with your hand several times to make sure that they are free on all sides to absorb the milk. Refrigerate 1 hour. The purpose of this operation is to draw out the blood and tenderize the meat.

After 1 hour, turn the liver into a colander placed in the kitchen sink, and drain well. (Save the milk only if you have a cat.)

2. The turnips: Peel the turnips and cut them into small sticks, about 1 inch in length and ¼-inch thick. Put them in a small casserole with 1½ tablespoons of the butter, sprinkle lightly with salt, and add just enough water to barely cover. Stirring frequently, cook the turnips over high heat until the water has completely evaporated. The turnips must stay white and slightly crunchy.

3. The radishes: (*For the most part, radishes grown in the United States are larger than those found in France. I suggest that you buy several bunches so that you can select only the smallest. Ed.*)

Trim the root ends of the radishes and cut off the leaves, but retain about 1 inch of green stem. Wash and drain.

Melt 1½ tablespoons of the butter in a small casserole, and when it begins to foam, add the radishes. Salt lightly and cook over low heat for 2 or 3 minutes. Then add them to the casserole with the turnips and cover to keep warm. Do not wash the casserole.

COOKING:

1. The sauce: Melt 1 tablespoon of the butter in the small casserole used to cook the radishes. Add the chopped onion and sauté over medium heat until soft but not browned. Then add the vinegar and cook until the vinegar is reduced to 1 tablespoon. Add the beef stock, and reduce again until syrupy (about 5 minutes). Set aside.

2. The calf's liver: Dry the strips of calf's liver well with paper towels, season with salt and freshly ground pepper, and dredge the liver in flour. Then, one by one, lay the strips out on your work surface and roll them with the palm of your hand.

Melt 2 tablespoons of the butter in a 14-inch skillet over high heat. When it sizzles, arrange the strips of liver side by side in the pan. Brown them quickly, turning the strips on all sides for even cooking. Keep them rare! When finished, place the strips in a thoroughly dry sieve or colander and keep them in a warm place. Wipe the skillet without washing it.

FINISHING THE SAUCE:

Return the casserole with the sauce to low heat. Then, using a wire whisk, stir in the remaining 3 tablespoons of butter, cut into tiny pieces. Do not let the sauce boil or it will separate. As soon as the butter is incorporated, remove the casserole from heat and stir in the mustard. Taste for seasoning and add a pinch of salt and freshly ground pepper.

Pass the sauce through a fine sieve into the skillet used to cook the liver. (*This refinement is optional. Ed.*) Return the liver to the skillet with the freshly chopped parsley, and bring just to a simmer, while turning the strips of liver to coat them with sauce.

TO SERVE:

Divide the liver between two hot plates and surround with the turnips and radishes which have been kept warm. (*Reheat briefly, if necessary. Ed.*)

Carré d'agneau rôti au poivre vert

ROAST RACK OF LAMB WITH GREEN PEPPERCORNS

To serve 2:

NOTE: *A rack of lamb—7 or 8 ribs composed of one side of the rib section—will easily serve 2 persons. However, if you wish to serve 4, purchase the whole rib section, split into 2 pieces, and double the other ingredients. The directions and cooking time will remain the same. Ed.*

1 rack of lamb, taken from the first 7 or 8 ribs, fat removed, but all bones and trimmings reserved (*see Note*)
Coarse salt
Freshly ground pepper
2 tablespoons softened butter, in all
1½ tablespoons green peppercorns (*poivre vert*), packed in water, drained
1 rounded teaspoon extra-strong Dijon mustard (*moutarde forte de Dijon*)
1 tablespoon freshly chopped parsley
1 egg white
½ lemon
A pinch fine salt
1 ounce (*⅓ cup*) fine fresh bread crumbs

NOTE: *After carefully trimming almost all fat from the lamb, have your butcher pare away the meat and gristle from the protruding rib bones so that they are clean and separated from one another, giving you smooth handles to facilitate carving and serving the meat later. (In the United States, this is often called "Frenching" the chops.)*

Then have him help you further by cracking the vertebrae between the ribs, taking care not to damage the meat. Discard the surplus of fat, but have your butcher save for you every bit of bone and trimmings from the meat. Ed.

COOKING THE LAMB:

The meat should stand at room temperature for at least an hour before roasting. Ed.

Preheat oven to 500° F.

Place the lamb in a shallow roasting pan, resting on its backbone with the trimmed ribs standing upright. Sprinkle with salt and freshly ground pepper and scatter the trimmings under and around the meat. Then spread the lamb with 1 tablespoon of the butter and roast 25 minutes, basting from time to time. (It is the custom to serve mutton somewhat rare, and lamb pink.)

After the meat has cooked, arrange it on an inverted plate that you have placed over a larger plate (to catch the juices), and cover it with a large mixing bowl (*or aluminum foil*). This will keep the meat warm while preventing it from stewing in its own juices, which would spoil the quality of the meat.

FINISHING THE LAMB:

Preheat the broiler to its maximum temperature.

Crush the drained green peppercorns with a fork; then blend them with the mustard and chopped parsley.

Beat the egg white until very stiff. Do this at the last moment so that the white will not revert to liquid.

NOTE: To be certain that the egg white will mount properly, make sure that there is not a trace of grease in your mixing bowl. To do this, rub the bowl with half a lemon, then rinse and dry it. Add a pinch of fine salt to the egg white, and lastly, the egg white must not be too cold.

Drain the cooking fat from the roasting pan into a small bowl and keep warm. Add ¼ cup of water to the pan, and over low heat, stir the bones and trimmings, also loosening the particles of juices that adhere to the bottom and sides of the pan. Then, leaving the bones and trimmings in the roasting pan, pass the juices through a fine sieve into a small saucepan. There should be 3 or 4 tablespoons. Add freshly ground pepper and stir in the remaining tablespoon of butter. Keep warm.

Carefully blend the green-peppercorn-mustard mixture into the beaten egg white, and using a metal pastry spatula or flexible knife, spread the flat side of the lamb with it, making a coating about ½-inch thick. Then sprinkle the coating with bread crumbs and baste it all over with the reserved cooking fat.

Lay the lamb carefully over the bones and trimmings remaining in the roasting pan, then pass the meat under the broiler grill for 3 or 4 minutes or until a golden crust has formed.

TO SERVE:

Carve through the chops and arrange them on a hot platter. Add all the lamb juices that have accumulated to the warmed pan juices and serve separately.

A rack of lamb, usually a simple dish, becomes an offering with real character when treated this way and served with very fine young string beans dressed with fresh butter.

Estouffade de gigot d'agneau avec les tartines d'ail 🌸
LAMB BRAISED IN RED WINE 🌿

To serve 6 or 8:

    One 6½-pound leg of lamb, boned (ask your butcher to do this for you)

    1 large onion (*about 8 ounces*), coarsely chopped

    4 cloves garlic, flattened and peeled

    1 pound tomatoes, about 4 ounces each

    Bouquet garni (1 small bunch parsley, 1 small stalk celery with leaves, 1 large bay leaf, 1 orange zest, and 2 large branches fresh or dried thyme, tied together)

    1 tablespoon bruised white peppercorns

    2 bottles (*6 cups*) robust dry red wine

    3 tablespoons olive oil

    ½ pound lean salt pork (unsmoked bacon), in one piece

    1 pork skin, about 10 ounces

    1 teaspoon coarse salt

    Beef stock (*about 4 cups*)

    1½ cups flour

PREPARATION (in the morning, or about 8 hours before serving):

1. Marinating the lamb: Make sure that all fat has been removed from the meat. Then cut it into large pieces about 3 ounces each. (*The boneless lamb should weigh about 4½ pounds. Ed.*)

Place the lamb in a very large 7- to 8-quart casserole of enameled cast iron or earthenware, with the chopped onion and flattened whole cloves of garlic.

Drop the tomatoes into boiling water, count to 10, then plunge them into cold water. Peel the tomatoes, remove the core, and cut them into large dice. Add the tomato to the lamb with the *bouquet garni* and bruised peppercorns.

Pour the wine over the meat and add the olive oil. Using a wooden spoon, turn the lamb in the wine, bringing the pieces of meat from the bottom of the casserole to the top. Let the lamb marinate 4 hours at room temperature, turning the meat from time to time.

2. The salt pork and pork skin: Cut the salt pork into *lardons,*

sticks the size of your thumb, and the pork skin into pieces about ¾-inch square. Place the salt pork and pork skin together in a saucepan with 1½ quarts of cold water and bring to a boil. Then reduce heat and simmer 5 minutes. Drain the *lardons* and pork skin in a sieve and rinse well under cold running water.

COOKING:

After the lamb has marinated 3½ hours, preheat oven to 325° F. After 4 hours, add the *lardons* and pork skin to the lamb with 1 teaspoon coarse salt and enough beef stock to cover the meat by ¾ of an inch.

Put the flour into a mixing bowl and moisten it with about ¾ cup cold water, added a little at a time. Knead the mixture until you obtain a soft dough. Use this dough to make an airtight seal around the lid of the casserole, so that no steam escapes during the cooking.

Place the sealed casserole in the oven and do not disturb for 3½ hours.

TO SERVE:

Only at the moment you are ready to serve the lamb, break the seal of the cover.

Discard the *bouquet garni* and use a cooking spoon to skim off any fat swimming on the surface of the sauce. Taste for seasoning and serve very hot in warmed deep plates or wide-rimmed soup bowls, accompanied by garlic toasts.

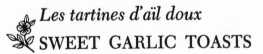

Les tartines d'ail doux
SWEET GARLIC TOASTS

To serve 6 or 8:
> 5 large heads new garlic, preferably the purple variety
> Coarse salt
> 3 tablespoons olive oil
> 1 or 2 loaves *pain-baguette* (*the long thin loaves of French bread; Ed.*)

PREPARATION OF THE GARLIC:

Separate 5 whole heads of garlic and peel each clove (*in this instance, you do not want to flatten the cloves; Ed.*). If there is a green sprout at the end of a clove, it is very important to split the garlic in half and remove it.

Drop the cloves into 2 quarts of cold lightly salted water and bring to a boil. Let the garlic boil vigorously for 5 minutes, then drain in a sieve.

Immediately begin the entire operation all over again—dropping the blanched cloves of garlic into 2 quarts of fresh cold salted water, and boiling them for 5 minutes. When the garlic has been brought to a boil in this manner 4 times (the cloves should be soft to the touch), drain, and purée them in a food processor or blender, or press them through a food mill, using the fine grate.

Incorporate 3 tablespoons of olive oil into the purée and add a pinch of salt to taste.

PREPARATION OF THE TARTINES:

Preheat the broiler at a low setting. (*If your broiler temperature is not adjustable, you will have to place the* tartines *as far from the heating element as possible. Ed.*)

Cut 1 or 2 long thin loaves of French bread into approximately 32 small rounds. Place the slices on an oiled baking sheet and toast them very lightly on both sides.

Then spread the toast liberally with the sweet garlic purée and return them to the broiler briefly, until glazed.

Serve the *tartines* with the *estouffade* of lamb. Soak them in the broth of the meat. And you will see. . . .

Blanquette d'agneau aux haricots et aux pieds d'agneau
LAMB WITH BEANS AND LAMB'S FEET

To serve 6:

½ pound dried *flageolets,* or other small dried beans (*see Note*)
One 3½-pound lamb shoulder, boned
2 onions, peeled
2 cloves
6 carrots
1 whole leek, washed and trimmed
3 small *bouquets garnis* (each composed of: 1 large sprig fresh thyme, 4 sprigs parsley, 1 stalk celery, and 1 bay leaf, tied together)
Coarse salt
3 lamb's feet (*If lamb's feet are unavailable, substitute 2 calf's feet, split. Ed.*)
2 lemons
1 tablespoon flour
4 teaspoons white peppercorns
3 quarts beef stock
1¼ cups *crème fraîche* (*or substitute heavy cream; Ed.*)
3 tablespoons Dijon mustard
4 egg yolks
Freshly ground white pepper (optional)
1 tablespoon chopped fresh parsley
1 tablespoon chopped fresh chervil (*If fresh chervil is unavailable, increase the quantity of parsley; Ed.*)

NOTE: *Flageolets* can be replaced by other varieties of dried white beans, or even by fresh *flageolets* (essentially a green shell bean). However, this dish is on the whole a winter recipe, so I have preferred to indicate the use of dried beans.

If you do use fresh beans, the quantity should be 2 pounds, shelled. Do not soak them, and reduce the cooking time to 30 minutes.

PREPARATION (12 hours in advance):

1. The dried beans: Soak the beans overnight in a large volume of cold water. They will absorb the water as they swell.

2. The lamb: Remove every bit of fat from the meat, then cut it into large cubes, about 1½ to 1¾ ounces each. Place the meat in a large basin and cover with ice water.

Refrigerate the meat 12 hours, changing the water once or twice. The reason for this procedure is to draw out the blood from the meat and to whiten it.

COOKING:

1. The dried beans: Drain the beans and put them in a casserole with 3 quarts of cold water. Add 1 onion stuck with 2 cloves, 2 whole carrots, the leek, and 1 *bouquet garni*.

Simmer the beans 2 hours over medium to low heat, skimming the surface frequently. After 15 minutes cooking time, add a good pinch of salt. The total cooking time will vary, depending on the variety and quality of the beans. I advise you to test them by tasting one from time to time.

2. The lamb's feet: While the beans are cooking, rub the lamb's feet with the juice of 1 lemon. Then plunge them into 3 quarts of rapidly boiling water. Let boil 10 minutes to blanch them, drain, and rinse under cold running water.

Use a small knife to cut off the nails, then put the feet into a clean casserole with 3 quarts of cold water and the juice of the second lemon. Add a tablespoon of flour that has been mixed separately with water, 2 whole carrots, 1 *bouquet garni*, and 2 teaspoons of the peppercorns. Simmer the lamb's feet about 2 hours, but do not overcook them.

When the lamb's feet have finished cooking, drain and rinse them, then bone them completely and cut the meat into morsels not too small in size.

3. The lamb: While the beans and lamb's feet are cooking, drain the cubes of lamb and put them into a large casserole with the beef stock, the 2 remaining whole carrots, peeled, the other whole onion, the remaining 2 teaspoons of peppercorns, and the last *bouquet garni*. Add a little salt, depending on the saltiness of the beef stock, and simmer the lamb 1½ hours over medium heat.

FINISHING THE BLANQUETTE:

1. The lamb: Use a skimmer to lift the cooked meat from the broth and place it in a clean casserole (preferably earthenware) with the meat from the lamb's feet. Cover them to keep warm while you finish the sauce.

Over high heat, boil down the stock until reduced to 1 quart, then set aside.

2. The sauce: In a small bowl, blend the cream with the mustard and egg yolks.

Stirring continuously with a wire whisk, pour the mustard-cream *liaison* into the reduced lamb broth. Warm the broth very gently over low heat while continuing to stir without stopping. Add salt and freshly ground pepper to taste.

At the first sign of a simmer, remove the sauce from heat and pour it through a sieve held over the casserole with the lamb.

Drain the beans (they must be very hot at this moment), discard their *garniture*, and mix with the lamb, turning them carefully in the sauce.

Let the *blanquette* return to a simmer, sprinkle with chopped parsley and chervil, and serve very hot.

Cul de lapereau à la crème de basilic
RABBIT WITH BASIL AND CREAM

To serve 2 or 4:

If you wish, you may use only the saddle and hind legs of the rabbit (about 2½ pounds) to serve 2, and save the rest of the meat for a Terrine of Rabbit in Aspic (*gâteau de lapereau en gelée du Moulin*, page 57), or you can use the whole rabbit (about 3¾ pounds dressed) to serve 4.

1 young 5-pound rabbit, about 3¾ pounds dressed
Coarse salt
Freshly ground pepper, preferably white

3 tablespoons butter, softened
1 large sprig fresh thyme (*or substitute* ½ *teaspoon dried thyme; Ed.*)
1 tablespoon chopped shallot
⅜ cup dry white wine
8 tablespoons heavy cream, in all
1 egg yolk
1 heaping tablespoon chopped fresh basil
1 heaping tablespoon chopped fresh parsley
½ lemon (optional)

PREPARATION OF THE RABBIT:

If you have a whole rabbit and wish to prepare this dish for only 2 persons, cut the rabbit in half crosswise, just behind the last ribs. Take care to make a clean cut and avoid splintering the bone. Save the rest of the meat for another dish.

With a small sharp knife, pierce the flesh above the joints of the hind legs to separate them. Then divide the saddle into large manageable pieces. If you are using the whole rabbit, proceed in the same manner with the front legs and rib cage. Season with salt and pepper.

COOKING:

Spread the softened butter over the bottom of a casserole just large enough to hold the pieces of rabbit, and arrange the meat within. Add a sprig of thyme, cover the casserole, and cook the rabbit about 30 to 40 minutes over very low heat.

Check the rabbit frequently to make sure that it does not brown. Also, if the butter shows signs of separating (it will become oily), add 2 tablespoons warm water and lower the heat further.

Keep the casserole covered throughout the cooking. To check that the rabbit is done, pierce the meatiest part of the leg with a fork. If the drops of juices that appear are white, the meat is done. If the juices are rosy, continue the cooking. When the rabbit is done, remove it from the casserole and wrap in aluminum foil to keep warm.

PREPARATION OF THE SAUCE:

Raise the heat underneath the casserole and add the chopped shallot.

Then, after a moment, add the white wine, and reduce it until only 3 tablespoons of liquid remain.

Add 4 tablespoons of the cream and bring to a simmer. Then, off heat, mix the egg yolk with the remaining 4 tablespoons of cream, and stir it into the casserole.

Return the casserole to the stove and bring the cream just to a simmer; then pass it through a fine sieve into a small heavy saucepan. Season with salt and freshly ground pepper.

TO SERVE:

Just before serving, stir freshly chopped basil and parsley into the sauce, and if you would like a degree of tartness, add the juice of ½ lemon. Nap the rabbit with sauce and serve at once.

Buttered pasta is a very good accompaniment to this dish.

I   *Individual spinach custards*
    Zucchini and tomato casserole
    Artichokes barigoule

2　*The little stuffed vegetables of Provence*

3   Terrine of rabbit in aspic

4 Warm rabbit salad with wild lettuces
Crayfish tails with butter sauce

Filet of veal with lemon
Raspberry, lemon, and orange ices

5   *Chicken baked in a salt crust*

6   *Fish cooked in cream with vegetables*

7 *Orange custard*
   Lemon custard tart

Snow eggs with pralines
Compote of winter fruits in wine

Les volailles & le gibier

POULTRY & GAME BIRDS

Fricassée de volaille aux herbes vertes du jardin
STEWED CHICKEN WITH GREEN HERB SAUCE

To serve 2 or 4:

NOTE: *If you use a larger chicken, this dish will serve 4 persons. No other changes in the recipe are necessary. However, if you do use a large chicken, it would be best to divide it into 8 pieces—separating the leg and thigh, and detaching the wings from the breast. Ed.*

1 chicken, about 3¼ to 3¾ pounds, dressed
1 bunch watercress, about 5 ounces
1 bouquet of chervil, about 1 ounce (*or substitute young flat-leafed parsley; Ed.*)
1 branch fresh tarragon
1 bouquet of young sorrel leaves, about 1½ ounces
7 ounces fresh young spinach leaves
5 tablespoons butter, in all
2 shallots, finely chopped
Salt
Freshly ground pepper, preferably white
1 egg yolk
½ cup heavy cream

HAVE READY:

1. The chicken: Clean and singe the fowl as you would for roasting; then quarter it. Make a slight incision between the leg and the body to facilitate the cooking, and cut off the wing tips.

2. The herbs: Wash all the herbs in several changes of water. Drain them thoroughly.

Detach and discard the stems from the watercress and chervil. Detach the tarragon leaves, but save the stem. (*Lightly packed, you should have about 2⅔ cups of leaves. Ed.*)

3. The sorrel: Working from bottom to top, strip off the stem and central vein from each leaf. Gather small bunches of leaves together, and roll each roughly into the shape of a cigar, then cut into thin shreds. This is called a *chiffonnade*.

Set the sorrel aside with the other herbs.

4. The spinach: Strip off the stems and wash the leaves in 3 or 4 changes of water. Then roll the leaves into cigars in the same manner used for sorrel, and cut them into a *chiffonnade*.

Together, the spinach and sorrel should make about 1 quart, tightly packed.

COOKING THE CHICKEN:

Liberally grease the bottom and sides of a large enameled cast-iron casserole with 3 tablespoons of the butter, softened, and distribute the shallots over all.

Sprinkle the chicken with salt and freshly ground pepper and arrange the pieces, skin side down, in the casserole. Add the tarragon stem, cover the casserole, and cook the chicken slowly, over low heat. The chicken must stay white—that is to say, the butter must remain creamy. This operation is called stewing (*étuver*) and it is indispensable that the casserole have a tightly fitting cover.

Cook the chicken about 35 minutes (*nearly 1 hour for a large bird; Ed.*), turning the pieces several times. Test for doneness by inserting the point of a knife near the top of the thigh bone. If the juices are pink, continue to cook the chicken. The meat is done when the juices run clear.

COOKING THE GREENS:

While the chicken is cooking, melt the remaining 2 tablespoons of butter in a 2-quart casserole. Drop in the spinach and stir with a wooden spoon until no more than a few drops of liquid remain on the bottom of the casserole. Then add the rest of the greens (sorrel, watercress, chervil, and tarragon).

Stirring constantly, cook over medium to high heat until all are limp. This will take only 2 or 3 minutes. (*The volume will decrease to about 2 cups. Take care that the greens do not scorch, and if necessary, add a small piece of butter. Ed.*) Set aside, uncovered.

PREPARATION OF THE SAUCE:

Mix the egg yolk with 2 tablespoons of the cream. Set aside.

When the chicken is done, remove it from the casserole and set aside on a hot serving platter, covered, to keep warm. There should be about $\frac{1}{2}$ cup of good cooking juices remaining in the casserole.

Add the rest of the cream to the casserole and return it to high heat. Boil the sauce 3 or 4 minutes, stirring constantly.

Add the greens and bring the sauce to a simmer, then remove from heat, and stir in the egg-yolk-cream *liaison*. Mixing with a wooden spoon, let the sauce thicken slightly; then taste for seasoning and add salt and freshly ground pepper.

TO SERVE:

Arrange the chicken on hot plates (*or serve it from the platter; Ed.*) and nap with the sauce. The garden will be on your table.

NOTE: *Hot buttered noodles are a perfect accompaniment to this dish. Ed.*

Fricassée de poulet au vinaigre de vin
CHICKEN IN RED WINE AND VINEGAR SAUCE

To serve 4:

> One 3¾-pound chicken, dressed and quartered (I prefer the white
> chickens of Allier which are raised on wheat)
> 1 pound yellow onions, thinly sliced
> 4 tablespoons butter, in all
> 2 ripe tomatoes, about 4 ounces each
> 2 cloves garlic, peeled
> *Bouquet garni* (1 small stalk celery with leaves, 1 large sprig fresh
> thyme, 1 bay leaf, and ½ bunch of parsley, tied together)
> Coarse salt
> Freshly ground pepper
> 1 cup red wine vinegar
> 1 cup dry red wine (preferably, the wine should be that which
> you plan to drink with the meal)

PREPARATION OF THE ONIONS AND TOMATOES:

Place the sliced onions in a large casserole with 1 tablespoon of the
butter and 2 tablespoons of water. Cover the casserole and cook the
onions over low heat for 30 minutes. Stir the onions from time to time
to make sure that they do not burn; if they should begin to color, add
another 2 tablespoons of water and lower the heat still further.

During this time, remove the core from the tomatoes, cut them in
half crosswise, and squeeze out the seeds and water. Then cut the
tomatoes into coarse pieces.

When the onions are ready, add the tomatoes and continue to
cook, covered, 5 minutes longer. Then take the casserole from heat
and press the garlic and *bouquet garni* into the midst of the vegetables. Set the casserole aside, covered.

PREPARATION OF THE CHICKEN:

Sprinkle the quarters of chicken with salt and freshly ground pepper.

Heat 2 tablespoons of the butter in another large casserole, and
over medium heat, brown the chicken slowly on both sides. (*Allow*

about 20 minutes for this operation, adjusting the heat as necessary to keep the butter from burning. Ed.)

Then arrange the chicken in the first casserole, over the bed of onions and tomatoes. Make sure that the chicken lies on top of the vegetables so that it will cook only by steam. Cover the casserole, and after the chicken has steamed 30 to 40 minutes, remove it (leave the vegetables in the casserole) and keep warm, covered, on a hot platter. *(Check the doneness by piercing the joint of the thigh with the point of a knife. If the juices run clear, the chicken is done; if they are pink, continue to cook. Ed.)*

PREPARATION OF THE SAUCE:

While the chicken is steaming, pour off and discard the cooking fat from the second casserole, and add the vinegar. Return the casserole to full heat and boil down the vinegar until it is reduced to a syrupy glaze. Then add the red wine and simmer until reduced to about 5 tablespoons. Set the casserole aside.

Remove the *bouquet garni* from the onions and tomatoes, and purée the vegetables in a food processor or blender, or use a food mill fitted with the fine grate. Turn the purée into the casserole with the vinegar-wine reduction, and stirring with a wooden spoon, bring it to a simmer. Then pass the sauce through a fine sieve, returning it to the first casserole. Add the chicken and its accumulated juices, and simmer about 5 minutes, while basting with the sauce.

Off heat, incorporate the remaining tablespoon of butter into the sauce. Taste for seasoning and add a pinch of salt and freshly ground pepper.

Serve the chicken steaming hot from the casserole.

This recipe brings back a recollection from Kenya. When I was there, one day I prepared a large banquet for a high-ranking Englishman whom I didn't know. I had ordered chickens from Allier. Inevitably, there was an airline strike (these things happen), so my chickens never arrived. Unhappily, the menu had been printed and it was out of the question to change it.

Desperately, I sent my helpers to the surrounding villages to raid the chicken supply. One hour later, I had dozens and dozens. However, they were scrawny and had the muscles of marathon runners. After cooking they revealed themselves not only to be hard as rocks, but the flesh was also as dark as that of game. They were far from my tender white chickens of Allier. Never have I had to cook anything so long as I did those birds. And in the end? The Englishman swore that positively nothing was as good as those delicious chickens from Allier.

Poulet grillé au citron
GRILLED LEMON CHICKEN

To serve 2: (*If you wish to serve 4 persons, double all the ingredients, but use 2 chickens rather than a larger fowl. All directions and the cooking time will remain the same. Ed.*)

    1 chicken, about 3¼ to 3½ pounds, dressed
    Coarse salt
    Freshly ground pepper
    1 teaspoon oregano
    1 sweet onion (preferably a new white onion)
    2 large lemons
    5 tablespoons olive oil, in all

PREPARATION (4 hours in advance):

Remove the feet, neck, and wing tips from the chicken; then lay it on its back on a chopping board. Using a large heavy knife, cleaver, or poultry shears, split the bird in half, following one side of the vertebral column. Then open the chicken and make a parallel cut through the other side of the vertebrae, taking out the entire backbone.

Make a small incision between the leg and thigh joints, then spread out the chicken, skin side up, and tap it with the side of a meat cleaver to flatten it slightly (but without crushing it!). Sprinkle both sides of the chicken with salt, freshly ground pepper, and oregano.

Peel and slice the onion and scatter it over the bottom of a shallow roasting pan (*preferably a terra cotta terrine; Ed.*). Lay the chicken on the bed of onion, skin side up.

Cut 1 of the lemons into very thin rounds and arrange them over the skin of the chicken. Brush 2 tablespoons of the olive oil over all. Cover with aluminum foil and marinate 4 hours in the refrigerator.

COOKING THE CHICKEN:

After marinating the chicken, preheat oven to 475°F and preheat broiler unit to the same temperature.

Remove the lemon slices from the chicken, but reserve them. Arrange the chicken on a separate shallow broiler pan, skin side up. Leave the onions in the first pan.

Baste the chicken with 1 tablespoon of the olive oil and place it under the broiler grill to brown. Then turn the bird and brown it on the other side, basting with the fat and juices that have accumulated. The chicken should be crisp. Allow about 10 minutes broiling time for each side.

Then take the chicken from the broiler pan and return it, skin side up, to the bed of onions in the first pan where it was marinated. Replace the slices of lemon over the crisp skin of the chicken, and brush the remaining 2 tablespoons of olive oil over all.

Bake the chicken in the 475°F oven for 30 to 35 minutes, depending on size. After 15 minutes, brush the chicken with the juice of the second lemon.

Check the chicken for doneness by making a small incision in the thigh. If the juices run clear, the chicken is done. If they are pink, cook a little longer.

TO SERVE:

Cut the chicken into 4 pieces and serve it very hot, still over the bed of onions and basted with the cooking juices.

Salade de tomates
TOMATO SALAD

A salad of tomatoes, cut into small quarters, is a marvelous accompaniment to the Lemon Chicken in the preceding recipe.

To serve 2:
   1 pound tomatoes, about 4 ounces each
   1 tablespoon fine salt
   Freshly ground pepper
   4 tablespoons wine vinegar
   5 tablespoons olive oil, in all
   1 tablespoon freshly chopped parsley

PREPARATION:

To make a good tomato salad, take 4 firm ripe tomatoes, weighing about 4 ounces each, core them, and cut each one into eighths.

Drop them into a bowl and mix with 1 tablespoon fine salt (yes, 1 tablespoon!), freshly ground pepper, the wine vinegar, and 2 tablespoons of the olive oil. When well combined, let stand 2 or 3 hours.

At the moment of serving, drain the tomatoes in a coarse sieve, discarding the juice. Turn the tomatoes into a salad bowl and toss with the remaining 3 tablespoons of olive oil. Sprinkle with chopped parsley and serve.

Poulet sous la croûte au sel
CHICKEN BAKED IN A SALT CRUST
(Color picture 5)

To serve 4:

 1 roasting chicken, about 4 pounds, dressed
 3 whole chicken livers
 2¼ pounds (6½ cups) flour
 2¼ pounds (4 cups) coarse sea salt (*gros sel de mer*)
 About 3 cups ice water
 Salt (*optional*)
 Freshly ground pepper
 1 large sprig fresh rosemary
 1 bay leaf
 4 cloves garlic, unpeeled (optional)
 Lettuce, wine vinegar, and walnut oil for accompanying salad

PREPARATION:

Preheat oven to 450°F.

1. The salt crust: Combine the flour and salt in a large mixing bowl. Add the ice water, ½ cup at a time, and knead until you have a well-blended workable dough.

Lay the dough on a lightly floured work surface, and using your hands, pat it and spread it out into a circle large enough to enclose the chicken.

2. The chicken: Rub the cavity of the chicken with salt (*optional*) and freshly ground pepper. Then slip inside the sprig of rosemary, bay leaf, and chicken livers (*and, if you like, 4 cloves of garlic; Ed.*).

Truss the bird simply with string (do not use skewers); then lay it breast down on the center of the dough. Wrap the dough completely around the chicken, enveloping it so that it will be hermetically sealed. Then turn the chicken over and lay it breast up on a baking sheet. Bake 1½ hours, undisturbed.

3. The salad: Prepare a salad seasoned with a good walnut-oil *vinaigrette* made with 1 tablespoon of wine vinegar to 4 tablespoons of oil.

TO SERVE:

Place the chicken, in its crust, on a large carving board, and bring it to the table.

All that remains is for you to break the crust with a strong heavy knife. Be forewarned, the crust is very hard. (*I suggest that you use a mallet to tap the knife gently through the crust, taking care not to pierce the chicken. Ed.*) Cut a circle around the top third of the crust, remove the lid, and lift out the chicken for carving.

Extract the 3 livers from the cavity, cut them into large slices, and mix them with the salad.

When a chicken is cooked in its own vapor this way, it keeps all its fullness of flavor, with just the slightest added aroma of rosemary and bay leaf.

NOTE: If you would like to prepare this dish in advance, it will keep very well for 30 to 40 minutes. But in this case, stop the cooking after 1 hour and 15 minutes, and do not open the crust until the moment of serving.

During the season of fresh truffles, you can slip 2 or 3 fine ones, weighing about 1¾ ounces each, inside the bird before wrapping it in the dough. The result is not bad, to say the least.

NOTE: *During one of several times that this recipe was prepared, I slipped an entire head of garlic inside the chicken. For myself, I found the result very satisfying. Ed.*

Le canard comme au Moulin
ROAST DUCK MOULIN-DE-MOUGINS

To serve 2:

NOTE: *If you wish to double the ingredients for this recipe—to serve 4 persons—it would be best to treat it initially as two separate operations, roasting each duck by itself in its own pan. After the meat is carved and the carcasses are cut into pieces, the remaining ingredients can be brought together in one casserole for the preparation of the sauce. Ed.*

One 6-pound Muscovy duck, about 5 pounds dressed (*see Note*)
Coarse salt
Freshly ground pepper
4 juniper berries, crushed slightly
1 branch fresh thyme (*or substitute ½ teaspoon dried thyme; Ed.*)
3 tablespoons butter, in all
1 cup robust dry red wine
4 shallots, coarsely chopped
1 teaspoon tomato paste
2 tablespoons cognac
Chicken stock (about 3 cups)

NOTE: It is preferable that the duck be killed by suffocation, not bled. (*This means that the duck should have its neck pulled, rather than cut, to allow the bird to retain its blood. The difference will distinguish this dish. Ed.*)

PREPARATION OF THE DUCK:

Preheat oven to 550°F (*or 500°F, if that is the highest temperature on your oven control; Ed.*).

After the duck has been plucked, remove any remaining quills and singe it. Then cut off the feet, wing tips, and neck. Using a meat cleaver, chop these pieces into small morsels. Clean the bird, but leave the liver, heart, and lungs in the cavity. Sprinkle the duck, inside and out, with salt and freshly ground pepper, and stick the juniper berries and thyme inside. Then truss the bird.

ROASTING THE DUCK:

Scatter the morsels of neck and wings over the bottom of a lightly greased roasting pan (*not aluminum*) just large enough to hold the duck. Spread the bird with 1½ tablespoons of the butter, softened, and lay it on its side in the pan.

Cook the duck 8 minutes on each side, then a final 10 minutes breast up. (*Each time you turn the duck, also turn the pieces of neck and wings. Ed.*) This hot searing will help to melt the excess fat in the skin. Remove the duck from the oven and let stand 20 to 30 minutes at room temperature.

171

Pour off all the cooking fat remaining in the roasting pan and replace it with the red wine. Stirring continuously, bring the wine to a boil, which will release the particles that adhere to the pan. Then set the pan aside.

After the duck has settled, detach the legs by cutting through the skin all around the joint with the point of a sharp knife. Pull on the leg to help release it.

Set the legs aside, covered, in a warm place (*such as the turned-off oven; Ed.*).

In the front part of the breast, near the base of the neck, you will find a triangular bone. With the point of a small sharp knife, remove it. Then carve each side of the breast into 5 long thin slices. These are called *aiguillettes*. Cover them to keep warm and set aside.

PREPARATION OF THE SAUCE:

Take the carcass of the duck and pull out the heart, liver, and lungs. Set them aside in a bowl. Also remove the juniper berries and branch of thyme, and add them to the roasting pan with the red wine.

Discarding any pieces of fat, use a meat cleaver to chop the bones of the carcass into small pieces. Heat the remaining 1½ tablespoons of butter in a casserole and add the bones. Over high heat, brown them well on all sides. Then add the shallots, and as soon as they are lightly browned, stir in the tomato paste. Add 2 tablespoons of warmed cognac and ignite. Stir the bones of the carcass until the flames extinguish themselves, then pour in the red wine with the juniper berries, thyme, and morsels of duck remaining in the roasting pan.

Bring the wine to a boil, and when it has reduced to ½ cup, add just enough chicken stock to barely cover the bones. Simmer the wine-stock about 20 minutes, or until the volume of liquid has been reduced by half.

During this time, place the heart, liver, and lungs on a cutting board and chop them very fine. If the liver is quite large, use only half (give the rest to the cat).

When the broth has reduced considerably, pour it, and the remains in the casserole, through a fine sieve into a clean casserole. Press down on the bones with a large cooking spoon. Skim off the fat; then reduce the broth again until there is barely ½ cup.

Add the chopped heart, liver, and lungs, and bring the sauce just to a boil. Then pass it through a fine sieve into the top of a double boiler (*bain-marie*). Press down very hard on the giblets to extract as much of their substance as possible, and scrape the bottom of the sieve from time to time. As you stir this *liaison* into the sauce, it will thicken. Add a partial turn of the pepper mill and taste for seasoning. The sauce should already be salty enough. Keep the sauce hot, stirring occasionally, but do not allow it to boil again.

FINISHING AND SERVING THE DUCK:

Preheat oven to 450°F.

Preheat the broiler at as low a temperature as possible, or with the broiler rack placed far from the heating element.

Just before you are ready to serve, sprinkle the duck legs with coarse salt and pass them under the broiler grill. Allow about 15 minutes to brown them. Stir any juices that have accumulated from the meat into the sauce.

When the legs are almost finished, divide the sauce between two very hot plates. Then distribute the *aiguillettes*, well displayed in a fan over the sauce. Spoon any juices that have accumulated over the meat, then place the plates in the hot oven for 1 minute before serving.

Serve the grilled legs on a separate hot plate, and accompany this dish with no more than a salad of curly chicory or escarole, seasoned with wine vinegar and walnut oil.

NOTE: This dish can be prepared in the morning, to be served in the evening. But you must never refrigerate the meat of the breast, or the legs, after they have been roasted, and do not add the *liaison* (heart, liver, and lungs) to the sauce until the last moment.

Canard en civet au vieux vin et aux fruits
DUCK IN RED WINE WITH WINTER FRUITS

To serve 2:

NOTE: *If you have a very large casserole—which will hold 2 ducks, quartered, and their* garniture—*you can increase this recipe to serve 4 persons. It is likely that you will need to add a larger quantity of wine to the marinade in order to cover the meat, but you should not have to adjust the proportions of any of the other ingredients. Ed.*

One 5- to 6-pound duck, about 4 pounds dressed (*a Muscovy duck is preferable, but not essential to this recipe; Ed.*)
1 carrot, thinly sliced
1 onion, thinly sliced
1 stalk celery, thinly sliced
3 cloves garlic, thinly sliced
Spices, tied together in a piece of cheesecloth:
    10 black peppercorns
    1 clove
    4 juniper berries
    1 branch fresh thyme (*or substitute ½ teaspoon dried thyme; Ed.*)
    1 orange zest (about ½ inch by 2 inches)
    4 sprigs parsley
4 cups robust red wine, such as a Burgundy, Côtes du Rhone, or an Algerian wine
10 large prunes, pitted
10 walnut halves
2 tablespoons butter, in all
Coarse salt
Freshly ground pepper
2 teaspoons flour
Chicken stock (optional)
1 Golden Delicious apple

In the morning or the evening of the day before you plan to serve the duck:

Remove any quills or pin feathers that you can find in the skin of the bird, then singe and clean it. Cut up the duck in the following manner:

Chop off the head and feet and discard them. Cut off and save the neck and wings. Detach the whole legs, and carve out the 2 meaty parts of the breast, each in one piece. Using a meat cleaver, chop up the bones of the carcass, and cut the reserved neck and wings into small pieces.

Arrange the meaty pieces of duck in a large bowl (*preferably glass or earthenware, not metallic; Ed.*), surrounded by the chopped-up bones, neck, and wings. Scatter the sliced vegetables over all. Stick the cheesecloth bag of aromatic spices deep into the center of the bowl and cover the contents with the red wine. (*Add more wine, if necessary. Ed.*)

Cover the bowl and marinate the duck at room temperature—about 10 to 12 hours, but not longer than 18 hours.

Soak the prunes in lukewarm water during this time.

COOKING THE DUCK:

Drain the duck, bones, and vegetables thoroughly in a large sieve placed over a 2-quart casserole to catch the wine. Also drain the prunes.

Place the prunes and walnut halves in the casserole with the wine marinade, and add the spice bag. Over low heat, bring the wine slowly to a simmer, skimming the surface as needed, and cook the fruits 15 minutes. Then set aside.

During this time, melt 1 tablespoon of the butter in a 5-quart enameled cast-iron casserole. Dry the meaty portions of legs and breast completely with paper towels, and sprinkle them on both sides with salt and pepper.

When the butter sizzles, arrange the pieces of duck, skin side down, in the casserole, and brown the meat very slowly so that the fat is rendered from the skin. Then turn the duck and brown the other side.

(Allow at least a full 15 minutes for this operation. If the meat is cooked too quickly, it will toughen before the fat is released. Ed.)

Set the well-browned pieces of meat aside on a plate, and add the chopped-up bones and vegetable *garniture* to the fat in the casserole. *(If you are cooking a lean Muscovy duck, there may not be as much fat as you need. In this case, add a little more butter. Ed.)* Raise the heat to medium and cook the bones and vegetables together until they are well browned. Then, holding them back with the cover to the casserole, tilt the casserole and pour off all the fat. *(If you are cooking a Muscovy duck, this may not be necessary. Ed.)*

Sprinkle the bones with the 2 teaspoons of flour and continue to cook 2 or 3 minutes, stirring and turning them constantly. Then return the browned meaty portions of duck to the casserole.

Pass the wine marinade through a fine sieve held over the duck and *garniture.*

Set aside the prunes and walnuts on a platter and keep them warm.

Return the spice bag to the duck, tucking it deep into the center of the casserole. If the contents of the casserole are not entirely covered by liquid, supplement the wine with warm chicken stock or water.

Over low heat, simmer the duck, covered, for about 1 hour. *(Check the state of the liquid occasionally to make sure that it does not come to a boil. Ed.)*

To assure yourself that the duck is perfectly cooked, pierce the leg with a fork. It should penetrate the flesh without resistance. When the duck is ready, remove the pieces of meat from the wine and set them aside on the platter with the prunes and walnuts.

Let the bones and vegetables remain in the casserole with the spice bag.

FINISHING THE CIVET:

Take the casserole from heat and set it at an angle (rest it on an inverted fork or spoon, etc.), so that in a short period of time the fat from the surface of the *civet* will run together and stabilize. Then you can lift it off easily with a spoon.

During this time, peel the apple, cut it in half, and remove the seeds. Then chop it into ½-inch dice.

Melt the remaining tablespoon of butter in a small skillet and when it begins to color, add the apple. Quickly brown the pieces of apple on all sides, then turn them into a sieve to drain. Set aside with the duck and other fruits.

After removing any fat from the surface of the wine-broth, return the casserole to the stove and boil down the liquid until reduced to about 1½ cups. Pass the sauce through a fine sieve into a 2-quart casserole, pressing down hard on the bones, vegetables, and spice bag before you discard them. Rinse and dry the first casserole and arrange the pieces of duck and fruits within. Taste the sauce for seasoning, and if needed, add a pinch of salt, and freshly ground pepper.

Pour the sauce over the duck, return the casserole to low heat, and let simmer about 5 or 10 minutes. Serve the duck from the casserole. (This dish is easily reheated.)

NOTE: *Because the* civet *does not suffer, and possibly even improves with reheating, allow more time than you think necessary for its lengthy preparation. Ed.*

This is an old recipe of our grandmothers' day which I have transformed only slightly—brightening it unelaborately with fruits.

The new *cuisine* does not consist of new inventions only and scorn for the old and traditional. On the contrary—except for some who simply are not serious people—the chefs of our era respect and admire the traditional cuisine of our provinces: real cream, good butter, and natural ingredients. What we try to do is make cooking more wholesome than it may have been in the past.

It follows that we avoid using flour in sauces, the way it was done not so very long ago. This is because flour absorbs the fats—which are not particularly digestible. In this recipe for *civet de canard*, the flour used represents less than a quarter of what you would find in one croissant. It is sufficient to thicken the sauce without holding the fats, which will float to the surface where they can be easily removed.

Poule faisane en salmis
ROAST PHEASANT WITH RED WINE SAUCE

To serve 2:

1 pheasant, about 2¼ to 2¾ pounds (*about 2 pounds dressed*)
Coarse salt
Freshly ground pepper
1 large sprig fresh thyme (*or substitute ½ teaspoon dried thyme; Ed.*)
3 juniper berries
4 tablespoons softened butter, in all
½ cup dry red wine (preferably, the wine should be that which you plan to serve with the meal)
2 shallots, chopped
½ teaspoon tomato paste
2 tablespoons cognac
Chicken stock (*about 2 cups*)

ADVICE FOR CHOOSING A TENDER PHEASANT:

There should not be any pronounced spurs on the feet. You should be able to twist the beak without resistance, and the tip of the breast bone must be very flexible. This advice applies to all birds.

To be sure that the pheasant was properly hung, run your fingers through the feathers. They should be totally dry. If they are moist where the quill is attached to the flesh, the bird was killed in the rain, and there is a risk that it will have a disagreeable taste. This can also mean that the bird was kept in a freezer or remained a long time in a cold room. This observation applies to any feathered game.

Lastly, check the eye. It should be clean and not running.

I suggest that you select a female bird rather than a male, because females are generally more tender and the flesh more delicate.

PREPARATION OF THE PHEASANT:

Preheat oven to 450°F.

Pluck, clean, and singe the bird. Pull out the heart, liver, and lungs, and wipe the interior with coarse salt and freshly ground pepper. Then

178

return the giblets to the cavity with the thyme and juniper berries. Truss the pheasant and lay it in a shallow roasting pan (*not aluminum*) or casserole.

Spread the bird with 2 tablespoons of the softened butter and place it in the preheated oven.

Roast the pheasant 30 minutes, basting frequently. Turn it from side to side every 5 minutes and onto its back for the final 10 minutes of roasting time.

PREPARATION OF THE SAUCE AND FINISHING THE PHEASANT:

Take the pheasant from the roasting pan and discard the cooking butter. Then pour the red wine into the pan and bring to a boil. Using a wooden spoon, scrape the particles of pheasant juices from the bottom and sides of the pan. Set aside.

Cut the pheasant into 4 pieces. Two parts each with a wing and half of the breast and 2 parts composed of a leg and thigh. Pull out all of the bones from the interior, leaving only the principal bones of the legs and wings. Reserve all the bones and the giblets.

Arrange the quarters of pheasant, skin side down, in a lightly buttered casserole, and sprinkle them with salt and freshly ground pepper. Cover the casserole tightly, and keep the meat warm over very very low heat. (*The warm turned-off oven where the pheasants were roasted would be ideal for this purpose, if you have another oven that you can use to bake the endives that will accompany this dish. Ed.*)

Using poultry shears or a meat cleaver, break up the reserved pheasant bones. Heat the remaining 2 tablespoons of butter in a casserole and brown the bones; then stir in the chopped shallots and a hazelnut-size dollop of tomato paste. When the shallots have softened, add the cognac, ignite, and when the flames have subsided, pour in the red wine waiting in the roasting pan.

Bring the wine to a simmer and cook until reduced to no more than 4 tablespoons. Then add just enough chicken stock to cover the bones, and cook 20 minutes over medium heat. Strain the wine-broth into a small clean casserole and reduce again, until only about ⅔ cup remains.

While the sauce reduces, chop the heart, liver, and lungs into a fine

179

paste. Add them to the sauce and return to a boil. Then press the sauce through a fine sieve held over the casserole containing the pheasant.

At the moment of serving, bring the casserole to a simmer. Taste for seasoning and add a pinch of salt and freshly ground pepper.

The recipe for endives to accompany the pheasant follows.

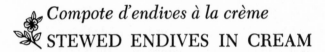

Compote d'endives à la crème

STEWED ENDIVES IN CREAM

To serve 2:

    4 large endives (*about 1½ pounds*)
    3 tablespoons butter
    Chicken stock (*about 2½ cups*)
    ⅓ cup heavy cream

PREPARATION:

After removing any bruised or withered leaves, trim the base of each endive. Then cut ½ inch off the tops, rinse briefly, and split the endive in two lengthwise.

Melt 2 tablespoons of the butter in a skillet, and over medium heat, sauté the endives on both sides. Allow 5 minutes for this.

Then arrange the endives side by side in a casserole just large enough to hold them. Add only enough chicken stock to barely cover the endives and dot with the remaining tablespoon of butter. Stew the endives over medium to low heat for about 20 minutes.

FINISHING THE ENDIVES:

Preheat oven to 450°F.

Place the stewed endives in a coarse sieve or colander and drain well. Then arrange them compactly together in an *à gratin* dish or shallow casserole.

Pour the cream over them and bake 15 minutes.

At this time the cream should be almost completely absorbed and the chicken stock should have seasoned the endives sufficiently. However, taste the sauce, and if you feel it necessary, add a pinch of salt and freshly ground white pepper.

TO SERVE:

Arrange the endives on two very hot plates, next to the serving of pheasant napped with its wine sauce. Baste the endives with their cream and serve at once.

The touch of bitterness from the endives compensates for the sweetness of the cream, and the full-bodied richness of the pheasant sauce gives you the joy of a dish as warming as the gold of autumn leaves.

Petites cailles en robe des champs
QUAIL IN BAKED POTATO NESTS

To serve 2: (*This simple dish can just as easily be prepared for 10 persons as for 2. Increase the quail, potatoes, and seasonings as you require. Ed.*)

    2 quail, either wild or domestic, dressed
    2 large Idaho potatoes, about 8 ounces each
    1½ teaspoons coriander seeds
    4 tablespoons butter
    Coarse salt
    Freshly ground white pepper

PREPARATION:

1. The potatoes: Preheat oven to 450°F.
Wash the potatoes well (*if you wish, you can grease the skin lightly with butter; Ed.*) and bake them in the hot oven for about 1 hour. To check that they are done, pierce one in the center with the point of a knife. If the knife does not meet resistance, the potatoes are ready.
If your butcher did not clean the quail, make use of this time to do so.

2. The coriander: Scatter the coriander seeds over the bottom of a dry skillet and heat them, shaking the pan continuously, until they are uniformly toasted.

Then place the seeds on a clean towel spread out over your work surface, and using a rolling pin, crush them to a powder. Place a fine sieve over a plate and strain as much of the crushed coriander through it as possible. (*The coriander seeds can also be pulverized with a mortar and pestle. Ed.*)

3. The quail: When the potatoes have only 15 minutes left to bake, sprinkle the quail, inside and out, with coarse salt and freshly ground pepper, and truss the legs with string.

Place 1½ tablespoons of butter in a small heavy cast-iron casserole and brown the quail, turning them on all sides. Then cover the casserole and cook 15 minutes. Set the casserole aside, covered, to keep the quail warm.

FINISHING THE QUAIL:

When the potatoes are done, remove them from the oven, but do not turn off the heat or change the temperature setting.

Make a lid the length of each potato, by cutting off a slice about ½-inch deep. Use a spoon to scoop out the inside of each lid and all the flesh inside the potatoes. Take care not to damage the skin. Set each potato shell aside with its corresponding lid.

Scrape the flesh of the potatoes into a warm bowl, and using a fork, incorporate the remaining 2½ tablespoons of butter, ½ tablespoon at a time. Mix in the powdered coriander and add salt to taste. Mash the potato with the fork until it becomes a smooth paste.

Using a spoon, spread the bottom and sides of the reserved potato shells with the mashed potato (*but do not fill the lids*). Press a warm quail into its nest, baste it with the casserole juices, and top with the reserved potato skin.

Return the stuffed potatoes to the hot oven for 5 minutes. Then turn off the oven and let them remain inside 5 minutes longer.

Serve the nests in a folded napkin, accompanied by a salad of lamb's lettuce (*mâche*), or a lettuce of the season.

As they say in Mougins: "Try and top this!"

Grives de vigne confites aux olives ❦
PRESERVED THRUSH WITH OLIVES ❦

To serve 2 or 3:

6 thrush (*see Note; you will use quail. Ed.*)

4 ounces imported black Niçoise olives (*select medium-size olives, not the tiny variety; Ed.*)

4 ounces lean salt pork, from the belly, in one piece

Coarse salt

Freshly ground pepper

2 cloves garlic, flattened and peeled

3 juniper berries, crushed slightly

1 large sprig fresh thyme (*or substitute ½ teaspoon dried thyme; Ed.*)

10 black peppercorns

2 tablespoons olive oil

1 tablespoon cognac

½ cup flour

NOTE: *In the United States, you will be unable to prepare this recipe with thrush. Instead, substitute 6 small quail. Pluck and clean them, and return the heart and liver to the breast cavity. Ed.*

PREPARATION:

1. The thrush: Pluck the birds, but do not remove the heads—which are most appreciated by connoisseurs. Clean them, or not, depending on your taste. For my part, I prefer not to clean them.

2. The olives: Remove the pits and drop the olives into a small casserole. (*An olive or cherry pitter will facilitate this operation. Ed.*)

3. The salt pork: Cut the salt pork into small *lardons*, sticks about 1 inch by ¼ inch, and put them together with the olives.

COOKING:

Preheat oven to 250°F.

Cover the olives and salt pork with 1 quart of cold water and bring to a boil. Simmer 2 minutes, then drain in a sieve and rinse under cold running water.

Sprinkle the birds with salt and freshly ground pepper, and arrange them side by side in a 1½-quart terrine for *pâté*.

Scatter the olives and *lardons* over and around the birds and add the garlic, juniper berries, thyme, and whole peppercorns. Baste the thrush with the olive oil, cognac, and 2 tablespoons of water. Cover the terrine with a tight-fitting lid.

In a small bowl, mix the flour with about 4 tablespoons of cold water to obtain a soft dough. Spread the dough around the cover of the terrine to seal it hermetically. Place the terrine in the low-temperature oven and forget about it for 4 hours. (*In spite of the seal around the cover of the terrine, after about 2 hours such a fantastic aroma persists in escaping that it is all but impossible to let your senses forget it. Ed.*)

TO SERVE:

After 4 hours, when the birds have finished cooking, bring the terrine to the table and break the seal. All of Provence will invite you to the table.

With the birds, serve a salad of curly yellow chicory and bitter red lettuce (*trévise*), seasoned with olive oil and wine vinegar.

NOTE: *It is also essential to the enjoyment of this dish to have a good crusty loaf of French bread at hand so that you can spread the birds on it, or to use to soak up the aromatic juices. Yes, the quail can be spread on bread or toast like a* confiture *and they have the richness of a moist* pâté. *Ed.*

I can tell you a story that will make the Society for the Prevention of Cruelty to Animals tremble, and bring cries of horror from old maids.

My friend F—— (if I mention his name, he will be arrested for poaching) is a true sportsman. From time to time, he traps small birds (robins, starlings, warblers . . . he allows himself to take what he wants).

He plucks them and roasts them; then he cuts a *pain-baguette* in half lengthwise, and brushes it with olive oil. There he carefully arranges the small birds, pours the cooking juices over them, and closes the sandwich, which he ties together with string. He then stores it in a cool place until the next morning when, as he leaves to go hunting, he puts it in his knapsack.

When it is time for his morning break, he stops in the shade of a cork-oak tree, takes out his bottle of red wine and his sandwich, cuts the string . . . and then, in spite of all the tenderness that you can feel for small birds, you cannot refrain from saying: "*Mon Dieu, that's good!*"

Les légumes

VEGETABLES

Comment choisir quelques légumes

HOW TO CHOOSE CERTAIN VEGETABLES

Artichokes (*les artichauts*): There are 2 kinds of artichokes—the large, fat, compact variety sometimes called "globe" artichokes (*known as* bretons *in France*), and the smaller, sometimes purple-tinged variety (*called* violets *or* poivrades) with long pointed leaves. If the points are thorny, don't take them; they are past their prime, in the act of going to seed, and will be tough.

Eggplants (*les aubergines*): Choose the smallest and make sure they are very firm. Those with a lighter purple coloring are more tender than those that are black.

Swiss chard (*les blettes*): The stalks should be very white and the leaves bright and shiny. The ends of the stalks, where they have been cut from their roots, should be white, not brown.

Carrots (*les carottes*): The freshness of the fernlike tops of the carrots guarantees the freshness of the vegetable. The carrots should be bright and without brown marks or blemishes. Little new carrots should have an almost transparent quality.

The carrots we find in the market in winter have usually been stored in silos. One can recognize this by the fine roots that spring forth. You can use these carrots in soups and sauces. They are stronger in taste than new carrots.

Cabbages (*les choux*): There are green, white, and red cabbages. They must all be very fresh in appearance—the leaves firm, and the base, where it was cut from the stalk, very white. After several days, a cut cabbage gives off a disagreeable odor.

Cauliflower (*les choux-fleurs*): Just like cabbage, its base, where it was cut from the stalk, should be very white. The head must also be completely white, without any touches of brown or gray.

Zucchini (*les courgettes*): Occasionally, one can still find the large yellow flower attached to the end of the vegetable. In this case, the zucchini must not even be peeled, but poached straightaway with the flower. Cook the zucchini, keeping it crisp, and serve it basted with only a little olive oil or butter.

For the zucchini without the flower, choose either the round or the long, bright in color, not too large, and above all, very firm.

Garlic (*l'ail*; plural: *les aulx*): It must be without any green sprouts and the cloves should be large and firm. New garlic is the best, because it is less strong and more delicate. The best-quality garlic has a slightly reddish purple coloring.

Onions (*les oignons*): Sweet new white onions are the least strong. The dark red and purple onions are sweeter than the yellow, which are the strongest. Onions must be very firm, without sprouts, and with dry paper-thin skins.

Shallots (*Les échalotes*): New shallots, still with their stems, are very sweet. The larger brownish-purple shallots are a little strong. The most preferable are little gray shallots (*échalotes grises*). The same rule applies as for onions: Choose them firm and without sprouts.

Lettuces (*les salades*): See the chapter on Salad Greens, page 30.

Snow peas (*les pois gourmands* or *pois mange-tout*): These mix wonderfully with other vegetables, but must be picked with their flower still attached. Otherwise they will be fibrous.

Peas (*les petits pois*): Like string beans and snow peas, they should still have their little white flower attached to the pod, guaranteeing their freshness. They must not be too plump and should always be bright and shiny. Don't hesitate to open a pod before buying them. The peas must be oblong, small, and with a young green color.

Potatoes (*les pommes de terre*): It is important to choose the type of potato which best lends itself to the preparation you have in mind.

1. The Idaho, which is most popular, adapts itself to almost all methods of preparation.

2. The white new potato is wonderful for purées, but often difficult to find.

3. The red potato is marvelous for salad.

One general rule is that potatoes must not be either withered or sprouting.

Sweet peppers (*les poivrons doux*): In my opinion, for salad you must choose either very large red bell peppers, or the smallest size green peppers, which are the most delicate. They should be fleshy, firm, and crunchy, a little shiny, and not at all withered.

Turnips (*les navets*): Turnips must be very white with slick and shining skins. It is preferable to buy them by the bunch, and their tops should appear very fresh.

Celery root and **yellow turnips** (*raves* and *navets ronds*): Choose the smallest and firmest, without roots, and preferably with their leaves.

Tomatoes (*les tomates*): Choose the smallest for a salad, the largest for chopping, and the oblong (plum) for sauce.

A guarantee of freshness is the stem end, which releases a strong fragrance when touched. Pick the firmest tomatoes and do not worry about any that are misshapen—it is usually a sign that they were cultivated naturally.

Broccoli (*les brocolis*): This delicious vegetable is seldom in demand in France, though it is greatly appreciated in Italy and the United States. Grown in France, it resembles a cabbage that hasn't arrived at maturity. I advise you to buy the broccoli that comes from Italy. It is very much greener and is sold in bunches. This way, all of it can be used.

Spinach (*les épinards*): Each leaf must be crisp, shiny, and dark green.

Asparagus (*les asperges*): They are eaten until June. In my humble opinion, the best are those with purple tips, then the green, followed by the white. Thin green wild asparagus are found in the woods of Provence and often in burned-out areas where there has been a fire. These are the best of all. In an omelette, they are a treat. Whatever their color, asparagus must be crunchy and not at all withered. Notice the tiny leaves that constitute the tip of the asparagus to make sure that they are tightly closed and not coming apart.

String beans (*les haricots verts*): Choose the firmest, most crackling, and without strings. However, the finest of the fine are the little green beans no larger than the tines of a fork, often with the little white flower still attached. These beans will toughen just in the hours of a morning. Don't wait for another daybreak to welcome this pleasure to your table. These little beans insist on care and loving attention: Don't cut them; only pinch off the ends delicately between your fingernails. Without waiting, drop the beans into boiling salted water (5 quarts of water for 1 pound of beans). Cook them, uncovered, 2 or 3 minutes; then extract a bean and taste it for doneness. They must remain crunchy to the bite. Drain the string beans quickly in a colander, then plunge them into a basin of ice water.

Lift the string beans out of the ice water by hand and place them in a colander to drain.

If you are serving the string beans in a salad, you can season them with a little vinegar and olive oil, a pinch of finely chopped shallot, and several snippings of fresh chervil. Or you can enjoy them with an addition of a heaping tablespoon of *crème fraîche* and the juice of a lemon. Lastly, these tiny little string beans are an admirable accompaniment to a number of other noble produces (see spring and summer salads in the chapter on Salad Greens).

Like string beans, *all* vegetables merit delicate treatment. However, most of the time they are treated like vulgar accessories. This is a profound error and a sacrilege. Nothing is more delicate, delicious, finer, more marvelous, than a true product of the earth. They suffer when they are piled in heaps and handled too much. Heat withers them and cold deadens them.

Treat vegetables with love. They will return it to you one hundredfold.

Les petits farcis de Provence
THE LITTLE STUFFED VEGETABLES OF PROVENCE
(Color picture 2)

In Provence, stuffed vegetables are a part of many family meals; they can be served hot, warm, or cold. They are easily reheated.

They can be served as an *hors d'oeuvre*, as a vegetable, as a main course, or as a *garniture*.

Arranged in rows by category, stuffed vegetables make an attractive presentation, but one can also do well with only one kind.

The most frequent combination is of tomato, zucchini, and onion. For the best presentation, I suggest that the different vegetables be of uniform size.

Coeurs d'artichauts farcis

ARTICHOKE BOTTOMS WITH HAM AND SPINACH

To serve 2 or 6:

This recipe will serve 2 persons as a separate first course. However, in case you wish to serve the artichokes as part of a composition of small stuffed vegetables, or as an accompaniment to roasted or grilled veal, they will serve 6.

6 medium-size artichokes, about 7 ounces each
Coarse salt
10 ounces fresh young spinach leaves
2 tablespoons butter, in all
1 egg yolk
4 tablespoons heavy cream
6 anchovy fillets, packed in olive oil
2 ounces *jambon de Paris*, minced (*use boiled ham; Ed.*)
Freshly ground pepper, preferably white

PREPARATION:

1. The artichokes: In a large heavy casserole or kettle (*not aluminum*), bring 5 quarts of water to a boil with 4 tablespoons of coarse salt.

Strip off the exterior leaves of the artichokes and break off the stems. When the water reaches a boil, plunge in the artichokes, and as soon as the water returns to a boil, cook 45 minutes, uncovered.

After 35 minutes, you can begin to test the artichokes for doneness. To do this, pull out a center leaf. If it detaches itself easily, the artichokes are ready for removal. Submerge them in ice water to stop the cooking and to preserve their color. When the artichokes are chilled, drain them upside down.

2. The spinach: While the artichokes are cooking, strip off the stems from the spinach and wash the leaves in 3 or 4 changes of water. Then drain the leaves thoroughly in a colander. (*If the leaves are large, tear them into smaller, more manageable pieces. Ed.*)

191

Melt 1½ tablespoons of the butter in a 3-quart casserole, and when it begins to color, add the well-drained spinach. Cook the spinach over high heat, stirring continuously with a wooden spoon, until all water has evaporated (about 10 minutes). Set the spinach aside in the warm casserole, uncovered.

3. The filling: In a small bowl, blend the egg yolk with the heavy cream, mixing well with a small wire whisk.

Melt 1 teaspoon butter in a small skillet and cook the anchovies for about 2 minutes over low heat, mashing them with a fork. Then stir the anchovies into the egg-yolk-cream mixture.

Return the casserole with the spinach to medium heat. Add the egg-yolk-cream-anchovy *liaison* and stir, without stopping, until slightly thickened. Then remove from heat, stir in the minced ham, add freshly ground pepper, and taste for salt. (*It may not be needed. Ed.*)

TO FINISH THE ARTICHOKES:

Preheat oven to 350°F.

Carefully pull off all the leaves from each artichoke, extract the fibrous choke, and trim the bottoms neatly.

Grease a shallow casserole or *à gratin* dish with the remaining ½ teaspoon butter (*use more if necessary; Ed.*). Fill the artichoke bottoms with the spinach mixture, pressing lightly with a fork; then arrange them in the casserole.

Bake the artichokes no more than 10 to 15 minutes and serve.

Aubergines farcies
SMALL STUFFED EGGPLANTS

These eggplants may be served as part of a composition of small stuffed vegetables, or as an accompaniment to roast leg of lamb.

To serve 6:

6 small eggplants, about 2 ounces each; or 3 eggplants, about 5 ounces each

3 tablespoons olive oil, in all

1¾ ounces pitted black olives (*use either oil-cured olives, or olives packed in water; Ed.*)

6 anchovy fillets

1 clove garlic, finely chopped

A pinch fresh thyme flowers, or fresh or dried thyme leaves

Freshly ground pepper

Coarse salt

NOTE: It is imperative that you prepare this dish with utensils that are glass, enameled cast iron, or stainless steel. If any metal such as aluminum contacts this vegetable, it will darken the flesh.

PREPARATION OF THE EGGPLANT:

Preheat oven to 450°F.

Pull off the green stem from each eggplant. (Do not cut it with a knife.) If you have 6 very small eggplants, cut off one long thin slice from end to end, removing a "lid." If they are larger, cut each eggplant in half lengthwise.

Scrape out the seeds from the interior with the point of a knife. Then, using a small spoon, remove the flesh. Be careful not to break the skin, and leave a shell about ⅛-inch thick.

Arrange the eggplant shells on a heat-proof serving platter and brush them with 2 tablespoons of the olive oil. Spread out the flesh of the eggplant over the bottom of a lightly oiled baking dish. Place both the shells and the flesh in the preheated oven.

Roast the shells about 15 to 20 minutes, and the flesh about 20 to

25 minutes—but do not let it burn! When they have both been removed from the oven, do not turn off the heat. The same temperature will be needed for the final cooking.

PREPARATION OF THE FILLING:

While the eggplant is cooking, remove the pits from the olives; then finely chop the olives and place them in a mixing bowl.

Heat the remaining tablespoon of olive oil in a small saucepan. Add the anchovies and crush them with a fork. As soon as they have dissolved into a paste, take them from the heat and mix with the chopped olives.

When the flesh of the eggplant has finished baking, mash it with a silver or stainless steel fork, then add it to the bowl with the olives and anchovies. Stir in the garlic and thyme, and add salt and freshly ground pepper to taste. The amount of salt you use will depend on the saltiness of the anchovies.

TO FINISH THE EGGPLANT:

Stuff the eggplant shells with the filling and smooth the surface. Return the eggplants to the oven for 5 to 10 minutes, or until just heated through. Serve hot.

NOTE: *Up to the point of the final reheating, the eggplants can be prepared several hours in advance, but do not refrigerate them.*

When they are ready to be served, you might want to add a small garniture of chopped parsley, or a piece of tomato for color. Ed.

Champignons blancs farcis 🌸
STUFFED MUSHROOMS 🌿

These mushrooms may be served as a *garniture* to a meat dish, or as part of a composition of small stuffed vegetables, or they can be passed with apéritifs. They are not to be considered as a dish by themselves.

To serve 6:

    6 very large white mushrooms of uniform size
    1½ ounces lean salt pork (unsmoked bacon), in one piece
    1 slice white bread
    3 tablespoons olive oil, in all
    1 tablespoon finely chopped onion
    1 clove garlic, finely chopped
    1 tablespoon finely chopped fresh parsley
    Coarse salt
    Freshly ground pepper

PREPARATION:

1. The mushrooms: If the stem end of the mushroom is caked with earth, shave it off, using a small knife. Detach the stems, pulling them out in their entirety to leave a hollow cap. Rinse and drain the caps and stems and gently pat them dry with a towel. Chop the stems and set aside.

2. The salt pork: Cut the salt pork into fine julienne strips. Place the strips in a small skillet, and over high heat, sauté them quickly. Allow about 3 or 4 minutes for this. Stir frequently and do not let the salt pork become crisp. Drain it in a sieve and set aside.

3. The bread crumbs: Cut the bread into very fine dice and sauté them in 1 tablespoon of the olive oil until golden brown. Set aside with the salt pork.

FINISHING THE MUSHROOMS:

Preheat oven to 400°F.

Heat 1 tablespoon of the olive oil in a 7-inch skillet. Add the chopped onion and cook, stirring continuously with a wooden spoon, until golden. Then add the chopped mushroom stems and garlic. Continue to stir until all the moisture in the mushrooms has evaporated. Then, off heat, combine them with the salt pork, bread crumbs, and freshly chopped parsley. Season with salt and a few turns of the pepper mill and mix well.

Fill the caps with the stuffing and arrange them on a baking sheet. Brush their tops lightly with the remaining tablespoon of olive oil and place them in the oven. Bake the mushrooms about 25 minutes without letting them brown. If they do begin to brown, sprinkle the baking sheet with a tablespoon of water.

Serve the mushrooms the moment they leave the oven.

Chou vert farci

GREEN CABBAGE LEAVES WITH HAM AND VEGETABLES

To serve 3 or 6:

These stuffed cabbage leaves can be served as an accompaniment to roast pork, or poached or braised pork shanks; or they can be served as part of a composition of small stuffed vegetables. (*They are also an excellent accompaniment to corned beef or other brined meats. Ed.*)

1 green cabbage (*preferably a Savoy*) about 2½ pounds (The leaves of the cabbage should not be too tightly closed.)
Coarse salt
1½ tablespoons butter
2 tablespoons finely diced carrots
1 tablespoon finely diced celery root
1 tablespoon finely chopped onion
4 ounces finely diced *jambon de Paris* (*use boiled ham; Ed.*), or you can also use cold roast pork

1 clove garlic, chopped
Freshly ground pepper
1 sprig fresh rosemary (*or substitute* ¼ *teaspoon dried rosemary;
   Ed.*)
1 cup chicken stock

PREPARATION:

1. The cabbage: Using the point of a small strong knife, work
through the bottom of the cabbage into the heart, cutting out the core
and tough fibrous parts of the leaves. Rinse the cabbage in several
changes of water, then drain.

Bring 3 or 4 quarts of water to a boil with 3 tablespoons coarse
salt. When the water is boiling rapidly, plunge in the cabbage, core
end down, and cook 5 minutes. Then cool the cabbage in a colander
held under cold running water.

Spread a towel over your work surface, place the cabbage on it,
and detach the large exterior leaves. Then cut out the hard part of
the core that extends into each leaf. Select 6 large perfect leaves, each
approximately the size of a dessert plate. (If the leaves are too small,
you will have to take 12 and put 2 together for each portion.)

2. The filling: Melt the butter in a small casserole over low heat.
Add the diced carrot, celery root, and chopped onion. Cook the *mire-
poix* 10 minutes, covered, stirring occasionally with a wooden spoon.
Then add the finely diced ham (or cold roast pork) with the chopped
garlic. Season with freshly ground pepper (*salt may not be necessary;
Ed.*) and cook, uncovered, 5 minutes longer.

TO FINISH THE CABBAGE:

Preheat oven to 350°F.

Divide the filling into 6 equal portions and place a mound of it
(*about 2 heaping teaspoons*) on each leaf. Then roll the leaves into
tight green balls.

Lay the sprig of rosemary on the bottom of a small baking dish or
casserole just large enough to hold the cabbage balls side by side.
Moisten the cabbage with enough chicken stock to reach ¾ of the way
up the sides of the baking dish; then bake the cabbage 30 minutes,
basting every 10 minutes.

🌺 *Courgettes farcies*
ZUCCHINI WITH HAM AND MUSHROOMS

To serve 2 or 6:

These zucchini will serve 2 persons as a main or first course, or they can serve 6 as part of a composition of small stuffed vegetables.

6 small zucchini, about 3 ounces each
Coarse salt
3 large white mushrooms
1 ounce *jambon blanc* (*use boiled ham; Ed.*)
4 tablespoons olive oil, in all
2 tablespoons finely chopped onion
3 sage leaves, preferably fresh, chopped
Freshly ground pepper

PREPARATION:

1. The zucchini: Scrub the zucchini, but do not peel them. Trim off the small crusty brown piece that once was the blossom end of the squash; then cut off a ¼-inch-thick slice lengthwise, from end to end. Keep the slices; they will be used later as "lids" to cover the stuffed zucchini.

Bring 2 quarts of water with 2 tablespoons of salt to a rapid boil. Plunge the zucchini and their "lids" into the boiling water and cook 6 minutes. Then drain in a colander placed under cold running water.

As soon as the zucchini are cool enough to handle, use a teaspoon to scoop out the interior. Take care not to break through the skin, and leave a shell about ¼-inch thick.

Place the pulp from the interior of the vegetable on a cutting board and chop it coarsely, then set aside in a sieve placed over a small mixing bowl so that the excess water can drain away.

2. The mushrooms: Clean the stems, then rinse the mushrooms briefly under cold running water. (*Do not allow them to soak. Ed.*) Dry thoroughly with a towel, then chop them coarsely and set aside.

3. The ham: Chop the ham into very small dice. Set aside.

COOKING:

Preheat oven to 400°F.

Heat 2 tablespoons of the olive oil in the casserole that was used to cook the squash. Add the onion and cook, over low heat, 7 or 8 minutes, stirring frequently with a wooden spoon.

When the onion is soft but not browned, add the chopped mushrooms, diced ham, and sage. Cook 5 minutes, stirring continuously; then add the chopped vegetable pulp and a pinch of salt. Regulate the heat so that the moisture from the vegetable pulp evaporates, and stirring continuously, watch that the mixture does not scorch or burn. When cooked, taste for seasoning and add a few good turns of the pepper mill.

TO FINISH THE ZUCCHINI:

Arrange the zucchini shells compactly in a shallow baking dish just large enough to hold them side by side. Sprinkle the interiors of the shells lightly with coarse salt.

Use a teaspoon to fill the zucchini with the ham-mushroom mixture, smoothing it down evenly. Then cover each zucchini with its reserved "lid" and brush them with the remaining 2 tablespoons of olive oil.

Bake the zucchini 35 minutes. Check them periodically as they cook. If they appear to be drying out or sticking to the pan, you may need to add 1 or 2 tablespoons of warm water.

✿*Oignons blancs farcis*
WHITE ONIONS WITH CHEESE AND CREAM

These onions may be served as an accompaniment to roast veal or pork, or as part of a composition of small stuffed vegetables.

To serve 6:

    6 medium-size sweet white onions, about 4 ounces each
    Coarse salt
    5 tablespoons *crème fraîche* (*or substitute heavy cream; Ed.*)
    1 egg yolk
    1 ounce Gruyère cheese, freshly grated
    Freshly ground white pepper
    1½ tablespoons butter, in all
    1 slice white bread, cut into small dice
    About 1 cup chicken stock

PREPARATION OF THE ONIONS:

There follow 2 methods for precooking the onions. You will need to allow a variable margin of cooking time, depending on the quality of the onions.

1. Roasting method for precooking onions: Preheat oven to 425°F for 20 minutes.

When the oven is hot, arrange the onions, unpeeled and untrimmed, on a baking sheet. Roast them undisturbed about 50 minutes. After 45 minutes, check for doneness by piercing an onion with a skewer. If the skewer penetrates easily, the onion is done. If it meets resistance, continue to cook the onions (*but do not roast them to the point where they collapse; Ed.*).

When the onions are done, take them from the oven and lower the heat to 350°F. Keep the oven ready at this temperature.

As soon as the onions are cool enough to handle, strip off their exterior skin. Then carefully trim off the root end at the base without detaching any layers of onion.

2. Boiling method for precooking onions: Peel the onions and carefully trim the roots. Bring 2½ quarts of water to a boil with 3 table-

spoons of coarse salt. When the water reaches a rapid boil, plunge in the onions and cook about 30 minutes. However, test for doneness after 20 or 25 minutes by piercing an onion with a skewer. If the skewer does not meet resistance, drain the onions in a colander and rinse them under cold running water.

PREPARATION OF THE FILLING:

After the onions have been precooked, use a very sharp knife to cut off the protruding stem end. (*The flesh of the onion will be very slippery and you do not want to break the exterior layers of the onion by grasping it too tightly. Ed.*)

Using a small teaspoon, scoop out the center of each onion. Leave enough of the outside layers to make a shell strong enough to support the filling. Take extreme care not to pierce the bottom of the shell, or to cut through the supporting exterior layers. If this should happen, the onion will not be usable.

Save the interior of the vegetable, chop it very fine, and place it in a small mixing bowl. Blend the onion with the *crème fraîche*, the egg yolk, and freshly grated Gruyère cheese. Season with salt and freshly ground pepper. Set aside.

TO FINISH THE ONIONS:

Choose a small casserole just large enough to hold the onions side by side, and grease it lightly with butter. Divide the filling among the onion shells and arrange them in the casserole.

Scatter the diced bread over the bottom of a small baking pan and toast briefly, either in the oven or under the broiler grill. Then affix the croutons evenly over the tops of the onions, followed by a hazelnut-size piece of butter.

Add just enough chicken stock to the casserole to immerse the onions halfway, then bake 30 minutes.

At the end of the cooking time, the liquid in the casserole should have reduced to 2 or 3 tablespoons. Baste the onions with this broth just before you serve them.

❧ *Pommes de terre farcies*
POTATOES WITH MUSHROOMS AND HERBS

To serve 2 or 6:

These potatoes will serve 2 persons as a main or first course, or they can serve 6 as an accompaniment or as part of a composition of small stuffed vegetables.

6 small new potatoes, about 3 ounces each, and of uniform shape (If small potatoes are not available, use 3 large ones cut in half crosswise and trimmed to the smaller size.)
5 ounces white mushrooms
3 tablespoons butter, in all
1 shallot, finely chopped
1 egg yolk
4 tablespoons heavy cream
2 teaspoons finely chopped parsley
2 teaspoons finely chopped chives
Coarse salt
Freshly ground pepper, preferably white
About 1¼ cups chicken stock

PREPARATION:

1. The potatoes: Peel and dry the potatoes. Then, using a small round spoon with sharp edges (*cuillère à pomme parisienne*), hollow them out, leaving a sturdy shell from ¼-inch to ⅜-inch thick.

Note: *If the potatoes need to wait for any length of time before being filled and baked, drop them into ice water. But be sure to dry them thoroughly, inside and out, before you fill them. Ed.*

2. The mushrooms: Clean and trim the mushrooms. Rinse them briefly under cold running water and wipe dry. Then chop the mushrooms very fine on a cutting board.

Melt 1½ tablespoons of the butter in a small casserole or skillet and add the chopped shallot. Cook the shallot about 2 minutes over

202

high heat, stirring constantly with a wooden spoon. Then add the chopped mushrooms and continue to stir until all of their moisture has evaporated.

Take the casserole from heat and stir in the egg yolk, first lightly beaten with the heavy cream. Return the casserole to very low heat and continue to stir for 1 or 2 minutes or until the mixture has thickened slightly.

Remove the casserole from heat and add the chopped parsley and chives. Season with salt and freshly ground pepper to taste, mix well, and set aside.

TO FINISH THE POTATOES:

Preheat oven to 425°F.

Choose a small roasting pan or casserole just large enough to hold the potatoes side by side, and grease it liberally with butter.

Dry the potatoes well with a towel and fill each one with the mushroom mixture. Tamp it down and smooth the surface with a fork. Arrange the potatoes in the baking dish and top each one with a hazel-nut-size piece of butter. Then add enough chicken stock to reach half-way up the sides of the potatoes.

Bake the potatoes 1 hour, and after the first 15 minutes, baste them frequently. At the end of the cooking time the broth should be almost totally reduced, but if this should happen too fast, add a little more stock.

Tomates farcies
TOMATOES WITH MEAT AND HERBS

To serve 2 or 6:

This recipe will serve 2 as a main course, or 6 as part of a composition of small stuffed vegetables.

6 round red tomatoes, about 3 ounces each (*larger tomatoes, about 6 ounces each, could also be used. In this case, double all the ingredients for the filling. Ed.*)

Coarse salt

3 ounces chopped meat: Use either leftover *daube de boeuf* (beef braised in wine), or *pot-au-feu* (boiled beef), or sausage. If you use either of the first two meats, reserve 2 tablespoons of their sauce or broth. If you are using sausage, the meat will be sufficiently moist.

2 tablespoons finely chopped sweet white onion

1 clove garlic, chopped

2 tablespoons chopped parsley

1 large pinch fresh thyme leaves (*or substitute a scant ¼ teaspoon dried thyme; Ed.*)

3 or 4 tablespoons olive oil, in all

Freshly ground pepper

2 slices (*1½ ounces*) white bread, cut into small dice

PREPARATION OF THE TOMATOES:

Wipe each tomato and cut out the core. Then cut a ½-inch-thick slice off the top of each tomato and set these "lids" aside. Press the tomatoes lightly to remove the seeds and water. Sprinkle the interior of the tomatoes with salt and turn them upside down to let the excess water drain.

PREPARATION OF THE FILLING:

Preheat oven to 400°F.

1. If you use beef from a *daube*: Cut the meat into fine dice the size of tiny peas. Add 2 tablespoons of the wine sauce, the chopped

onion, chopped garlic, parsley, and thyme. Mix with a wooden spoon until well-blended, and season to taste with salt and freshly ground pepper.

2. If you use meat from a *pot-au-feu:* Proceed in the same manner as above, except add 2 tablespoons of broth instead of sauce.

3. If you use sausage: Heat 1 tablespoon of the olive oil in a skillet, and when it begins to smoke, open the sausage casing and add the meat, crumbled. As it cooks, stir the sausage with a fork to break up any lumps. After 4 or 5 minutes, drain the meat in a sieve held over a bowl, and when it has drained, stir in the same seasonings as for the other meats and mix well.

4. The croutons: Scatter the diced bread over the bottom of a skillet to which a little olive oil has been added. Sauté the bread until crisp and lightly browned. Set aside.

TO FINISH THE TOMATOES:

Stuff the tomatoes with the filling and top each one with a *garniture* of toasted croutons. Return the "lids" to the tomatoes, and arrange them in a roasting pan just large enough to hold them side by side.

Brush the tomatoes with 2 tablespoons of the olive oil and bake them in the preheated oven for 20 minutes.

This dish can be prepared in advance, but it must not be cooked until just before serving.

I remember my mother preparing a large platter of these stuffed tomatoes—but using much larger ones—which she alternated with medium-size potatoes, hollowed out and filled in the same way.

We carried the platter to the bakery to be cooked. It made me hungry just to carry it there. I don't ever recall being given the job of bringing it back after it was cooked. This was prudent! For I certainly would have offered myself a quick snack on the way home. I loved this dish and I still do.

Petits artichauts violets à la barigoule
ARTICHOKES BARIGOULE
(Color picture 1)

To serve 2 or 4, depending on the size of the artichokes:

8 small artichokes, about 4 to 6 ounces each
1 lemon
4 cloves garlic, peeled
1 sprig fresh basil (*about 5 large leaves*)
1 tablespoon freshly chopped parsley
3 tablespoons olive oil
1 medium-size sweet onion, thinly sliced
1 young carrot, thinly sliced
1 sprig fresh thyme (*or substitute ¼ teaspoon dried thyme; Ed.*)
1 small bay leaf
Coarse salt
Freshly ground pepper, preferably white
⅜ cup dry white wine

PREPARATION:

1. The artichokes: Trim the stems of the artichokes, leaving about 2 inches. Use a heavy chopping knife to cut approximately 1 inch off the tops. Tear away several layers of outside leaves close to the base, and trim the bottoms smoothly and evenly with a small sharp knife. (*The exposed flesh should be a pale green, almost white. Ed.*) Rub the artichokes well with half a lemon to prevent the flesh from darkening, and set them aside in a basin of cold water to which the juice of the remaining half lemon has been added.

2. The fresh herb mixture: Chop 2 of the 4 cloves of garlic together with the basil leaves and parsley. Set aside.

COOKING:

Heat the olive oil in an enameled cast-iron or other nonmetallic casserole just large enough to hold the artichokes side by side. Add the onion and carrot, and sauté the vegetables over medium to low heat for about 10 minutes or until soft but not browned. Then add the thyme, bay leaf, and remaining 2 whole cloves of garlic.

Arrange the artichokes on top of the vegetables and sprinkle with salt and freshly ground pepper. Pour in ⅜ cup of dry white wine and add just enough water to barely submerge the artichokes. Cover the casserole, bring the liquid to a simmer, and cook 15 minutes over medium heat. Then uncover the artichokes, raise heat to high, and boil down the broth until only a few tablespoons of syrupy juices remain. (*This reduction will take about 15 minutes. Turn the artichokes periodically during this time. Ed.*)

Remove the casserole from heat and add a pinch of salt and freshly ground pepper. Carefully stir in the chopped garlic-basil-parsley mixture and serve.

If necessary, this dish may be reheated; but in that case do not add the fresh herb mixture until the last moment before serving.

La ratatouille niçoise à ma façon
PROVENÇAL VEGETABLE RAGOUT VERGÉ

To serve 6:

1½ pounds ripe tomatoes
⅔ pound sweet white onions, preferably new onions
2 thick-fleshed sweet (*bell*) peppers, about 6 ounces
1¼ pounds small eggplants, preferably long and very firm
1¼ pounds small zucchini, about 4 of uniform size
13 tablespoons olive oil, in all
Coarse salt
Freshly ground pepper
A pinch of thyme flowers, or fresh or dried thyme leaves
3 cloves garlic, finely chopped
10 large fresh basil leaves, chopped
1 tablespoon chopped fresh parsley

PREPARATION OF THE VEGETABLES:

1. The tomatoes: Drop the tomatoes into boiling water, count to 10, then plunge them into a basin of cold water. This will make them

easy to peel. Remove the core and peel the tomatoes; then cut them in half crosswise and gently squeeze out the seeds and water. Cut the tomatoes into large dice and set aside.

2. The onions: Peel the onions and cut them into thin slices. Set aside.

3. The sweet peppers: Split the peppers in half lengthwise and scrape out the seeds. Remove the core and any remnants of white membrane. Then cut the peppers into long thin slices and set them aside with the onions.

4. The eggplants: Remove the stem end and peel the eggplants completely. Then cut them into pieces the size of your thumb. Set aside. (*Optional: If you wish, you can sprinkle the pieces of eggplant with salt and place them in a colander to release any bitter juices. Ed.*)

5. The zucchini: Scrub the zucchini, then peel them lengthwise at ⅜-inch intervals, making stripes of green and white. Cut the zucchini crosswise into 1½-inch lengths, then cut these in half lengthwise. Set aside.

COOKING:

Now that the drudgery of preparing the vegetables is finished, move on to the cooking.

Pour 3 tablespoons of the olive oil into each of 2 skillets and heat until almost smoking. Drop the onions and peppers into one skillet and the tomatoes into the other. Season both skillets with salt and freshly ground pepper, and add a pinch of thyme flowers to the tomatoes.

Cook the tomatoes 2 or 3 minutes over high heat, then turn them out onto a plate.

Cook the onions and peppers over low heat for about 15 to 20 minutes without letting them color, then turn them out onto the plate with the tomatoes.

Pat the pieces of eggplant dry with a towel. Pour 5 tablespoons of the olive oil into a 10-inch skillet, and over high heat, brown the pieces of eggplant on all sides. Turn them frequently. Allow about 8 to 10 minutes for this operation, and as soon as the eggplant has browned, drain it in a coarse sieve or colander held over a bowl to catch the oil.

Return the oil that has drained from the eggplant to the skillet and add 2 more tablespoons of fresh oil. When the oil is hot, add the quarters of zucchini and cook over high heat for 7 to 8 minutes or until lightly browned. Place the zucchini with the eggplant in the sieve to drain.

TO FINISH THE RATATOUILLE:

Just before you are ready to serve the *ratatouille*, mix all the vegetables together in a 3- to 4-quart casserole. Heat the vegetables while stirring carefully with a wooden spoon.

Season the *ratatouille* with salt and freshly ground pepper; then, at the last moment, stir in the chopped garlic, basil, and parsley.

Serve this dish as an accompaniment to roasted or grilled meats.

Usually a *ratatouille* creates itself during a long slow cooking, taking about 2 to 3 hours. But in this version, I give you the advantage of keeping the freshness and texture of the individual vegetables. I can also give you an excellent recipe which utilizes *ratatouille*:

Les oeufs au plat niçois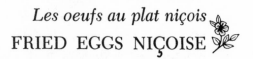
FRIED EGGS NIÇOISE

To serve 1:

Grease a small porcelain, enameled cast-iron, or Pyrex egg dish with olive oil.

Heat 5 tablespoons of *ratatouille* and spread it over the bottom of the dish. Using the back of a soup spoon, make 2 deep imprints in the *ratatouille*. Break 2 fresh eggs and slide 1 into each indentation. Sprinkle with salt and freshly ground pepper.

Heat the egg dish 2 minutes on top of the stove, then finish the eggs by baking them 2 to 3 minutes (or until the whites have set) in a preheated 425°F oven.

It is all simple and delicious.

Tian de courgettes et tomates
ZUCCHINI AND TOMATO CASSEROLE
(Color picture 1)

To serve 4:

1 large onion, about 6 ounces
5 tablespoons olive oil, in all
5 small zucchini, about 1¼ pounds
5 or 6 small firm ripe tomatoes, about 1½ pounds
1 large clove garlic, peeled
Coarse salt
Freshly ground pepper
½ teaspoon thyme leaves, fresh or dried

PREPARATION OF THE VEGETABLES:

1. The onion: Peel the onion and cut it into very thin slices. Heat 2 tablespoons of the olive oil in a small skillet, and over low heat, cook the onion until soft but not browned.

2. The zucchini: The zucchini should be long, firm to the touch, and dark green. Wash them and then, using a vegetable peeler, peel off long strips of skin down the length of each squash. The strips should be about ⅜-inch wide and at ⅜-inch intervals, leaving alternating green and white bands of skin and flesh. With the help of a *mandoline* or other slicing device, cut the zucchini into thin even rounds, ⅛-inch thick at most. Discard the stem and blossom ends.

3. The tomatoes: With a small knife, remove the core from each tomato, then cut them vertically into slices of the same thickness as the zucchini. Set aside.

COOKING:

Preheat oven to 475°F.

Rub the bottom and sides of a 9- to 10-inch *à gratin* dish (or other shallow casserole) with the clove of garlic, pressing down hard to release its juices. Then line the dish evenly with a layer of cooked onion. Over the bed of onion, arrange long overlapping rows of zucchini and tomatoes—forming alternating bands of red and green.

Season with coarse salt and freshly ground pepper. Scatter thyme leaves over all, and brush the vegetables with 2 tablespoons of the olive oil.

Place the dish in the hot preheated oven and bake 30 to 35 minutes. After the first 15 minutes, baste with the remaining tablespoon of olive oil and, after 20 minutes, with the rendered vegetable juices. Tilt the dish to catch them.

When finished cooking, the vegetables should be soft and lightly browned.

This dish is also quite good sprinkled with grated *comté* (*or Gruyère; Ed.*), and it is a perfect accompaniment to Roast Rack of Lamb with Green Peppercorns (*carré d'agneau rôti au poivre vert*, page 150).

It is equally delicious if, using the back of a spoon, you press little nests into the cooked vegetables and then break a fresh egg into each one. Cook them on top of the stove first, then finish the eggs in a hot oven, taking care not to overcook the yolks.

You can also serve this dish cold, but it must not be refrigerated.

La fricassée du jardin de mon père
BRAISED YOUNG VEGETABLES WITH SALT PORK

Truly, the ideal situation would be to have a kitchen garden and to be able to pick your own vegetables before sunrise or after sunset. However, if you live in the city do not despair. Find the vendors with the best produce and go to market early in the morning so that you can take your pick of the finest they have.

To serve 4:

    12 small new spring onions (*these look like bulbous scallions; Ed.*)
    4 small young lettuces with delicate leaves (*such as Bibb, Boston, or butter lettuce*)

2 bunches tiny new carrots with their leaves (about 30 carrots the size of your index finger)

2 bunches tiny turnips, the same size as the carrots

3 pounds tiny young peas in their shells (if you can, choose those that still have their little white flower attached)

3 cups to 1 quart tiny new potatoes, barely out of the ground (one peels these potatoes by rubbing them with the tips of the fingers under cold running water)

5 tablespoons cold butter, in all

5 ounces lean meaty salt pork (from the belly), in one piece (Remove the skin and cut the pork into *lardons*, sticks the size of your little finger.)

1 teaspoon coarse salt

PREPARATION OF THE VEGETABLES:

1. The onions: The onions should have their first skin removed—the one that has had contact with the earth. Cut off the root end and the stem. Wipe the onions with a towel, but do not wash them.

2. The lettuces: Rinse the lettuces carefully under cold water. Drain, then dry them with a towel. Leave the lettuces whole.

3. The carrots: Scrape them with the point of a small knife to remove the fine skin. Cut off the root end and the leaves. Wipe the carrots without washing them and leave whole.

4. The turnips: Scrape them with the point of a small knife to remove the fine skin. Cut off the root end and the leaves. Wipe the turnips without washing them and leave whole.

5. The peas: Shell the peas and discard any that are too large. Do not wash them.

6. The potatoes: Under cold running water, wipe the skins from the potatoes. Dry them immediately, and above all, do not let them soak.

COOKING:

Over medium heat, melt 2 teaspoons of the butter in a heavy 3-quart casserole. Add the *lardons* and cook 2 or 3 minutes, turning them frequently with a wooden spoon. Only sear the *lardons*; do not let them brown.

Add all the vegetables except the lettuce, with 4 tablespoons of cold water and the teaspoon of coarse salt. Then arrange the lettuces on top, spreading them carefully over all.

Cover the casserole and cook the vegetables 20 to 30 minutes over medium heat. To test for doneness, check the potatoes. They should be cooked enough so that they will not offer resistance when pierced with the point of a knife. The other vegetables will be ready at the same time.

The moment the potatoes are ready, stir in the remaining cold butter, cut into tiny pieces. Taste for seasoning and serve at once.

I advise you to serve this dish as a first course, because any accompaniment would interfere with the delicacy of these young vegetables.

Aspic de légumes frais avec son coulis de poivrons doux
VEGETABLES IN ASPIC WITH SWEET PEPPER SAUCE

To serve 4 or 8:

NOTE: *The quantity of the ingredients in this recipe is substantial. Depending on the rest of your menu, or the number of persons you wish to serve, each portion could be divided. However, do not attempt to use smaller molds—there are too many separate ingredients, and the stunning visual effect created with a 2-cup mold would suffer. Ed.*

THE VEGETABLES:

2 large artichokes (preferably "globe" artichokes), about
   7 ounces each
½ lemon
Coarse salt
7 ounces small young zucchini, about 3 of uniform size
Sugar

7 ounces carrots
7 ounces young white turnips
4 ounces small young string beans
1¼ pounds medium-size asparagus, about 24 stalks
4 branches fresh basil leaves
Freshly ground white pepper

THE ASPIC:

(In France, one can purchase aspic ready-made from the local char-cuterie. In the United States, you will have to prepare it yourself. Ed.)

4 cups strong greaseless cold chicken or veal stock
2 envelopes (2 tablespoons) unflavored powdered gelatin
3 egg whites, and their shells
½ lemon
A few sprigs fresh parsley, or thyme
1 bay leaf
¼ teaspoon peppercorns

THE SAUCE (*coulis de poivrons doux*):

2 large sweet red bell peppers
4 tablespoons olive oil
2 medium-size white onions, about 6 ounces each, thinly sliced
2 tomatoes, about 6 ounces each
2 cloves garlic, flattened and peeled
Bouquet garni (1 small stalk celery with leaves, 1 large sprig
    thyme, and 4 large sprigs parsley, tied together)
Coarse salt
Freshly ground pepper

PREPARATION OF THE VEGETABLES (the day before):

Place four 2-cup bowls in the refrigerator to chill.

1. The artichokes: Wash the artichokes and cut off the stems. Then wipe the bottoms with half a lemon to prevent them from darkening.

Bring 2 quarts of salted water to a rapid boil. Plunge in the artichokes and cook, uncovered, for 45 minutes. To make sure that they are perfectly cooked, pull off a leaf. If it detaches itself easily, the artichokes are done.

Drain the artichokes, and when they are cool enough to handle, remove the leaves and the choke. Wipe the bottoms with lemon and set them aside on a towel spread over a large baking sheet.

2. The zucchini: Wash the zucchini and trim the ends. Then peel them lengthwise in ⅜-inch bands, leaving alternating stripes of white flesh and green skin. Then cut the zucchini into ¼-inch slices.

Place the zucchini slices in a small saucepan with a pinch each of coarse salt and sugar, and add enough cold water to barely cover them. Cover the saucepan and cook the zucchini until the water has evaporated. By this method, the juices will remain concentrated in the vegetables. (*Allow about 7 minutes for this. Stir the zucchini frequently to make sure that it does not scorch. Ed.*)

Set the zucchini aside, arranged separately, on the towel with the artichoke bottoms.

3. The carrots and turnips: Peel the vegetables and cut them into ¼-inch slices. Place them in separate saucepans, each with a pinch of coarse salt and sugar. Add just enough cold water to barely cover the vegetables. Cover the saucepans and cook the vegetables until the water has evaporated. (*Allow about 7 minutes for the turnips and 8 or 9 minutes for the carrots. Stir frequently to be sure that the vegetables do not scorch or overcook. Ed.*)

Then set the carrots and turnips aside, separately, with the artichoke bottoms and zucchini.

4. The string beans: Nip off the ends of the beans and drop them into 2 quarts of boiling salted water. (*Allow about 6 to 7 minutes, depending on size. Ed.*) When they are cooked, yet still remain firm, drain, and quickly plunge them into cold water. When chilled, drain again, and set them aside with the other vegetables.

5. The asparagus: Cut the asparagus into even lengths, taking only the first 4 inches of each spear. Peel them, if necessary; then tie the asparagus into several small bundles and drop them into a casserole with 2 quarts of boiling salted water. Cook about 6 or 7 minutes; the time will depend on the size of the asparagus. Be sure to keep them firm.

When they are cooked, carefully lift the asparagus out of the casserole and plunge them into cold water. When chilled, remove the string and arrange the asparagus on the towel.

PREPARATION OF THE ASPIC:

Pour 3 cups of the cold stock into a 4-quart casserole. In a small bowl, soften the gelatin over the remaining cup of cold stock.

Using a wire whisk, beat the egg whites to a froth; then stir them, with their crushed shells, into the casserole with the stock. Add the juice of ½ lemon, the herbs, peppercorns, and softened gelatin. Stirring constantly with a wire whisk, bring the stock slowly to a boil. When a foam develops and the stock rises up—as if to boil over—remove the casserole from heat, and let stand undisturbed 10 minutes.

Saturate a clean dish towel or cloth with cold water. Wring it out and use it to line a fine sieve, placed over a large deep bowl. After the stock has had a 10-minute rest, pour it slowly through the sieve, letting it strain undisturbed into the bowl. The result should be a totally clear liquid aspic. Let cool at room temperature. Ed.

ASSEMBLING THE MOLDS:

All the vegetables should be cooked and ready, arranged separately on the towel before you begin:

1. Prepare the molds: Remove the chilled bowls from the refrigerator. Pour 2 tablespoons of cooled aspic into each, and tilt the bowl from side to side to allow the gelatin to slide over the interior, lining it with a bright clear coating.

2. The asparagus: Pour ½ cup liquid aspic into a deep plate or soup bowl. Add the asparagus tips and turn them in the gelatin until thoroughly impregnated. Then divide the asparagus into 4 parcels, and place 1 parcel on the bottom of each mold.

3. The artichoke bottoms: Cut the artichoke bottoms into thin slices. Saturate them with aspic, adding more as needed, and arrange the slices in a layer over the asparagus.

4. The zucchini: After coating the slices with aspic, arrange a ring of zucchini around the interior of each bowl. Reserve any extra slices.

5. The carrots and turnips: Soak the slices of carrots and turnips in aspic. Then arrange them, standing upright and slightly overlapping, in the shape of a crown around the inside of each bowl. (Alternate the colors, so that you have a disc of orange carrot followed by

one of white turnip, and so forth.) Thanks to the aspic, they will adhere easily.

If there are any excess vegetables (carrots, turnips, or zucchini), arrange them neatly in the center of the mold.

6. The string beans: Finish with the string beans, distributing them evenly over all the vegetables.

7. The basil leaves: Detach the basil leaves. Pressed down, there should be about 1 cup. Chop them coarsely and mix with the remaining aspic.

The aspic must remain liquid, slippery, and cold throughout this entire operation. Above all, do not allow it to set.

Season each bowl of vegetables with freshly ground white pepper. Cover with the remaining basil-flavored aspic, and chill overnight in the refrigerator.

PREPARATION OF THE SAUCE (*coulis de poivrons doux*):

1. Prepare the peppers: Stick 2 skewers through each pepper (*or use a long-handled cooking fork; Ed.*) and hold it over a gas flame or fire until the skin is completely charred. (If you have an electric stove, place peppers under the broiler grill, heated to maximum temperature, and turn them until charred on all sides.)

When each pepper is totally blackened, hold it under cold running water and peel off the skin. This is very easy—simply rub it with your fingers. Then split the pepper in half, remove the core, and scrape out the seeds. Cut the peppers into thick strips.

2. Cooking the sauce: Heat the olive oil in a large saucepan or casserole and add the sliced onions. Sauté the onions over medium heat until soft and golden. Stir frequently.

Meanwhile, drop the tomatoes into boiling water, count to 10, then plunge them into cold water. Remove the core, peel them, and cut each one into 8 pieces. Carefully scrape out the seeds, but do not press out the water.

Add the tomatoes to the onions with the strips of pepper, garlic, and *bouquet garni*. Season with a little salt and simmer the sauce for 30 minutes.

Then discard the *bouquet garni*, and purée the sauce in a food processor or blender, or press it through a food mill using the fine grate. Taste the sauce for seasoning, add freshly ground pepper, and pass it through a fine sieve. (*I did not feel that this additional refinement was absolutely necessary. Ed.*) Place the sauce in the refrigerator to chill.

TO SERVE:

When ready to serve the vegetable molds, spread the sweet pepper sauce over the bottom of a chilled serving platter, or spread it over 4 individual plates. Pour the rest of the sauce into a sauceboat.

Soak each bowl of vegetables in a basin of hot water to help release the gelatin (no longer than 1 minute); then slide a small knife around the rim and reverse the bowl, unmolding the vegetables onto the serving platter. You will discover a beautiful mosaic of brilliant colors beneath the glittering aspic.

NOTE: *After unmolding the vegetables, it is preferable to return them to the refrigerator for a few minutes before serving. Ed.*

This dish is long in preparation time, but can easily be made the day before you wish to serve it. Serve the vegetables as an accompaniment to cold roast lamb adorned with some of its slivers of garlic—and there you have a great summer dish, and also a good idea for a supper.

Dariole d'épinards
INDIVIDUAL SPINACH CUSTARDS
(Color picture 1)

To serve 4:

6 ounces young spinach leaves (*see Note*)
Salt
2 eggs
½ cup milk
½ cup heavy cream
Freshly ground white pepper
Freshly grated nutmeg
2 tablespoons butter, in all

NOTE: *If you would like to surround the* darioles *with a garniture of spinach, as shown in the color picture, increase the quantity of spinach to 12 ounces, and just before serving, cook the additional 6 ounces separately in 1½ tablespoons of butter. Ed.*

PREPARATION:

1. The spinach: Wash the spinach well in several changes of water. Strip off the stems and drain the leaves in a colander.

Bring a large casserole of salted water to a boil. Drop in the spinach and cook it, uncovered, 1 minute. Drain the spinach quickly and plunge it into a basin of cold water. When chilled, drain thoroughly in a colander or coarse sieve.

2. The custard: Break the eggs into a 2-quart mixing bowl. Pour in the milk and cream; add salt, freshly ground pepper, and 2 or 3 gratings of nutmeg. Mix the ingredients well with a wire whisk and set aside.

COOKING:

Preheat oven to 350°F.

Melt 1½ tablespoons of the butter in a small skillet. When it foams, add the cooked spinach—thoroughly drained and gently squeezed dry. Over medium to low heat, stir the spinach with a fork for about 5 minutes. Then combine the spinach with the custard mixture.

Using a brush, or your index finger, grease the bottom and sides of 4 small individual soufflé or custard molds with the remaining ½ tablespoon of butter. Make sure that they are well greased, using more butter if necessary. Then, with the help of a small ladle, divide the spinach-custard mixture among the molds.

Line the bottom of a small roasting pan with a piece of parchment paper that is slightly larger than the pan, turning up the sides. Cut a cross in the center of the paper (*see Note*) and arrange the molds within. Fill the pan with enough hot water to reach ¾ of the way up the sides of the molds. The roasting pan becomes a *bain-marie*.

NOTE: Lining the pan is not absolutely essential, except for this reason: It prevents communication of direct heat from the pan to the molds and the risk of the water coming to a boil. This could cause small bubbles in the texture of the custard. The reason for cutting a cross in the paper is to keep it from inflating and tipping over the small molds.

Bake the *darioles* about 30 minutes or until the custard appears set.

NOTE: *They can remain in their hot bath for an additional 15 minutes before serving, but I suggest that you keep them (in their bath) on the oven rack, with the oven door open, until ready to serve. Ed.*

At the moment of serving, all that remains to be done is to slip a small knife around the rim of each mold and invert the custard onto your serving plate.

NOTE: If you wish, you can add 1 tablespoon of yellow raisins to the uncooked custard mixture. However, before adding them, first bring them to a boil in 2 cups of cold water. Drain, refresh them with cold water, then drain again thoroughly in a sieve.

Or you can also add 1 tablespoon of lightly toasted slivered almonds, which harmonize very well with these ingredients.

Dariole de pommes aux poireaux

INDIVIDUAL POTATO AND LEEK CUSTARDS

To serve 4: *(Though this recipe is for 4 individual servings, I found the custard mixture sufficient to fill five 4-ounce molds. Ed.)*

1 large Idaho potato, about 7 ounces
1 leek
1 small Idaho potato, about 3 ounces
1 tablespoon butter, in all
½ cup milk
½ cup heavy cream
2 eggs
Salt
Freshly ground white pepper
Freshly grated nutmeg

PREPARATION:

1. The large potato: Preheat oven to 450°F.

Scrub the potato and bake it 1 hour. To check that it is done, insert the point of a knife into the center of the potato. If it does not meet resistance, the potato is ready.

2. The leek: Cut off the root end and remove any blemished exterior leaves. Split the leek in half and wash it well, making sure that there is no trace of sand. Cut the white and yellow part of the leek into julienne strips about 1½ inches long. Discard the coarser dark green part of the leek.

Place ½ tablespoon of butter in a small saucepan with 2 tablespoons of water. Add the leek and cook, covered, over medium heat, about 10 minutes or until the water has evaporated completely. *(Stir frequently to make sure that the leek does not scorch. Ed.)* Set aside.

3. The small potato: Wash and peel the potato and cut it into very fine dice. Then place the diced potato in a sieve and hold it under cold running water to rinse off some of the starch. Drain thoroughly.

FINISHING THE CUSTARD:

Warm the milk and cream together in a small saucepan, but do not let them actually get hot.

When the large potato has finished baking, remove it from the oven and lower the temperature to 350°F.

Cut the hot potato in half, and using a teaspoon, scoop out the flesh. Then quickly press it through a food mill placed over a mixing bowl. Mix in the warm milk and cream, a little at a time.

Beat the 2 eggs together and add them to the potato purée. When well blended, season with salt, freshly ground pepper, and 2 or 3 gratings of nutmeg. Stir in the cooked leek and diced raw potato.

Using a brush, or your index finger, grease the bottom and sides of 4 or 5 small soufflé or custard molds with the remaining ½ tablespoon of butter. Add more, if necessary. Using a small ladle, fill each mold with the custard mixture.

Line the bottom of a small roasting pan with a piece of parchment paper that is slightly larger than the pan, turning up the sides. Cut a cross in the center of the paper (*see Note*) and arrange the molds within. Fill the pan with enough hot water to reach ¾ of the way up the sides of the molds. The roasting pan becomes a *bain-marie*.

NOTE: Lining the pan is not absolutely essential, except for this reason: It prevents communication of direct heat from the pan to the molds and the risk of the water coming to a boil. This could cause small bubbles in the texture of the custard. The reason for cutting a cross in the paper is to keep it from inflating and tipping over the small molds.

Bake the *darioles* 30 to 35 minutes, or until the custard appears set.

NOTE: *The custards can remain in their hot bath for an additional 15 minutes before serving, but I suggest that you keep them (in their bath) on the oven rack, with the oven door open, until ready to serve. Ed.*

At the moment of serving, all that remains to be done is to slip a small knife around the rim of each mold and invert the custard onto your serving plate.

Galette de pommes de terre
CRISP POTATO CAKE

To serve 2 or 3: (*The ingredients for this dish may be increased to serve a larger number of persons. If you wish to do so, see the Note at the end of the recipe. Ed.*)

> 3 potatoes, about 6 to 8 ounces each
> Coarse salt
> 8 tablespoons (*1 stick*) butter
> Fine salt

PREPARATION:

I will give you two different ways of preparing this recipe. Neither is more difficult or more time-consuming than the other.

1. The potatoes: Peel and wipe the potatoes and slice them into paper-thin rounds—the same thickness as for potato chips.

Or cut them into very thin julienne strips, the size of matchsticks.

Spread the potatoes out on a towel and dry them well, then sprinkle with coarse salt.

2. The butter: In a small saucepan, gently melt 1 stick of butter over very low heat. Skim off any white milky particles from the surface. Then, off heat, keep the butter warm.

3. The skillet: Drop a small handful of fine salt into a heavy 9-inch skillet. Keeping the skillet dry, use a rag to wipe it clean. Discard the salt when you are finished.

Pour 2 tablespoons of warm clear butter into the skillet. Be careful to take only the clarified butter from the top without disturbing the white sediment that will have settled on the bottom of the saucepan. Tilt the skillet to coat it completely.

TO ASSEMBLE AND COOK THE POTATOES:

1. Round slices of potato: Cover the bottom of the buttered skillet with thin slices of potato. Arrange them in a circular pattern, slightly overlapping. Baste each layer with a spoonful or two of clarified butter. Then cover the last layer with all the remaining butter, taking care to avoid any of the white sediment.

Place the skillet over medium heat, and using two large metal spatulas or skimmers, press down on the potatoes while shifting them ever so slightly with short jerks of the wrist, to prevent them from sticking to the pan. As the potatoes cook, press down on them forcefully with the back of your spatula to saturate them with butter.

2. Julienne strips of potato: Hold the potatoes in a towel and squeeze them in your hands to extract any water. Then spread the potatoes out over the bottom of the buttered skillet and pour all the remaining butter over them. Take care to avoid any of the white sediment. Cook these potatoes in the same manner as described above for round slices of potato.

TO FINISH COOKING:

After cooking either preparation of potato about 10 to 15 minutes on one side, slip a spatula under the bottom of the cake and lift it slightly to check that it has become a crisp golden brown. Then, using two large spatulas, carefully turn the cake, reversing it onto its other side. Continue to cook the potatoes 10 to 15 minutes longer, until the second side is also crisp and golden brown.

TO SERVE:

Just before serving, tilt the skillet, and holding the potatoes in place with the back of a spatula, pour off any cooking butter.

Then slide the crisp potato cake onto a hot serving plate and serve at once.

NOTE: *If you wish to serve 4 persons, or 6 at most, use six 7-ounce potatoes, 12 tablespoons (1½ sticks) butter, and a 10-inch skillet. To use a larger number of potatoes would require a larger skillet and might result in a potato cake too difficult to turn. Ed.*

Pommes purées
MASHED POTATOES

To serve 4:

2 pounds Idaho potatoes (use farinaceous potatoes, not waxy or
   new potatoes)
5 tablespoons butter
Salt
About ½ cup milk

PREPARATION:

Peel the potatoes, cut them into large cubes (about 2 ounces each),
and rinse in cold water.

Put the potatoes in a 2-quart casserole, and cover by an inch or
more with cold water. Add salt and place the casserole over medium
heat. After the water comes to a boil, allow about 20 minutes cooking
time. When the potatoes can be pierced easily with the point of a
knife, they are done. Be sure not to overcook them or they will absorb
the water and disintegrate.

Just before the potatoes have finished cooking, warm the milk in
a saucepan but do not let it come to a boil. Keep the warm milk covered to prevent it from forming a skin.

When the potatoes are done, pour them all at once into a food mill
held over the kitchen sink. As soon as they are thoroughly drained,
press the potatoes through the food mill into the same warm casserole
used to cook them. Place the casserole over very low heat and add
the butter, cut into small pieces. Using a wooden spoon, mix the
potatoes well until the texture is smooth and glossy.

Then add the milk, a little at a time, until you obtain the desired
consistency. (The exact quantity of milk depends on the nature of
the potatoes.) Taste for seasoning (you can probably add a pinch of
salt) and serve at once.

You may think that it is pretentious, or ridiculous, to tell you how to
make mashed potatoes. Everyone knows how! But no, everyone does
not know how. In fact, very few people do it well. Try my instructions

and you will see the difference. This is a dish that is treated with negligence but that really requires the utmost attention.

ONE MUST:

1. Peel the potatoes just before cooking them, or they will harden.
2. Cook them in cold water, and do not allow them to fall apart.
3. As soon as they are done, drain them without waiting, or they will become gluey.
4. Blend them with butter and do not stop until they are completely smooth and glossy.
5. Never add the milk all at once, because you risk adding too much liquid.
6. Finally, you must serve the purée immediately. The potatoes cannot wait and cannot be reheated.

Pommes cendrillon
BAKED POTATOES WITH HERBS AND CHEESE

To serve 4: (*This is a flexible recipe that can be easily divided to serve 2 persons, or increased to serve 6 or 8. Ed.*)

4 Idaho potatoes, about 8 ounces each and of uniform shape
4 tablespoons butter
6 tablespoons heavy cream, in all
Salt
Freshly grated nutmeg
2 tablespoons freshly chopped parsley
2 tablespoons freshly chopped chives
1 egg yolk
2 tablespoons coarsely grated Gruyère cheese

PREPARATION:

Preheat oven to 450°F.

Scrub the potatoes well under cold running water. Then bake them in the preheated oven for about 1 hour. Check that they are

226

done by poking them with the point of a small knife. If the knife penetrates the potatoes without resistance, they are done. Take them from the oven, but do not turn the oven off. Keep it hot at the same temperature.

With a small knife, make an incision around the top of each potato, removing a "lid" about ¼-inch thick. Use a teaspoon to scrape out all the flesh of the potato, taking care not to pierce the shell. Discard the lids.

Collect the pulp in a warmed mixing bowl and mash it with a fork. Then work in the butter, followed by 4 tablespoons of the cream, and salt, nutmeg, and fresh herbs. Fill the potato shells with this preparation.

TO FINISH THE POTATOES:

In a small bowl, mix the remaining 2 tablespoons of cream with the egg yolk and freshly grated Gruyère cheese. Spread a tablespoon of this mixture over each potato.

Arrange the potatoes on a baking sheet and return them to the hot oven for 5 to 10 minutes, or long enough to obtain a golden crust. Serve at once.

This recipe may be prepared a little ahead of time, but it is indispensable that you scoop out the flesh of the potatoes and mix it with the butter, cream, and spices as soon as the potatoes leave the oven. If they are prepared in advance, do not ever refrigerate them, and do not cover them with the cream-egg-yolk-cheese mixture until just before they are to go into the oven.

Le risotto au safran
SAFFRON RICE

To serve 4:
  7 tablespoons butter, in all
  2 tablespoons chopped onion
  1 cup short-grain rice, rinsed and well-drained
  1½ cups chicken stock
  1 sprig fresh thyme (*or substitute ¼ teaspoon dried thyme; Ed.*)
  A pinch of saffron (*⅛ teaspoon powdered saffron or ¼ teaspoon saffron threads*)
  ¾ pound well-ripened tomatoes
  4 tablespoons dry white wine
  3 heaping tablespoons freshly grated Parmesan cheese
  Coarse salt
  Freshly ground white pepper

PREPARATION:

Melt 3 tablespoons of the butter in an enameled cast-iron casserole. Add the chopped onion, and over low heat, cook 5 minutes without allowing the onion to brown. Add the rice and continue to cook, stirring frequently, until the rice is as translucent as the onion.

Add the chicken stock, a sprig of thyme, and a pinch of saffron, and bring the liquid almost to a simmer. Stir once, cover the casserole, and cook 20 minutes over very low heat. Then remove the casserole from heat, and without disturbing the cover, let stand 5 minutes.

Drop the tomatoes into boiling water, count to 10, then plunge them into cold water. This will make them easy to peel. Cut out the core and peel the tomatoes, then cut them in half crosswise and press out the seeds and water. Chop the tomatoes into small dice.

TO FINISH THE RISOTTO:

After the rice has settled for 5 minutes, remove the cover of the casserole and add the chopped tomatoes and white wine. Return the casserole to low heat, and simmer the rice, uncovered, for 2 minutes.

Then stir in the remaining 4 tablespoons of butter, 1 tablespoon at a time, followed by the cheese. Mix well, adding salt and freshly ground pepper to taste.

This *risotto* must be creamy. Serve it from the casserole.

Nouilles fraîches à la crème de pistou
FRESH NOODLES WITH BASIL AND CREAM

To serve 2: (*These ingredients can easily be doubled to serve 4. Ed.*)
  10 ounces fresh noodles, or 8 ounces of the best-quality imported
    dry noodles
  Salt
  1 tablespoon olive oil
  1 clove garlic
  15 large fresh basil leaves
  1½ tablespoons butter
  2 heaping tablespoons *crème fraîche* (*or substitute 4 to 5 table-
    spoons heavy cream; Ed.*)
  Freshly ground white pepper
  4 ounces freshly grated Parmesan cheese

  PREPARATION:
In a large casserole, bring 3 quarts of salted water to a boil. When the water is boiling vigorously, add the olive oil and drop in the noodles. Disperse them with the tines of a large cooking fork to make sure that they do not stick together. Maintain the water at a rapid boil for 8 to 10 minutes.

NOTE: *Depending upon thickness and quality, fresh pasta will often become perfectly cooked within only a few minutes. I suggest that you check a strand of pasta after 3 minutes, and intermittently there-after, to make sure that it remains slightly* al dente. *Ed.*

229

While the pasta is cooking, flatten and peel the clove of garlic. Then chop it as finely as possible, together with the basil leaves. Set aside.

FINISHING THE NOODLES:

When the pasta has finished cooking, drain it quickly in a colander, then return it to the same warm casserole that it was cooked in.

With 2 forks, blend in the butter, *crème fraîche*, and the chopped garlic-basil mixture, one at a time. Taste for salt and add a generous amount of freshly ground pepper. Take care not to crush or break the noodles—but do mix and serve the pasta as quickly as possible. Pass a bowl of freshly grated Parmesan cheese separately.

If fresh basil is not available, you can replace it with a large handful (3 to 4 tablespoons) of freshly chopped parsley. It's then altogether another dish of course—but never mind, you will still have the perfume of the garlic.

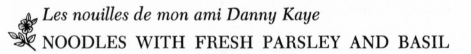

Les nouilles de mon ami Danny Kaye

NOODLES WITH FRESH PARSLEY AND BASIL

To serve 2: (*These ingredients can easily be doubled to serve 4. Ed.*)
  ½ pound fresh noodles, or 7 ounces of the best-quality dry noodles, made with eggs
  Salt
  5 tablespoons pungent imported virgin olive oil, in all
  ½ lemon
  3 heaping tablespoons freshly chopped parsley
  6 large fresh basil leaves, chopped
  Freshly ground white pepper

PREPARATION:

In a large casserole, bring 3 quarts of salted water to a boil. Add 2 tablespoons of the olive oil, drop in the noodles, and maintain the water at a rapid boil until the noodles are cooked. The cooking time depends on the quality of the noodles. After 3 minutes, test one from time to time.

While the noodles are cooking, pour the remaining 3 tablespoons of olive oil into a large bowl, and add the juice of ½ lemon and the chopped parsley and basil.

When the pasta has finished cooking, drain well in a colander; then quickly turn the noodles into the bowl with the olive oil and herbs. Season with salt and freshly ground pepper, and with the help of two forks, toss the noodles like a salad. Serve at once.

Danny Kaye's pasta is only one of a number of dishes that I had the pleasure of tasting (with an excellent California wine: Chenin Blanc) at his beautiful home in Beverly Hills.

I shall take advantage of this occasion to pay homage to Danny Kaye, who is not only a marvelous actor and hilarious companion, but who is also a great friend of the children of the world. This man of innumerable talents uses his astonishing love of cooking to express his passion for everything that is beautiful and true.

He is a chef of great talent, particularly in Chinese *cuisine*. In this domain, he is certainly equal to the finest of Chinese chefs.

As for the noodles—being a perfectionist, he of course makes them himself. The recipe is simple, delicious, but not particularly economical. You judge: 2 pounds of flour, 3 *dozen* egg yolks, plus a small measure of olive oil!

Les fromages

CHEESES

Picodons marinés à l'huile d'herbes sèches

GOAT CHEESE MARINATED WITH DRIED HERBS

To serve 6:

6 *picodons*, or 1 pound *chèvre* (*see Note*)
1 large sprig thyme (*about 1 teaspoon thyme leaves*)
1 large sprig rosemary (*about 1 teaspoon rosemary leaves*)
1 large sprig savory (*about 1 teaspoon savory leaves*)
10 whole black peppercorns
12 whole coriander seeds
1 large clove garlic, peeled
2 cups imported virgin olive oil

NOTE: Picodons *are small firm discs of goat cheese* (chèvre) *with a variegated powdery-blue to golden exterior. They are not commonly found in this country. However, you can substitute either* crottins de Chavignol *or simply the driest* chèvre, *sold in bulk, available. In the last instance, purchase a 1-pound piece from a "log" of* chèvre *with a diameter of about 2½ inches. And of course, if fresh herbs are available, do not hesitate to use them. Ed.*

232

PREPARATION:

Cut the cheese into slices about ¾-inch thick. (*If you are using a 1-pound piece from a log, there should be 6 slices. Ed.*) Arrange the herbs and cheese in layers in a wide-rimmed 1-quart jar that can be hermetically sealed.

Strew the peppercorns and coriander seeds over the cheese and add the whole clove of garlic. Pour in enough olive oil to completely cover the cheese. Add more than the 2 cups, or less, as needed.

Seal the jar tightly and let the cheese marinate for no less than 1 week and no more than 1 month. The jar should be kept unrefrigerated, at a cool to mild temperature. (If you hold the cheese any longer than 1 month, the oil will become rancid.)

TO SERVE:

Serve the cheese with hot toasted slices of French bread, brushed with the oil from the marinade.

Assiette de fromage blanc aux fruits frais du jardin
WHITE CHEESE WITH FRESH SUMMER FRUITS

To serve 4:

21 ounces *fromage blanc* (*substitute 3 packages farmer's cheese; see Note*)
10 tablespoons buttermilk (*see Note*)
8 prunes
1 small cantaloupe, about 1 pound
2 white peaches
8 fresh apricots
12 almonds, freshly shelled
12 perfect strawberries
2 pears

Lemon
24 unblemished young lettuce leaves, from the heart of a Boston
   or butter lettuce
4 sprigs fresh mint (8 leaves in all)
Heavy cream

NOTE: *Fromage blanc* is a bland fresh white cheese, not unlike cottage cheese. If you cannot find it, which is highly probable, you can
obtain a white cheese with nearly the same character by adding buttermilk to farmer's cheese. Beat the buttermilk into the cheese, a
little at a time, until the consistency of the farmer's cheese is light
and creamy, with a slight tartness. Ed.

HAVE READY:

1. The prunes: Soak the prunes 4 hours in a bowl of warm water.
2. The cantaloupe: Cut the melon into quarters and scrape out
the seeds. Then peel the melon and cut each quarter into 4 long slices.
3. The peaches: Drop the peaches into boiling water. Count to 10,
then plunge them into cold water. This will make them easier to peel.
(*With ripe peaches, this usually isn't necessary. Ed.*)
   After pulling off the skin, cut the peaches into long thin slices.
4. The apricots: Remove the pits and cut the apricots into quarters.
5. The almonds: Shell the almonds and blanch them 1 minute in
boiling water. Then drain and slip off the brown skins.
6. The strawberries: Rinse and hull the berries.
7. The pears: Peel and quarter the pears and remove the core and
seeds. Then cut them into long thin slices and wipe gently with lemon
juice.
8. The lettuce: Separate and wash the lettuce leaves, discarding
any that are bruised or withered. Dry them gently on a towel.

ASSEMBLING THE PLATES:

Place a neat mound of *fromage blanc* in the center of each of four
very large plates. (*Choose flat plates rather than those with rims. Ed.*)
   Make a crown of 6 lettuce leaves in the center of each plate, and
over the lettuce compose a circle of the different fruits, alternating

their colors. Stick a small sprig of fresh mint on the top of each mound of cheese. Split the 12 blanched almonds in half, and arrange 6 of the halves in the shape of a star around each sprig of mint.

Serve the plates of fruit well chilled and accompanied by a bowl or sauceboat of heavy cream.

This is a dish that is refreshing and light, to be served, for example, as a summer lunch around the swimming pool.

Fromage blanc aux herbes
WHITE CHEESE WITH HERBS

To make about 1 pint:

10½ ounces *fromage blanc* (*substitute 1½ packages farmer's cheese; see Note*)
4 tablespoons buttermilk (*see Note*)
4 tablespoons *crème fraîche* (*or substitute heavy cream; Ed.*)
1 tablespoon wine vinegar
2 tablespoons walnut oil
1 tablespoon chopped fresh parsley
1 tablespoon chopped fresh chervil (*or substitute fresh basil or chives; Ed.*)
1 teaspoon minced shallot
Salt
Freshly ground white pepper

NOTE: *Fromage blanc is a bland fresh white cheese, not unlike cottage cheese. If you cannot find it, which is highly probable, you can obtain a white cheese with nearly the same character by adding a little buttermilk to farmer's cheese. It will lighten the consistency of the cheese and give it a slight tartness. Ed.*

PREPARATION:

Using a fork, blend the buttermilk into the farmer's cheese, a tablespoon at a time. Then, switching to a wire whisk, beat in the cream, followed by the remaining ingredients. Mix well after each addition. Refrigerate the cheese and serve as is.

If you happen to have a garden with some young garlic plants, pick 2 or 3 tender shoots from the heart of a plant, chop them, and add them to the preparation.

Ah! Those summer evenings under the great linden tree where my father put out the table for dinner. Night came late, but there was already a peaceful silence numbing the bourbonnais countryside.

I was 5 years old, 8 years old, or perhaps 15—of little importance, since my mother's movements were always the same when she brought out the large tureen of fresh milk from which she had removed the thick layer of cream. We began our dinner with big bowls of milk into which we dipped pieces of week-old country bread. It smelled so good, this bread, that we never ate it until it was at least two days old. To the last spoonful of milk, we continued dipping our bread.

Then there was a bowl of *fromage blanc*, like the one in this recipe. Hers came straight from the cellar, fresh and aromatic. Our only accompaniment was small new potatoes, cooked in their jackets in salted water.

That was all of our dinner, but it was delicious. It is good to remember these things.

Tartines de roquefort aux noix
ROQUEFORT WITH WALNUTS ON HOT TOAST

To serve 6:
   5 tablespoons butter, softened
   3½ ounces freshly shelled walnuts (*about 1 cup*), coarsely
      chopped
   7 ounces Roquefort cheese
   2 tablespoons Armagnac or cognac
   Freshly ground pepper, preferably white
   1 *pain de campagne* (*a round loaf of coarse-textured French
      country bread; Ed.*), 3 or 4 days old

PREPARATION:

Place the butter in a 2-quart mixing bowl, and using a wooden spoon, work it into a paste. Then mix in the chopped walnuts.

Put the Roquefort on a soup plate and mash it well with a fork. Then blend in the Armagnac and add 4 to 5 good turns of the pepper mill. Combine the cheese with the butter and nuts, mixing until all ingredients are thoroughly incorporated.

TO SERVE:

Either in your oven or under the broiler grill, toast thick slices of stale *pain de campagne*. While the bread is still hot, spread it with cheese and serve at once.

You can accompany these cheese toasts with celery hearts and radishes. They also marry well with grapes and with quarters of pears wiped with lemon juice to prevent their darkening.

In the country in the heart of France, a soup accompanied only by these Roquefort *tartines* often composes a meal.

Tartines de rigottes de Condrieu au thym
MELTED CHEESE ON TOAST WITH THYME

For each serving:
    1 *rigotte de Condrieu,* about 3 ounces (*see Note*)
    4 thin slices *pain-baguette* (*a long thin loaf of French bread; Ed.*)
    2 tablespoons olive oil
    A pinch dried thyme leaves
    Freshly ground pepper

NOTE: *A* rigotte *is a small cylinder of cow cheese weighing about 3 ounces. If you cannot find this exact cheese, a good* Port-Salut *makes a fine substitute. Cut the cheese to fit your bread. Ed.*

PREPARATION:

Preheat the broiler.

Brush 4 slices of bread with 1 tablespoon of the olive oil. Place them under the broiler grill until lightly browned.

Cut the cheese into 4 slices the same dimensions as your bread. Lay a slice of cheese on each piece of toast, then sprinkle with thyme and freshly ground pepper. Brush with the remaining tablespoon of olive oil.

TO SERVE:

Just before serving, run the toasts under the broiler grill for a few minutes, or until the cheese is lightly browned and bubbly.

These *tartines* may be served as a separate cheese course or they can also be offered with apéritifs.

NOTE: *Accompanied by a salad, I found that these* tartines *make a perfect light meal. Ed.*

Les desserts
DESSERTS

Les sorbets de fruits frais
FRESH FRUIT ICES

Fresh fruit ices are the most pleasing of desserts. But they must be a pure reflection of the fruit and kept altogether natural. Use only fresh fruits of the finest quality, and sugar. *Sorbets* are reasonably priced and simple to make, and many fruits lend themselves well to this preparation.

One indispensable element is quite clearly an ice-cream maker (*sorbetière*). You can find them in housewares stores; they are small and inexpensive.

In every case, it is preferable not to make the ices until a short time before you plan to serve them. This is to preserve the flavor and quality of the fruit juice.

NOTE: *Lacking an ice-cream maker, you can still prepare all of these sorbets, and quite easily, too, but their texture will be coarser. Pour the fruit purée into a shallow metal pan and place it in your freezer. After 1 hour, stir the mixture frequently with a fork. After several hours, the result will be a coarse granular ice. Though not of the same texture as a* sorbet *prepared in an ice-cream maker, the fresh flavor will be the same. Ed.*

Sorbet à l'abricot
APRICOT ICE

To serve 4:

> 1⅓ pounds fresh apricots (*see Notes*)
> 1 large juicy lemon
> ¾ to 1 cup sugar (preferably powdered sugar, which dissolves more easily)

NOTE: The season for fresh apricots being brief, this *sorbet* can also be made with canned apricots. (*See Note at the end of the recipe. Ed.*)

PREPARATION:

Gently pull apart each apricot and remove the pit. Purée the fruit (unpeeled) in a food processor or blender, or pass it through a food mill, using the fine grate.

Add the juice of 1 lemon, followed by the sugar. Mix well, tasting for sweetness. The amount of sugar will vary depending on the quality of the apricots.

FINISHING THE ICE:

Pour the purée into the container of an ice-cream maker and prepare it according to the manufacturer's instructions.

When the *sorbet* is ready, form it into large balls, using a soup spoon dipped in hot water.

Serve the *sorbet* in ice-cold glass bowls or goblets.

NOTE: *If you are using canned apricots, you will need two 17-ounce cans of apricot halves packed in heavy syrup. Drain the apricots in a sieve and reserve ⅓ cup of the syrup.*

Purée the apricots as directed, adding the lemon juice. Then pour in the reserved ⅓ cup of syrup, but do not add sugar. Mix well and finish the sorbet in the manner described. Ed.

Sorbet à l'ananas
PINEAPPLE ICE

To serve 4:

1 fresh well-ripened pineapple, about 3 pounds
8 tablespoons sugar (preferably powdered sugar, which dissolves
   more easily)

PREPARATION:

Cut off the top of the pineapple. Save it, with the leaves, and keep it
in the refrigerator.

Using a sharp medium-size knife, carve out the flesh of the pineapple, leaving a sturdy shell about ⅜-inch thick. Place the shell in
the freezer compartment of your refrigerator.

Remove the hard core running through the flesh of the fruit; then
chop the rest of the pineapple into small pieces.

Purée the pineapple in a food processor or blender, or pass it
through a food mill. Then press the pineapple through a fine sieve.
Add the powdered sugar and mix well with a wire whisk. (*Taste for
sweetness; pineapples will vary. Ed.*)

FINISHING THE ICE:

Pour the purée into the container of an ice-cream maker and prepare
it according to the manufacturer's instructions.

With the help of a spoon dipped in hot water, scoop the *sorbet* into
the frozen pineapple shell. Decorate with the reserved top of the
pineapple and serve.

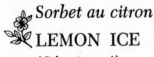

Sorbet au citron

LEMON ICE

(Color picture 4)

To serve 4:

> About 1½ pounds juicy lemons (*to yield 1 cup lemon juice*)
> 10 sugar tablets (1¾ ounces)
> 2 cups water (It is preferable to use bottled mineral water, but not a sparkling water. Tap water too often has the unpleasant scent of chlorine.)
> ¾ cup powdered sugar

PREPARATION:

Rub the skin of the lemons with the sugar tablets until the tablets are saturated to the point that they become a bright, translucent yellow and are totally impregnated with the perfume of the zest. Then drop the tablets into a saucepan with the 2 cups of water, add the powdered sugar, and heat just until the sugar is dissolved. Let cool.

Cut the lemons in half, squeeze them, and strain their juice through a fine sieve into the cooled sugar syrup.

FINISHING THE ICE:

Stir the syrup and juice together until well combined, then pour into the container of an ice-cream maker and prepare according to the manufacturer's instructions.

Serve the *sorbet* in ice-cold glass bowls or goblets, forming it into balls with the help of a soup spoon dipped in hot water.

Sorbet à la fraise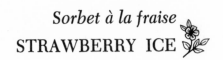
STRAWBERRY ICE

To serve 4:

- 1 pound strawberries (*To be sure that you have enough choice berries, it would be safer to buy 3 pints rather than 2. Ed.*)
- ¾ cup sugar (preferably powdered sugar, which dissolves more easily)
- 1 lemon
- 1 or 2 tablespoons superfine sugar

PREPARATION:

Set aside 4 perfect strawberries with their stems intact.

Wash the rest of the berries, drain, and hull them. Then, crush the berries in a blender or food processor, or press them through a food mill, using the fine grate. Gather the purée in a bowl and add the powdered sugar and the juice of 1 lemon. Mix well with a wire whisk.

FINISHING THE ICE:

Pour the purée into the container of an ice-cream maker and prepare it according to the manufacturer's instructions.

When the *sorbet* is ready, form it into balls with the help of a soup spoon dipped in hot water, and drop them into ice-cold glass bowls or goblets.

Lightly moisten the 4 reserved strawberries with water, then roll them in a small mound of superfine sugar. This will give them a glossy, crystalized look. Place a strawberry on top of each ice and serve at once.

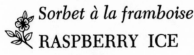

Sorbet à la framboise

RASPBERRY ICE

(Color picture 4)

To serve 4:

1 pound raspberries (*2 to 3 half-pints*)
1 small lemon
¾ cup sugar (preferably powdered sugar, which dissolves more easily)

PREPARATION:

Pick through the berries (*do not wash them*), then crush them in a blender or food processor, or press them through a food mill, using the fine grate. Gather the purée in a bowl and add the juice of a small lemon and the sugar. Mix well with a wire whisk. (*Taste for sweetness; depending on the quality of the berries, they might need a little more sugar. Ed.*)

FINISHING THE ICE:

Pour the purée into the container of an ice-cream maker and prepare it according to the manufacturer's instructions.

When the *sorbet* is ready, serve it in ice-cold glass bowls or goblets, forming it into balls with the help of a soup spoon dipped in hot water.

Sorbet au melon
CANTALOUPE ICE

To serve 4:

- 3 small cantaloupes, about 1 pound each (*see Note*)
- 2 lemons
- 6 tablespoons sugar (preferably powdered sugar, which dissolves more easily)
- A pinch fine salt
- 4 strawberries

NOTE: *If you wish, you can also use a larger melon, or melons, and forgo using the hollowed out melon rinds as serving bowls. Ed.*

PREPARATION:

Cut each melon in half crosswise, and scrape out the seeds. Then, with the help of a teaspoon, remove all the flesh of the melon, leaving only a sturdy shell. Take care not to break through the shell or to take any of the green part of the rind. Keep the 4 most nearly perfect melon halves and place them in the freezer compartment of your refrigerator.

Crush all the melon pulp in a food processor or blender, or pass it through a food mill, using the fine grate. Gather the purée in a bowl, add the juice of 2 lemons, the sugar, and a pinch of salt. Mix well with a wire whisk.

FINISHING THE ICE:

Pour the purée into the container of an ice-cream maker and prepare it according to the manufacturer's instructions.

When the *sorbet* is ready, form it into balls, using a soup spoon dipped in hot water. Mound the balls in the 4 frozen melon halves and crown each portion with a strawberry.

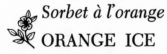

Sorbet à l'orange

ORANGE ICE

(Color picture 4)

To serve 4:

- 4 large juicy oranges, about 2 pounds (*to yield 1½ cups orange juice*)
- 10 sugar tablets (*1¾ ounces*)
- ½ cup water (it is preferable to use bottled mineral water, but not a sparkling water. Tap water too often has the unpleasant scent of chlorine.)
- 5 tablespoons sugar (preferably powdered sugar, which dissolves more easily)

PREPARATION:

Rub the skin of the oranges with the sugar tablets until the tablets are saturated to the point that they become a translucent orange and are totally impregnated with the perfume of the zest. Then drop the tablets into a small saucepan with the ½ cup of water and the powdered sugar, and heat just until the sugar is dissolved. Let cool.

Cut the oranges in half, squeeze them, and strain their juice through a fine sieve into the cooled sugar syrup.

FINISHING THE ICE:

Stir the syrup and juice together until well combined, then pour it into the container of an ice-cream maker and prepare it according to the manufacturer's instructions.

Serve the *sorbet* in ice-cold glass bowls or goblets, forming it into balls with the help of a soup spoon dipped in hot water.

Sorbet à la poire william
PEAR ICE

I advise you to use William pears for this recipe, because they have more flavor than other pears and the flesh of the fruit is better suited to this preparation. (*In this order, substitute Bartlett, Comice, or Anjou pears. Ed.*)

To serve 4:

> 1½ pounds firm ripe pears
> 4 lemons
> ¾ cup sugar

PREPARATION:

Peel the pears, cut them in half, and remove the core and seeds. Cut 2 of the lemons in half and use them to wipe the flesh of the pears on all sides to prevent them from darkening.

Arrange the pears in a heavy casserole just large enough to hold them side by side. Add the sugar and enough cold water to barely cover the pears (*about 1½ cups*).

Bring the water to a boil, reduce heat, and gently simmer the pears 10 to 15 minutes. Then, using a slotted spoon, lift the pears from the casserole and set aside on a plate.

Reduce the cooking syrup to about ¾ cup, or until it begins to thicken slightly. But above all, do not let it take on color. Then return the pears to the syrup and chill them in the refrigerator.

FINISHING THE ICE:

Add the juice of the remaining 2 lemons to the cold pears, then purée the fruit with the syrup in a food processor or blender, or pass it through a food mill, using the fine grate.

Pour the purée into an ice-cream maker and prepare it according to the manufacturer's instructions.

When the *sorbet* is ready, serve it in ice-cold glass bowls or goblets, forming it into balls with the help of a soup spoon dipped in hot water.

Parfait glacé à la liqueur d'anis
ANISE-FLAVORED ICE CREAM

If you wish, the anise liqueur can be replaced by another liqueur, or by coffee.

To serve 4 or 6:

    11 tablespoons sugar, in all
    6 egg yolks
    1 cup heavy cream
    3 tablespoons *Pastis* or *liqueur d'anis* (*or you can use Ricard, Pernod, or any anise-flavored apéritif. Ed.*)

PREPARATION:

In a small casserole, heat 9 tablespoons (*½ cup plus 1 tablespoon*) of the sugar with 5 tablespoons of water. Boil until the sugar is completely dissolved and the liquid is clear. Remove from heat, but cover to keep the syrup warm.

Drop the egg yolks into a large mixing bowl and beat them with a wire whisk until thick.

Return the syrup to a boil, then pour it into the egg yolks in a slow steady stream. Place the bowl over a pan of hot water (*bain-marie*) and continue to beat until the egg yolks are thick and foamy. This will take about 7 or 8 minutes. (*The consistency should be thick enough to coat the wires of the whisk. Ed.*) Then remove the bowl from the *bain-marie* and continue to beat until the custard has cooled completely.

Pour the cream into a well-chilled bowl (*preferably stainless steel*) and beat with a wire whisk until thick and voluminous. Then add the remaining 2 tablespoons of sugar and continue to beat until the cream is firm (*but take care not to turn it into butter; Ed.*).

Take the first bowl with the custard mixture, and beat it over ice until it is the same temperature as the whipped cream. Stir in the anise liqueur.

Using a large wooden spoon or spatula, fold the cream into the custard. When thoroughly incorporated, scrape the mixture into a well-chilled mold of your choice.

Place the mold in the freezer for at least 6 hours.

TO SERVE:

Shortly before you are ready to serve, dip the mold into hot water; then turn the ice cream out onto a serving plate. Return the ice cream to the freezer briefly, to set the surface.

Pruneaux confits au thé de lotus et à la crème fraîche
PRUNES WITH BUTTER-CREAM

To serve 4:

- 12 extra-large prunes (preferably the French from the town of Agen), about ¾ pound, pitted
- 4 Orange Pekoe tea bags
- ½ cup sugar
- 4 tablespoons unsalted sweet butter, softened
- 1 cup heavy cream
- 1 tablespoon powdered sugar
- 3 tablespoons sliced almonds

PREPARATION OF THE PRUNES (12 hours in advance):

Place the prunes in a bowl with enough warm water to cover. Let stand at room temperature for 2 hours.

Meanwhile, bring 2 cups of water to a boil and pour it over the tea bags. Let the tea infuse for 15 minutes, then remove the bags and add the ½ cup sugar.

Return the tea to a boil, then simmer the syrup 15 minutes. During this time, remove any scum that forms on the surface. Let the syrup cool.

After 2 hours, when the prunes have swelled, drain, and place them in the tea syrup to macerate in the refrigerator for at least 8 to 10 hours.

FINISHING THE CONFECTION:

Place a deep serving plate in the freezer compartment of your refrigerator.

Preheat the broiler.

Shortly before serving, beat the softened butter until creamy. Beat the cream until very thick; then incorporate the whipped butter and the tablespoon of powdered sugar. Chill the mixture in the refrigerator 10 minutes to firm it.

During this time, lightly toast the sliced almonds on an ungreased baking sheet under the broiler grill. Watch the almonds carefully and toss them frequently. (*This operation will only take about 2 minutes. Ed.*) Set the toasted nuts aside.

TO SERVE:

Dip a tablespoon into a bowl of warm water and then into the cold butter-cream mixture to form 12 balls of cream. Do this very quickly, placing each ball of cream on the ice-cold serving plate just taken from the freezer.

Top each ball of cream with a prune, and nap with a teaspoon of the syrup. Sprinkle the toasted almonds over all and serve immediately, very cold.

Gratin d'orange

 BROILED ORANGE SEGMENTS WITH SABAYON SAUCE

To serve 4:

    6 large navel oranges (except for bitter oranges, other varieties may be used if you remove the seeds)

    6 tablespoons sugar, in all (*see Note*)

    3 egg yolks

    2 tablespoons heavy cream

PREPARATION OF THE ORANGES:

Using a vegetable peeler, remove all of the zest (*orange skin*) from 1 of the oranges, without including any trace of white pith. Stack portions of the peelings together and, using a scissors, snip them into fine julienne strips.

Place the strips of zest in a small saucepan with ½ cup of cold water and bring to a boil. Simmer the zest 2 to 3 minutes, then drain in a sieve and refresh under cold running water. Let the zest remain in the sieve and set aside to drain thoroughly.

Finish peeling the orange, cutting close to the flesh and removing every trace of white pith; then peel the remaining 5 oranges in the same way. Using a small, very sharp knife, separate the segments of fruit from the membrane encasing them. Do this while holding the fruit over a bowl to catch all of the juices. Then place the fruit in another bowl, sprinkle with 3 tablespoons of the sugar (*see Note*), and place in the refrigerator to chill. Reserve the juices.

NOTE: *If you are using good sweet navel oranges, you may wish to omit this addition of sugar. Ed.*

PREPARATION OF THE SABAYON SAUCE:

Drop the egg yolks into the top part of a double boiler (*bain-marie*). Add the remaining 3 tablespoons of sugar, 4 tablespoons of reserved orange juice, and the heavy cream. Place the mixture over boiling water, and beat continuously with a wire whisk until it is frothy and just thick enough to coat the wires of the whisk. Remove the sauce from heat (separating the double boiler) and stir in the julienne strips of zest. Let cool.

TO FINISH THE GRATIN:

Preheat the broiler to its maximum temperature.

Divide the chilled orange segments among 4 heat-resistant dessert plates and spread the *sabayon* sauce over them. (*See Note.*)

At the last moment before serving, slide the plates under the hot broiler, close to the heating element. Keep the dessert there only briefly—just until the sauce is lightly glazed. (*If you leave it under the heat too long, the* sabayon *will separate. Ed.*)

251

You can replace the oranges with raspberries or strawberries, napping them with the same orange-flavored *sabayon*.

NOTE: *If you do not have heat-resistant individual plates, this confection can be presented on a platter and served at the table. Ed.*

 Soupe de fruits des isles aux fleurs
STRAWBERRY SOUP WITH EXOTIC FRUITS

To serve 6:
> 2 ripe red bananas (*or substitute 3 yellow bananas to make about 1 pound; Ed.*)
> Juice of 1 lemon
> 1 tablespoon powdered sugar
> 1½ tablespoons unsalted sweet butter, well-softened
> 1¼ cups heavy cream
> 18 sugar tablets (3 ounces)
> ½ teaspoon orange-flower water
> 1 pound (about 2 pints) strawberries
> 18 litchis (*if necessary, preserved litchis can be substituted; Ed.*)
> 2 ripe kiwis
> 1 fresh ripe pineapple

At a certain time of the year, one does not find in France, nor in Europe in general, the makings of a basket of fruit—other than the always available oranges, tangerines, pears, apples, and so on.

And it is at exactly this moment that in our markets, as if picked the evening before, one finds the most unusual collection of exotic fruits with the colors and exciting fragrances of far-off islands. Therefore, I devised this simple and original recipe to make use of all of them.

PREPARATION OF THE BANANA MOUSSE:

Press the bananas through a food mill, using the fine grate. Then stir in the lemon juice and powdered sugar.

Beat the butter until smooth and combine it with the banana purée, adding the purée to the butter a little at a time. Keep the mixture at room temperature—in a warm spot, if necessary—so that the butter remains soft.

Pour the heavy cream into a chilled metal bowl set inside a larger bowl containing ice cubes and a little water.

Beat the cream with a wire whisk until voluminous and slightly firm. Then incorporate the banana purée. As soon as this is accomplished, stop the beating, or you will risk turning the cream into butter.

Place the banana mousse in the refrigerator to firm.

NOTE: *Later, just before you are ready to assemble the* soupe, *you might transfer the mousse to the freezing compartment of your refrigerator for only a brief period. This will help you to form the mousse into ovals of a more uniform shape. Ed.*

PREPARATION OF THE STRAWBERRY PURÉE:

In a small saucepan, bring ¾ cup of water to a boil with the sugar tablets. Add the orange-flower water and let cool.

Rinse and hull the strawberries, then press them through a food mill, using the fine grate, or purée them in a food processor or blender. When the syrup has cooled, combine it with the strawberry purée. The purée will be the consistency of a sauce—not too thick.

Place the purée in the refrigerator to chill.

ASSEMBLING THE SOUP:

Shell the litchis and peel the kiwis.

Cut the pineapple crosswise into round slices. You need at least 4 slices. Peel each slice and remove the "eyes." Then divide each piece into thirds and cut out the hard center core.

Choose a large round serving platter with some depth and chill it in the refrigerator. Then cover the bottom of the platter with the strawberry purée.

First dipping 2 large tablespoons (or soup spoons) into hot water, form 6 plump ovals of banana mousse, and arrange them in a star-shaped design over the strawberry purée.

Decorate each oval of mousse with 3 litchis (*if the litchis are large, use only 1 or 2; Ed.*).

Then slice the kiwis into rounds and distribute them in a neat pattern over the strawberry purée.

Arrange the fan-shaped slices of pineapple, partially overlapping, around the rim of the platter, tucked slightly underneath each scoop of mousse. Serve the *soupe* ice-cold.

Crème renversée à l'orange
ORANGE CUSTARD
(Color picture 7)

To serve 4:
  ⅞ cup superfine sugar, in all
  2 seedless oranges, preferably navel
  2 cups milk
  ½ vanilla bean
  3 eggs
  3 egg yolks
  2 tablespoons orange liqueur

PREPARATION OF THE CARAMEL:

Place ½ cup of the sugar in a small heavy saucepan with 2 tablespoons of water. Cook over medium to low heat until the sugar syrup takes on a clear brown color. Then, off heat, quickly stir in 3 tablespoons of cold water. (*The syrup will hiss and sizzle! Ed.*) This is to prevent the caramel from hardening and sticking to the bottom of the saucepan.

Pour the syrup into a warmed 2-quart soufflé dish, tilting it so that the caramel completely coats the bottom of the mold.

Cut 1 of the oranges into very thin slices and press them into the caramel. Set aside. (*If necessary, divide the slices so that they line the bottom of the mold completely. Ed.*)

PREPARATION OF THE CUSTARD:

Preheat oven to 350°F.

Pour the milk into a heavy saucepan with 3 tablespoons of the sugar and the ½ vanilla bean. Over low heat, bring the milk to a simmer.

Break 3 whole eggs into a mixing bowl, adding 3 egg yolks, the remaining 3 tablespoons of sugar, and the grated zest of the second orange. Beat these ingredients together with a wire whisk.

When the milk reaches a simmer, remove the vanilla bean, and while beating continuously, pour the hot milk over the egg mixture. When thoroughly combined, strain through a fine sieve into a 2-quart bowl.

Stir in the orange liqueur, then pour the custard mixture into the prepared soufflé mold. Set the mold inside a *bain-marie* (*a larger pan half-filled with hot water; Ed.*). Then carefully place it in the preheated oven.

Bake the custard about 40 minutes, checking occasionally to see that the water in the *bain-marie* does not evaporate too fast. Add more water if necessary.

FINISHING THE CUSTARD:

When the custard is done, let it cool at room temperature in its water bath. Then remove it from the pan and chill in the refrigerator for at least 2 hours.

When ready to serve, unmold the custard, first releasing it by sliding a small knife around the inside edge of the soufflé dish. Then hold a serving plate over the mold and invert the custard onto it.

Compote de fruits d'hiver au vin
COMPOTE OF WINTER FRUITS IN WINE

(Color picture 7)

To serve 4:

    4 pears (Bartlett, Anjou, or Comice), or 8 to 12 small red Seckel
        pears
    16 large California prunes
    24 whole walnuts (48 halves)
    1 large orange, preferably a navel
    1 cinnamon stick
    1 vanilla bean
    2 cloves
    2 small bay leaves
    4 tablespoons sugar
    1 bottle (*3 cups*) Côtes du Rhone, or other robust red wine

PREPARATION:

1. The pears: Peel the pears, leaving them whole with their stems intact. But do cut out the small hard piece at the bottom of the fruit.

2. The prunes: Soak them 10 minutes in a bowl of lukewarm water.

3. The walnuts: Shell the walnuts, opening them carefully with a knife and separating the 2 kernels without breaking them.

4. The orange: Cut the orange crosswise into round slices ¼-inch thick. Discard the two ends.

COOKING:

Arrange the pears, stem end up, in a small nonmetallic casserole just large enough to hold them side by side. Drain the prunes and disperse them, with the walnut halves, around the pears.

Add the cinnamon stick, vanilla bean, cloves, bay leaves, and sugar. Cover with the orange slices and pour the wine over all. If there is not enough wine to cover the fruits, add cold water.

Cover the casserole and cook the fruits over low heat, just barely maintaining a simmer, for about 30 minutes.

TO SERVE:

After cooking the fruit, let it stand in a cool place for about 2 hours. Before serving, remove the cinnamon stick, vanilla bean, cloves, and bay leaves.

Arrange the fruits in a small glass bowl and baste them with the wine-syrup.

Serve chilled, but not ice-cold. This is a dessert that warms the palate.

Figues fraîches rafraîchies aux framboises
FRESH FIGS WITH RASPBERRIES

To serve 4: (*If you wish, you can easily divide this recipe to serve 2. Ed.*)

12 fresh purple figs, ripe but not too soft
8 ounces fresh raspberries
4 tablespoons red currant jelly
6 heaping tablespoons very cold *crème fraîche* (*or substitute 1 cup heavy cream, whipped over ice until thick; Ed.*)
2 tablespoons *eau de vie de framboise* (*a clear raspberry alcohol*)
2 tablespoons powdered sugar
12 crystalized violets (*available at fine gourmet and confectionary shops; Ed.*)

PREPARATION:

1. The figs: Barely stroking the flesh of the fruit, use a small sharp knife to pull back the skin. Cut off the stem, stand each fig upright, and cut a cross at the stem end, splitting the fruit through to the middle. Then, with a slight pressure of your thumb and index finger, open the fruit like a blossom with 4 petals.

Arrange the figs on a plate and keep them cold in the refrigerator.

2. The raspberries: Hull and pick over the berries and drop them into a bowl.

Melt the red currant jelly, without letting it become hot, and gently stir it into the raspberries. Set aside in the refrigerator.

3. The *crème fraîche*: Just before you are ready to serve, combine the *crème fraîche* with the *eau de vie de framboise* and powdered sugar. Mix with a wire whisk until thickened.

TO SERVE:

Spread equal portions of *crème fraîche* over the centers of 4 chilled dessert plates. Then arrange 3 figs on each plate—bursting open like flowers. Place a heaping tablespoon of raspberries glazed with the red currant jelly in the center of each fig, and decorate with a crystalized violet.

Pamplemousse rose grillé au miel
BROILED PINK GRAPEFRUIT WITH HONEY

To serve any number of persons:
  1 pink grapefruit per person
  2 tablespoons solid lavender honey per grapefruit (*see Note, page* 277)

NOTE: Be sure that the honey you choose is very, very thick. If you use clear, flowing honey, it will brown and run off the grapefruit without caramelizing. I choose lavender honey for this recipe, and I prefer pink grapefruit because they are both pungent and more flavorful.

PREPARATION:

So that the grapefruit may stand upright without tipping, cut off a very thin piece of skin from each end, without penetrating the flesh. Then cut each fruit in half crosswise.

Slip a serrated knife between the flesh and the membrane of each section and loosen the segments from the skin with a curved knife.

COOKING:

Preheat the broiler to its maximum temperature.

Spread each half of grapefruit with 1 tablespoon of thick honey, and when the broiling unit is very hot, slide the grapefruit underneath, close to the heating element.

Broil the grapefruit 7 to 8 minutes, or until the surface is lightly caramelized. Serve sizzling hot.

This recipe is also delicious served as a first course.

Cocktail de melon aux groseilles

MELON AND RED CURRANTS IN WINE

To serve 4:

  2 small melons, about 2 pounds each
  14 ounces (*1 pint*) fresh red currants (*If fresh currants are un-
    available, you could substitute fresh blueberries. Ed.*)
  2 tablespoons superfine sugar
  ⅝ cup Sauternes or Barsac, preferably the same dessert wine that
    you will drink with the fruit

PREPARATION:

1. The melons: Cut the melons in half and scrape out the seeds.

Using a melon-ball cutter or a small spoon with sharp edges, carve out the flesh of the melon, forming small uniform pieces. Drop them into a mixing bowl.

Then scrape out the flesh that remains, taking care not to remove any green from the rind, and leaving a smooth sturdy shell. Divide this part of the flesh equally and return it to the 4 melon shells.

2. The currants: Pick over the berries and wash and drain them. If possible, set aside 4 perfect clusters of berries with their leaves.

Pull the remaining berries from their stems and add them to the bowl with the melon balls.

Pour the Sauternes or Barsac over the melon balls and berries. Then mix the fruit gently with sugar, and divide it among the melon halves. Decorate each serving with a cluster of berries.

These simple elements together have a perfect harmony of color and taste.

Oeufs à la neige, aux feuilles de pêcher et aux pralines
SNOW EGGS WITH PRALINES
(Color picture 7)

To serve 6:
>   2 cups milk
>   6 fresh peach leaves (*see Note*)
>   5 eggs, separated
>   10 tablespoons sugar, in all
>   1 vanilla bean
>   Salt
>   1¾ ounces pralines (*about ½ cup crushed; see Note*)

Before you begin to prepare this recipe, there are certain simple rules to follow:

1. Neither the egg whites nor the bowl that you beat them in should be cold.

2. There must be not even the slightest trace of yolk in the egg white.

3. The bowl and the wire whisk must be absolutely clean.

4. Add a pinch of salt to the whites.

5. The ideal beater is a good old-fashioned wire whisk. However, you can use a manual or electric beater satisfactorily—if you start slowly and progressively increase the speed.

The peach leaves give this cream a faint almond perfume, but you can replace them with a vanilla bean split in half lengthwise, or 3 tablespoons of finely ground coffee, such as powdered Turkish coffee. (Let it steep for 10 minutes, covered, in the boiling hot milk.)

NOTE: *Fresh peach leaves are not that difficult to come by when local peaches are in season. There are always a number of leaves in the baskets or bins of peaches at the fruit stands. However, if the peach leaves are not fresh and are not moist and shiny dark green, either increase the number of leaves or substitute 1/4 to 1/2 teaspoon almond extract. Or use one of the other flavorings suggested. Ed.*

PREPARATION OF THE CUSTARD SAUCE:

Pour the milk into a 1-quart casserole, add the peach leaves, and bring to a simmer. Just as the milk is about to boil over, remove the casserole from heat, cover, and let steep 5 minutes.

Meanwhile, separate the egg yolks from the whites. Set the whites aside, but not in the refrigerator.

Using a wire whisk, beat 8 tablespoons of the sugar into the egg yolks, a tablespoon at a time. Continue to beat until they become a very pale yellow. Then strain the hot milk through a sieve into the yolks, and mix to blend.

Pour the custard mixture into a heavy casserole or saucepan, and over low heat, stir continuously with a wooden spoon until thickened. You can test the sauce, to see if it has reached the desired thickness, by pressing a finger against the back of the cream-coated spoon. If your imprint remains, the custard is cooked.

Be careful! The custard must never reach a boil. If it does, it will curdle. If this seems imminent, beat the custard rapidly, off heat, or else cool it by pouring it into a bottle and shaking it vigorously.

Pour the custard sauce into an ice-cold bowl and whisk it until well chilled.

PREPARATION OF THE WHITES:

Pour 2 quarts of water into a large casserole 12 inches in diameter. Add the vanilla bean and a pinch of salt. Bring the water to a boil, then reduce heat to below a simmer.

Meanwhile, beat the egg whites with a pinch of salt until almost stiff. When they increase in volume and begin to hold their shape, slowly add the remaining 2 tablespoons of sugar. Then continue to beat until the whites are firm and glossy.

With the help of a large spoon, form the whites into egg-shaped ovals and drop these into the simmering water. Cook the egg whites 7 to 8 minutes, turning them several times. Then remove the "eggs" with a skimmer and lay them on a towel to dry.

TO SERVE:

Pour the cold custard into a large wide-rimmed glass bowl. Arrange the "eggs" on top and place the bowl in the refrigerator until ready to serve.

Using a rolling pin or bottle, crush the pralines coarsely in a towel. Just at the moment of serving, sprinkle the pralines over all.

This dessert can be prepared 3 or 4 hours in advance. However, do not add the pralines until the last moment. Be sure to keep the dessert cold.

NOTE: *If pralines are not available, they are very simple to prepare: Roast 1 cup blanched almonds in a 350°F oven until lightly browned. Dissolve ½ cup sugar in 3 tablespoons water in a heavy saucepan and cook, swirling the pan, until caramelized.*

Stir in the almonds, then quickly spread the praline out on an oiled baking sheet to harden. After 30 minutes, crack the praline into manageable pieces. Ed.

Mousse au chocolat amer

BITTER CHOCOLATE MOUSSE

To serve 4 or 6:

4½ ounces unsweetened chocolate
1 tablespoon unsweetened powdered cocoa
3 tablespoons strong hot coffee, preferably espresso
½ lemon
8 egg whites, at room temperature
A pinch of salt
4 tablespoons superfine sugar

PREPARATION:

Place the unsweetened chocolate, cocoa, and hot coffee together in the top of a double boiler (*bain-marie*). Melt the chocolate over low heat, blending it with the other ingredients as it dissolves. When the mixture becomes a homogenous paste, remove the chocolate from heat, separating the double boiler, and set aside.

Wipe the interior of a large mixing bowl with ½ lemon. Rinse with cold water and dry thoroughly. Break the egg whites into the bowl, making sure there is not a trace of yolk, and begin to beat them with a wire whisk, slowly at first, then increasing the speed as they begin to come together.

Add a pinch of salt, and as the whites begin to hold their shape, add the sugar a little at a time, beating continuously until the whites are stiff and glossy.

Using the whisk, mix one quarter of the egg whites with the chocolate. When thoroughly incorporated, carefully fold in the rest of the whites, not using the whisk, but with a rubber or wooden spatula. Fold from top to bottom, so that the whites do not collapse.

Scrape the mixture into a 1½-quart glass dessert compote, and refrigerate 1 hour or longer.

This mousse, which is very light and only faintly sweetened, must be served the same day that it is prepared. (*The next day, the whites will begin to deflate and the mousse will sink, becoming watery. Ed.*)

Sauce au chocolat amer
BITTER CHOCOLATE SAUCE

This sauce is to accompany vanilla or coffee ice cream; Frozen Coffee Mousse (*Mousseux glacé au café*, page 266); meringues with ice cream; poached pears with vanilla ice cream; and so on.

To serve 6:

3½ ounces unsweetened baking chocolate
⅞ cup milk
2 tablespoons heavy cream
1 teaspoon sugar
1½ tablespoons butter

PREPARATION:

Melt the chocolate in a double boiler (*bain-marie*) over very low heat.

Pour the milk into a heavy saucepan, add the cream and sugar, and bring to a simmer. When the sugar is dissolved, slowly pour the milk into the melted chocolate, and using a wooden spoon, stir together over low heat. (*At first, the chocolate will become thick and lumpy, then it will gradually incorporate itself into the milk. Ed.*)

When the sauce is smooth and well-blended, remove it from heat, stir in the butter, and let cool slightly, stirring from time to time.

NOTE: *If this sauce is allowed to cool completely, it will become hard. However, if you wish to return it to a smooth flowing consistency, it can be gently reheated. Ed.*

Meringues
MERINGUES

Meringues may be used in a number of ways: served *au naturel*, by themselves; in portions of two pieces held together with whipped cream or ice cream; with Bitter Chocolate Sauce, page 264; Bitter Chocolate Mousse, page 263; Frozen Coffee Mousse, page 266; etc.

To make 5 snail meringues, 6 inches in diameter; or 10 individual shells:

Melted butter (about 1½ tablespoons)
Flour
½ lemon
5 egg whites, at room temperature
A pinch of salt
1¾ cups superfine sugar

PREPARATION:

Preheat oven to 200°F.

Using a brush, paint two baking sheets with melted butter, or if you prefer, line them with parchment paper. Dust the pans lightly with flour, tilting them to make sure that the entire surface is covered. Then turn the pans upside down and tap them lightly to shake off any excess.

Using any small pointed implement, trace in the flour the size and placement of the meringues to use as a guide when you form them.

Wipe the interior of a large mixing bowl with ½ lemon. The juice will remove any traces of grease which would prevent the egg whites from mounting properly. Then rinse the bowl with cold water and dry thoroughly.

Break the egg whites into the bowl, making sure that there is not a trace of yolk.

Beginning slowly, but increasing your speed, beat the egg whites from top to bottom with a wire whisk. (*You can also use an electric mixer. Ed.*) As you put air into the whites (after about 4 or 5 minutes), they will begin to hold together. At this time, add salt and, while continuing to beat, half of the sugar.

When the whites have become stiff, add the remaining sugar in a slow steady stream, without interrupting the rhythm of beating. The whites should be very stiff so that they will hold their shape.

When you have finished beating, spoon the meringue into a pastry bag, and using a large tube opening, pipe it into the shape you wish to make.

Place the meringues in the low oven and bake them 2½ hours. They must not take on any color. If you notice this happening, you could take the precaution of covering them with aluminum foil. (*It is unlikely that they will color, unless your oven temperature is incorrect. Ed.*)

Take the finished meringues from the oven, but let them cool before removing them from the baking sheet. Keep them in an airtight container in a warm dry place. They should remain fresh and crisp for several days.

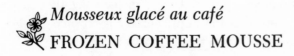

Mousseux glacé au café
FROZEN COFFEE MOUSSE

To serve 6:
    3 tablespoons powdered instant coffee, preferably espresso
    3 cups cold heavy cream
    4 tablespoons superfine sugar
    2 small meringues, prepared to the size of your mold (page 265)
    Additional meringue shells
    Bitter Chocolate Sauce (*sauce chocolat amer*, page 264)

PREPARATION OF THE COFFEE MOUSSE:

As you would prepare cocoa, dissolve the powdered coffee in a little of the cream, stirring briskly with a wire whisk. Then pour in the rest of the cream and begin beating it.

NOTE: *The cream must be very cold, but it also helps to beat the cream in a chilled metal bowl embedded in a larger bowl of ice or ice water. After adding the first cup of cream, let the cream thicken slightly before each further addition, adding approximately ½ cup at a time. Ed.*

When the cream is thick and voluminous, slowly incorporate the sugar in a fine steady stream. Continue beating until the cream is very firm, but be careful not to let it turn into butter. Set aside in the refrigerator.

NOTE: *Do not refrigerate the cream for any long period. Set it aside only for the length of time necessary to trim and arrange your meringues. Ed.*

ASSEMBLING THE MOUSSE:

Take two uniform snail meringues, and if necessary, trim them so that they will fit the diameter of your mold. Save the trimmings.

NOTE: *A suitable receptacle for this dessert would be a 2½-quart soufflé dish or charlotte mold.*
While the coils of the meringue cannot be separated without crumbling, they can be trimmed quite easily with a knife. Using a shaving motion, follow the curve of the meringue. Ed.

Crumble the trimmings, along with 2 or 3 cups of additional crumbled meringue, into the coffee mousse. Fold in with a wooden or rubber spatula until well mixed.

Place one of the meringues, inverted with the best side down, on the bottom of your mold. Then fill the mold with the coffee mousse and cover with the second circle of meringue.

Place the mousse in the freezer for at least 4 hours, or preferably overnight.

TO SERVE:

When ready to serve, dip the mold into a basin of hot water, then invert the frozen mousse onto a serving plate. Cover with Bitter Chocolate Sauce.

NOTE: *Because the meringue prevents the cream from freezing against the bottom of the mold, I found the frozen mousse easy to remove. First run a long thin table knife or flexible metal spatula around the inside wall of the mold; then, when it is inverted, the mousse should slide right out. Ed.*

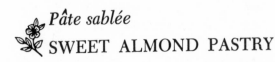

Pâte sablée
SWEET ALMOND PASTRY

In some respects, this dough is easier to work with when it is not freshly made. It keeps very well divided into smaller portions and wrapped in sheets of plastic. It can remain in the refrigerator for 1 week, to be taken out 20 minutes before you use it. Or you can keep it in the freezer and take it out 1 hour in advance.

You will find this pastry used in the following tarts: lemon custard, page 269; strawberry or raspberry, page 271; red currant, page 272; cherry custard, page 273; prune custard with Armagnac, page 274; West Indian coconut custard, page 275; and walnut and honey, page 277.

Quite obviously, this pastry can be used for all fruit tarts.

To make 2½ pounds pastry dough (enough for 12 small individual tartlets, or four 10- to 11-inch pastry shells):

4 ounces (*¾ cup*) almonds
3½ cups flour
Grated zest of 1 lemon
⅔ cup superfine sugar
⅛ teaspoon salt
¾ pound (*3 sticks*) softened butter
1 egg
2 egg yolks
3 tablespoons white rum

PREPARATION OF THE ALMONDS:

Blanch the almonds by dropping them into a quart of boiling water. Let stand 30 seconds, then drain in a sieve. While the almonds are hot, pinch off the brown skins. Then spread out the almonds on a baking sheet and place them in a low oven for 10 to 15 minutes to dry.

Grind the almonds into a powder, using a food processor or blender.

PREPARATION OF THE DOUGH:

Mix the almond powder with the flour, lemon zest, sugar, and salt. Then make a well in the center and add the butter (cut into large pieces), the whole egg, egg yolks, and rum.

Knead these ingredients together until they are all completely incorporated, but do not work the dough beyond this extent.

If you have the good fortune to have an electric mixer with a dough hook, you can use it to knead the pastry. Proceed in the same order as directed, using the slow speed. Stop as soon as the dough is blended.

Gather the dough into a ball, then divide it into 4 smaller balls. They should weigh approximately 10 to 11 ounces each. Wrap them in sheets of plastic and store in the refrigerator or freezer.

Croûte au citron
LEMON CUSTARD TART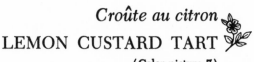
(Color picture 7)

To serve 6:

¼ recipe (about 10 ounces) Sweet Almond Pastry (*pâte sablée*, page 268)
Flour
3 tablespoons softened butter
⅓ cup superfine sugar
2 eggs
1 or 2 lemons, depending on their juiciness

PREPARATION OF THE PASTRY:

Preheat oven to 425°F.

Sprinkle your work surface lightly with flour. Then, using a rolling pin, expand the dough into a circle about 12 to 14 inches in diameter. Lay the piece of dough evenly over a round 10-inch tart mold, pressing the pastry lightly against the sides. Then run the rolling pin across the top of the mold, cutting off any excess. The bottom and sides of the pastry shell should be of the same thickness, without a border.

Prick the surface all over with the tines of a fork and refrigerate the pastry at least 15 minutes before baking.

Bake the pastry shell 12 to 15 minutes, or until lightly browned. Then let cool.

PREPARATION OF THE LEMON CUSTARD:

While the pastry shell is cooling, blend the softened butter with the sugar in a small heavy casserole or saucepan. When well-combined, mix in the 2 whole eggs.

Grate the zest of 1 lemon and add it to the mixture, followed by the juice of the lemon (*or lemons; there should be ¼ cup lemon juice; Ed.*).

Place the casserole over low heat, and using a wire whisk, stir without stopping until the first sign of a simmer. (*At this point the custard will begin to thicken rapidly. Ed.*) At that moment, take the casserole from heat and rest the bottom of it in a bowl of cold water. Stop the cooking by beating the custard continuously until slightly cooled.

Using a pastry spatula, spread the lemon cream over the bottom of the tart shell. Let the custard cool completely (*1 hour or longer*) before serving.

Croûte aux fraises de jardin, fraises des bois ou framboises
STRAWBERRY, WILD STRAWBERRY OR RASPBERRY TART

To serve 6:

¼ recipe (about 10 ounces) Sweet Almond Pastry (*pâte sablée,* page 268)

Flour

1¼ pounds (*about 2 pints*) strawberries, wild strawberries, or raspberries

4 tablespoons red currant jelly

PREPARATION OF THE PASTRY:

Preheat oven to 425°F.

Sprinkle your work surface lightly with flour. Then prepare and bake a pastry shell following the instructions on page 270.

PREPARATION OF THE BERRIES:

Hull the fruits, handling them gently and as little as possible—especially wild strawberries or raspberries. If you are using cultivated strawberries, rinse them with cold water and drain.

Over low heat, melt the red currant jelly without letting it come to a boil.

Using a brush, paint a thin glaze of the jelly over the bottom of the cooled pastry shell. Distribute the berries, stem end down, evenly over all. If you are using large strawberries, slice them in half vertically and lay them cut side down.

Brush the remaining jelly over the fruits and let stand 10 minutes before serving.

Croûte aux groseilles fraîches
RED CURRANT TART

To serve 6:

¼ recipe (about 10 ounces) Sweet Almond Pastry (*pâte sablée,* page 268)
Flour
1¼ pounds (about 1½ pints) red currants (*see Note*)
4 tablespoons red currant jelly

NOTE: *If fresh red currants are not available, fresh blueberries can be substituted. Ed.*

PREPARATION OF THE PASTRY:

Preheat oven to 425°F.

Sprinkle your work surface lightly with flour. Then prepare and bake a pastry shell following the instructions on page 270.

PREPARATION OF THE RED CURRANT FILLING:

Pick over the berries, pull them from their stems, and drop them into a bowl.

Over low heat, melt the red currant jelly without letting it come to a boil. Then mix it with the berries, taking care not to crush them. Fill the cooled pastry shell with the fruit.

Let stand 15 to 20 minutes before serving.

Clafoutis aux cerises noires 🌸
CHERRY CUSTARD TART 🌿

To serve 6:

¼ recipe (about 10 ounces) Sweet Almond Pastry (*pâte sablée*, page 268)

Flour

1¼ pounds fresh cherries, pitted (black, Bing, Queen Anne, or morello)

2 eggs

3 tablespoons finely ground blanched almonds

3 tablespoons vanilla sugar (*see Note*)

1 tablespoon Kirsch

4 tablespoons heavy cream

1½ tablespoons butter, melted

NOTE: To make vanilla sugar: In a large jar with an airtight lid, bury 4 fresh vanilla beans in 2 pounds of superfine sugar. Seal the jar tightly and do not use for at least 1 week.

PREPARATION OF THE PASTRY:

Sprinkle your work surface lightly with flour. Then, using a rolling pin, expand the dough into a circle about 12 to 14 inches in diameter. Lay the piece of dough evenly over a round 10-inch springform tart mold, pressing the pastry lightly against the sides. Then run the rolling pin across the top of the mold, cutting off any excess. The bottom and sides of the pastry shell should be of the same thickness, without a border.

Prick the surface all over with the tines of a fork and refrigerate the pastry thoroughly before baking.

PREPARATION OF THE FILLING:

Preheat oven to 425°F.

1. The cherries: Using a cherry pitter, stone the cherries. Then arrange them in one layer over the bottom of the tart shell. (*The cherries should fill the pastry completely; use more if necessary. Keep*

*the shell under refrigeration until the last moment before baking.
Ed.)*

2. The custard: Beat the eggs, then add the ground almonds,
vanilla sugar, Kirsch, and heavy cream. Melt the butter gently in a
small saucepan and pour it into the egg mixture. Mix thoroughly until
the ingredients are well blended.

FINISHING THE TART:

When the oven is hot, take the pastry shell from the refrigerator and
pour the custard mixture over the cherries.

Bake the tart about 25 minutes. Then, after giving it a few minutes
to settle, remove the tart form and slide the *clafoutis* onto a round
serving platter.

Serve as soon as possible, while the *clafoutis* is still slightly warm.

La tourte de pruneaux à l'Armagnac
PRUNE CUSTARD TART WITH ARMAGNAC

To serve 4:

¼ recipe (about 10 ounces) Sweet Almond Pastry (*pâte sablée*,
    page 268)
Flour
½ pound pitted prunes, from California or the French town of
    Agen
3 tablespoons finely ground blanched almonds
4 tablespoons vanilla sugar (page 273)
2 eggs
5 tablespoons heavy cream
2 tablespoons orange-flower water
2. tablespoons melted butter
4 tablespoons Armagnac

PREPARATION OF THE PASTRY:

Sprinkle your work surface lightly with flour. Then prepare a pastry shell following the instructions on page 270, and refrigerate the pastry thoroughly before baking.

PREPARATION OF THE FILLING:

Preheat oven to 425°F.

1. The prunes: If necessary, remove the pits from the prunes; then soak them 15 minutes in a bowl of lukewarm water.

2. The custard: While the prunes are soaking, put the ground almonds into a 2-quart mixing bowl with the vanilla sugar, eggs, cream, and orange-flower water. Using a wire whisk, beat the ingredients together until thoroughly incorporated. Over very low heat, melt the butter in a small saucepan, then stir it into the custard mixture.

FINISHING THE TART:

After the prunes have soaked 15 minutes, drain, and dry them with a towel.

When the oven is hot, take the pastry shell from the refrigerator and distribute the prunes evenly over the bottom. Then pour the custard over them and bake the tart 25 minutes.

As soon as the tart has finished baking, remove it from the oven, and while very hot, saturate the surface with the Armagnac.

Serve lukewarm.

Tourment d'amour
WEST INDIAN COCONUT CUSTARD TART

To serve 6:

¼ recipe (about 10 ounces) Sweet Almond Pastry (*pâte sablée*, page 268)
Flour
1 cup freshly grated coconut, loosely packed
6 tablespoons vanilla sugar (page 273)

¼ teaspoon powdered cinnamon
3 eggs
½ cup heavy cream
6 tablespoons dark rum or *rhum vieux* (*an aged rum, such as Myers's Jamaican rum; Ed.*)

There are two kinds of rum: agricultural, which is the pure product of distilling the fresh juice of sugar cane; and industrial, which comes from the distillation of molasses and in which only the sugar residue is drawn from the cane juices.

In both kinds, there is a white rum (resulting directly from the distillation) and also a brown rum. In the industrial quality, the brown color is more often (or always?) obtained by the addition of burnt sugar or caramel.

But old brown agricultural rum deserves its name—*rhum vieux*. It is, in effect, aged in oak casks originally made in the Limousin, as are the casks that hold cognac and Armagnac. It is the wood, and its tannin, from which the old rum takes its amber color. In reality, with the effects of the climate and temperature of the environment, the rum is rarely able to stay in the casks more than 3 or 4 years, because the beautiful amber color then rapidly turns to a brownish gray. But nevertheless, there are some remarkable exceptions, and certain old rums can rival excellent Armagnac. It is true, however, that to judge the quality of alcohols is a delicate matter that requires experience.

PREPARATION OF THE PASTRY:

Sprinkle your work surface lightly with flour. Then prepare a pastry shell following the instructions on page 270, and refrigerate the pastry thoroughly before baking.

PREPARATION OF THE CUSTARD:

Preheat oven to 425°F.

Stir the coconut, vanilla sugar, and cinnamon together in a 2-quart mixing bowl. Add the eggs, one at a time, mixing well after each addition. Then add the cream and 2 tablespoons of the rum.

FINISHING THE PASTRY:

When the oven is hot, take the tart shell from the refrigerator, and after a final stir, pour the custard into the pastry. Immediately place the tart in the oven and bake 25 minutes.

When the tart is finished, take it from the oven, and while it is still very hot, sprinkle the custard with the remaining 4 tablespoons of rum. (*At first the rum will float on the surface; then it will be quickly absorbed. Ed.*)

If possible, serve the tart while it is still warm.

Croûte aux noix et au miel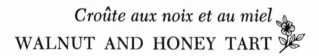
WALNUT AND HONEY TART

To serve 6:

¼ recipe (about 10 ounces) Sweet Almond Pastry (*pâte sablée,* page 268)
Flour
7 ounces (*2 cups*) freshly shelled walnuts
12 sugar tablets (*2 ounces*)
5 tablespoons solid lavender honey (*see Note*)
3 tablespoons *crème fraîche* (*or substitute heavy cream; Ed.*)

NOTE: *Imported solid lavender honey* (miel solide de lavende), *though hard to find, is available in the United States. However, if you cannot find it, substitute another fragrant honey that you happen to like. But be sure that the honey is thick and opaque, not the thin clear variety one is more accustomed to. "Honey spreads," solid in appearance, produced by regional beekeepers, have an ideal consistency. Ed.*

PREPARATION OF THE PASTRY:

Preheat oven to 425°F.

Sprinkle your work surface lightly with flour. Then prepare and bake a pastry shell following the instructions on page 270.

PREPARATION OF THE WALNUT FILLING:

Chop the walnuts coarsely, so that each half is broken into no more than 4 pieces.

Put the sugar tablets into a heavy saucepan with 2 tablespoons of cold water. Cook the sugar over medium heat until it becomes caramel-colored. Then, using a wooden spoon, quickly stir in the walnuts, coating them with the syrup. Off heat, before the mixture has a chance to harden, stir in the honey, followed by the cream. Continue stirring until the mixture is well blended and has cooled slightly.

Then, using a metal pastry spatula, spread it over the tart shell. Let the tart stand 1 hour or longer before serving.

Index

Agneau
carré d', rôti au poivre vert, 150–152
estouffade de gigot d', avec les tartines
d'aïl, 153–155
aux haricots et aux pieds d'agneau, blanquette d', 156–158
*Aiguillettes de foie de veau aux radis et aux
navets*, 148–150
Almond
pastry, sweet, 268–269
soup, 22
Anchovy(ies)
condiment with olives, capers and, 50–51
sauce, 85
for crudités, 49–50
scrambled eggs with, 68–69
Anchoyade, l', 49–50
Anise-flavored ice cream, 248–249
Antillaise crème (soup), 23–24
Appetizers, *see* First courses
Apricot ice, 240
Armagnac, prune custard tart with, 274–
275
Artichoke(s)
barigoule, 206–207
bottoms, with ham and spinach, 191–192
choosing, 186
soup, cold, 13–14
Asparagus, choosing, 189
Aspic
terrine of beef and vegetables in, 52–55
terrine of rabbit in, 57–60
vegetables in, with sweet pepper sauce,
213–218
Aubergines, les, 186
farcies, 193–194
Avocado, tomato and mushroom salad, 47–
48

Barbe de capucin, 30
Basil
butter, spiny lobster grilled with, 101–
102
marinated raw salmon with oil and, 120–
122
noodles with cream and, 229–230
noodles with parsley and, 230–231
omelette with tomato and, 66–67
rabbit with cream and, 158–160
Bass, striped, wrapped in green lettuce
leaves, 115–117
Batavia, 30, 32
Bay leaves, baked fish with citrus sauce
and, 112–114
Beans, dried, lamb and lamb's feet with,
156–158
Beef
filet of, with raisin and pepper sauce,
139–141
rib of, with shallot and vinegar sauce,
137–139
and vegetables in aspic, terrine of,
52–55
wine sauce for, 83
Belons au champagne, gratin de, 89–91
Beurre blanc, 80–81
petite nage de queues d'écrevisses au,
86–89
Beurre fondu, 79
Bocuse, Paul, 129
Bourride agathoise, petite, 130–134
Boursette, 31
Brillat-Savarin, Anthèlme, 30
Broccoli, choosing, 188–189
Brochet de mon ami Paul, le, 128–129
Butter
basil, spiny lobster grilled with, 101–102

Index

Butter (*cont.*)
  sauce, 79
    crayfish tails with, 86–89
    foamy white, 80–81
  -wine sauce, salmon and shellfish in, 122–125

Cabbage
  choosing, 187
  green leaves stuffed with ham and vegetables, 196–197
Calf's liver, with radishes and turnips, 148–150
Canard
  en civet au vieux vin et aux fruits, 174–177
  comme au Moulin, 170–173
Cantaloupe ice, 245
Capers, condiment with olives, anchovies and, 50–51
Carrots, choosing, 186–187
Casserole
  fish and spiny lobster, 130–134
  zucchini and tomato, 210–211
Cauliflower, choosing, 187
Celery root, choosing, 188
Champagne sauce
  oysters with, 89–91
  shellfish in, 91–92
Champignons
  blancs farcis, 195–196
  courgettes farcies, 198–199
  pommes de terre farcies, 202–203
  salade Mikado, 47–48
Cheese(s), 232–238
  baked potatoes with herbs and, 226–227
  goat, marinated with dried herbs, 232–233
  layered omelette with tomato, spinach and, 63–65
  melted, on toast with thyme, 237–238
  Roquefort
    sauce for salads, 36–37
    with walnuts on hot toast, 236–237
  white
    with fresh summer fruits, 233–235
    with herbs, 235–236
  white onions stuffed with cream and, 200–201
Cherry custard tart, 273–274
Chervil, cucumber salad with cream and, 41–42
Chicken, 161–170
  baked in a salt crust, 169–170
  grilled lemon, 166–167
  in red wine and vinegar sauce, 164–166
  stewed, with green herb sauce, 161–163
Chicken liver pâté, 55–56
Chicorée frisée, 31, 32, 33
Chicory, 31, 32, 33
Chicou, le, 32
Chiffonnade, 106, 162

Chocolate, bitter
  mousse, 263
  sauce, 264
Citrus sauce, baked fish with bay leaves and, 112–114
Clafoutis aux cerises noires, 273–274
Coconut
  spinach soup with, 23–24
  West Indian custard tart, 275–277
Coffee mousse, frozen, 266–268
Compote of winter fruits in wine, 256–257
Condiment, olive, anchovy and caper, 50–51
Cornette, 31, 32
Côte de boeuf aux échalotes et au vinaigre, 137–139
Crab meat and grapefruit salad, 45–46
Crayfish tails with butter sauce, 86–89
Cresson, 31
Croûte
  au citron, 269–270
  aux fraises de jardin, fraises des bois ou framboises, 271
  aux groseilles fraîches, 272
  aux noix et au miel, 277–278
Croutons, fish soup with, 26–28
Crudités, anchovy sauce for, 49–50
Cucumber salad with chervil and cream, 41–42
Curry, fresh pea soup with, 15–16
Custard(s)
  orange, 254–255
  potato and leek, individual, 221–223
  spinach, individual, 219–220
  tart
    cherry, 273–274
    lemon, 269–270
    prune with Armagnac, 274–275
    West Indian coconut, 275–277

Dandelions, 32
Darioles
  d'épinards, 219–220
  de pommes aux poireaux, 221–223
Daurade royale rôtie au laurier avec sa fondue d'orange et de citron à l'huile d'olive, 112–114
Desserts, 239–278
  almond pastry, sweet, 268–269
  anise-flavored ice cream, 248–249
  bitter chocolate sauce, 264
  compote of winter fruits in wine, 256–257
  figs (fresh) with raspberries, 257–258
  fruit ices, 239–247
    apricot, 240
    cantaloupe, 245
    lemon, 242
    orange, 246
    pear, 247
    pineapple, 241
    raspberry, 244

strawberry, 243
melon and red currants in wine, 259–260
meringues, 265–266
mousse
  bitter chocolate, 263
  frozen coffee, 266–268
orange custard, 254–255
orange segments, broiled, with sabayon sauce, 250–252
pink grapefruit broiled with honey, 258–259
prunes with butter-cream, 249–250
snow eggs with pralines, 260–262
strawberry soup with exotic fruits, 252–254
tarts
  cherry custard, 273–274
  lemon custard, 269–270
  prune custard with Armagnac, 274–275
  raspberry, 271
  red currant, 272
  strawberry, 271
  walnut and honey, 277–278
  West Indian coconut custard, 275–277
  wild strawberry, 271
Doucette, 31
Duck
  in red wine with winter fruits, 174–177
  roast Moulin-de-Mougins, 170–173

Écrevisses au beurre blanc, petite nage de queues d', 86–89
Eggplants
  choosing, 186
  small stuffed, 193–194
Eggs, 61–71
  fried
    Niçoise, 209
    with wine vinegar, 70–71
  omelettes
    layered, with tomato, cheese and spinach, 63–65
    Swiss chard and onion, 61–63
    tomato and fresh basil, 66–67
    zucchini, 67–68
  scrambled, with anchovies, 68–69
  snow eggs with pralines, 260–262
Endive, 31
  compote d', à la crème, 180–181
Endives stewed in cream, 180–181
Escarole, 32
Estouffade de gigot d'agneau avec les tartines d'ail, 153–155

Fennel sauce, 78–79
Field salad, 31
Figs, fresh, with raspberries, 257–258
Figues fraîches rafraîchies aux framboises, 257–258
Filberts, *see* Hazelnuts

Filet de boeuf aux raisins à la mathurini, 139–141
Filets mignons de veau au citron, les, 141–143
First courses, 38–60
  anchovy sauce for crudités, 49–50
  chicken liver pâté, 55–56
  olive, anchovy and caper condiment, 50–51
  salads
    cucumber with chervil and cream, 41–42
    grapefruit and crab meat, 45–46
    rabbit with wild lettuce, warm, 38–41
    string bean with hazelnuts and cream, 42–44
    tomato, avocado and mushroom, 47–48
  terrines
    of beef and vegetables in aspic, 52–55
    of rabbit in aspic, 57–60
Fish, 105–134
  baked fish with bay leaves and citrus sauce, 112–114
  baked with potatoes, onions and tomatoes, 110–112
  cooked in cream with vegetables, 107–110
  soup
    with croutons, 26–28
    of the Midi, 24–26
    and spiny lobster casserole, 130–134
  See also names of fish
Flageolets, 156
Fricassée du jardin de mon père, la, 211–213
Fromages, les, 232–238
  assiette de fromage blanc aux fruits frais du jardin, 233–235
  fromage blanc aux herbes, 235–236
  oignons blancs farcis, 200–201
  omelette arlequin, 63–65
  picodons marinés à l'huile d'herbes sèches, 232–233
  pommes cendrillon, 226–227
  sauce au roquefort, 36–37
  tartines
    de rigottes de Condrieu au thym, 237–238
    de roquefort aux noix, 236–237
Fruits
  exotic, strawberry soup with, 252–254
  fresh summer, white cheese with, 233–235
  ices, 239–247
    apricot, 240
    cantaloupe, 245
    lemon, 242
    orange, 246
    pear, 247
    pineapple, 241
    raspberry, 244
    strawberry, 243

Index

Fruits (*cont.*)
 winter
  compote of, in wine, 256–257
  duck in red wine with, 174–177
 See also names of fruits

Galette de pommes de terre, 223–224
Game birds, 178–185
 preserved thrush with olives, 183–185
 quail in baked potato nests, 181–182
 roast pheasant with red wine sauce,
  178–180
Garlic
 choosing, 187
 and saffron mayonnaise, 28–29
 toasts, 154–155
 vinaigrette sauce with cream and, 35
 and vinegar sauce, pike with, 128–129
Goat cheese marinated with dried herbs,
  232–233
Grapefruit
 and crab meat salad, 45–46
 pink, broiled with honey, 258–259
Green peppercorns, roast rack of lamb with,
  150–152
Green salads, 30–37
 greens for, 30–33
 Roquefort sauce for, 36–37
 vinaigrette sauce for, 33–35
  with garlic and cream, 35
  traditional, 34–35
Grives de vigne confites aux olives, 183–185

Ham
 artichoke bottoms with spinach and,
  191–192
 green cabbage leaves stuffed with
  vegetables and, 196–197
 zucchini stuffed with mushrooms and,
  198–199
Hazelnuts, string bean salad with cream
  and, 42–44
Herbs, 33
 baked potatoes with cheese and, 226–
  227
 dried, goat cheese marinated with,
  232–233
 green sauce, chicken stewed with,
  161–163
 potatoes stuffed with mushrooms and,
  202–203
 tomatoes stuffed with meat and, 204–
  205
 white cheese with, 235–236
Homard
 en civet de vieux Bourgogne, 95–98
 à la crème de Sauternes, fricassée de,
  93–95
Honey
 broiled pink grapefruit with, 258–259
 and walnut tart, 277–278

Ice cream, anise-flavored, 248–249
Ices, fruit, 239–247
 apricot, 240
 cantaloupe, 245
 lemon, 242
 orange, 246
 pear, 247
 pineapple, 241
 raspberry, 244
 strawberry, 243

Jamaican baked pork chops, 135–137

Kaye, Danny, 231
Kidneys, veal
 in mustard sauce, 143–144
 and sweetbread in cream with spinach,
  145–147

Laitue, 31
Lamb
 with beans and lamb's feet, 156–158
 braised in red wine, 153–154
  garlic toasts for, 154–155
 roast rack of, with green peppercorns,
  150–152
Lamb's lettuce, 31, 32, 33
Langouste
 grillée au beurre de basilic, 101–102
 petite bourride agathoise, 130–134
 au poivre rose, 98–100
Lapereau
 à la crème de basilic, cul de, 158–160
 gâteau en gelée du Moulin, 57–60
 salade de râble, aux feuilles de mesclun,
  38–41
Leek(s)
 and potato custards, individual, 221–223
 and sea scallops in cream, 102–104
Légumes, les, 186–231
Lemon
 chicken grilled with, 166–167
 custard tart, 269–270
 filet of veal with, 141–143
 ice, 242
Lettuce, 31
 lamb's, 31, 32, 33
 striped bass wrapped in leaves of,
  115–117
 wild, 31
  warm rabbit salad with, 38–41
Lobster
 with Sauternes and cream, 93–95
 simmered in red wine, 95–98
 spiny
  and fish casserole, 130–134
  grilled with basil butter, 101–102
  with paprika cream sauce, 98–100

Mâche, 31
Mayonnaise, 77–78
 garlic and saffron, 28–29
Melon and red currants in wine, 259–260

Index

Meringues, 265–266
Mesclun, 31–32
   salade de râble de lapereau aux feuilles de, 38–41
Mikado, salade, 47–48
Monk's whiskers, 30
Mousse
   bitter chocolate, 263
   frozen coffee, 266–268
Mousse au chocolat amer, 263
Mousseux glacé au café, 266–268
Mushrooms
   potatoes stuffed with herbs and, 202–203
   salad with tomatoes, avocado and, 47–48
   stuffed, 195–196
   zucchini stuffed with ham and, 198–199
Mussels, sole in saffron cream sauce with, 125–127
Mustard sauce, veal kidneys in, 143–144

Noix de Saint-Jacques aux poireaux, 102–104
Noodles
   with basil and cream, 229–230
   with parsley and basil, 230–231
Nougat de boeuf de ma tante Célestine, 52–55
Nouilles
   fraîches à la crème de pistou, 229–230
   de mon ami Danny Kaye, 230–231

Oeufs, les, 61–71
   brouillés aux filets d'anchois, 68–69
   omelettes
      arlequin, 63–65
      aux rouelles de courgettes, 67–68
      à la tomate fraîche et aux feuilles de basilic, 66–67
      trucca cannoise ou Trouchia, 61–63
   au plat avec la giclée de vinaigre de vin, 70–71
   au plat niçois, 209
Oeufs à la neige, aux feuilles de pêcher et aux pralines, 260–262
Oils for salads, 33
Olives
   condiment with anchovies, capers and, 50–51
   preserved thrush with, 183–185
Omelettes
   layered, with tomato, cheese and spinach, 63–65
   Swiss chard and onion, 61–63
   tomato and fresh basil, 66–67
   zucchini, 67–68
Onion(s)
   choosing, 187
   fish baked with potatoes, tomatoes and, 110–112
   and Swiss chard omelette, 61–63
   white, stuffed with cheese and cream, 200–201

Orange
   custard, 254–255
   ice, 246
   sauce, panfried red mullet with, 117–120
   segments, broiled with sabayon sauce, 250–252
Oysters with champagne sauce, 89–91

Pamplemousse
   au crabe, salade de, 45–46
   rose grillé au miel, 258–259
Paprika cream sauce, spiny lobster with, 98–100
Parfait glacé à la liqueur d'anis, 248–249
Parsley, noodles with basil and, 230–231
Pastry, sweet almond, 268–269
Pâté, chicken liver, 55–56
Pâté fin de foies de volaille, 55–56
Pâté sablée, 268–269
Pea(s)
   choosing, 188
   soup, with curry, 15–16
Pear ice, 247
Pepper and raisin sauce, filet of beef with, 139–141
Peppercorns, green, roast rack of lamb with, 150–152
Petites cailles en robe des champs, 181–182
Petites entrées, les, 38–60
   l'anchoyade, 49–50
   gâteau de lapereau en gelée du Moulin, 57–60
   nougat de boeuf de ma tante Célestine, 52–55
   pâté fin de foies de volaille, 55–56
   salades
      de concombres à la crème de cerfeuil, 41–42
      de haricots verts à la crème et aux noisettes, 42–44
      Mikado, 47–48
      de pamplemousse au crabe, 45–46
      de râble de lapereau aux feuilles de mesclun, 38–41
   tapenade, 50–51
Petits farcis de Provence, les, 190–205
Petits rougets de mon ami Pierrot, les, 117–120
Pheasant, roast, with red wine sauce, 178–180
Physiology of Taste (Brillat-Savarin), 30
Picodons marinés à l'huile d'herbes sèches, 232–233
Pike with garlic and vinegar sauce, 128–129
Pineapple ice, 241
Pink grapefruit broiled with honey, 258–259
Pissenlit, 32
Pistou
   nouilles fraîches à la crème de, 229–230
   soupe au, 17–20
Pois frais au curry, soupe de, 15–16

Poissons, les, 105–134
  soupe de
    du Moulin, 24–26
    Parisienne, 26–28
Pork chops, Jamaican baked, 135–137
Potato(es)
  baked
    with herbs and cheese, 226–227
    quail in nests of, 181–182
  cake, crisp, 223–224
  choosing, 188
  fish baked with onions, tomatoes and,
    110–112
  and leek custards, individual, 221–223
  mashed, 225–226
  stuffed with mushroom and herbs, 202–
    203
Poule faisane en salmis, 178–180
Poulet, 161–170
  fricassée
    de volaille aux herbes vertes du jardin,
      161–163
    au vinaigre de vin, 164–166
  grillé au citron, 166–167
  sous la croûte au sel, 169–170
Poultry, 161–177
  See also Chicken; Duck
Pralines, snow eggs with, 260–262
Provençal
  tomato relish, 74–76
  vegetable ragout Vergé, 207–209
  vegetable soup, 17–20
Prune(s)
  with butter-cream, 249–250
  custard tart with Armagnac, 274–275

Quail in baked potato nests, 181–182

Rabbit
  in aspic, terrine of, 57–60
  with basil and cream, 158–160
  salad with wild lettuce, warm, 38–41
Radishes, calf's liver with turnips and,
    148–150
Ragout, Provençal vegetable, Vergé, 207–
    209
Raisin and pepper sauce, filet of beef with,
    139–141
Raspberry(ies)
  fresh figs with, 257–258
  ice, 244
  tarts, 271
Ratatouille niçoise à ma façon, la, 207–209
Red currant(s)
  and melon in wine, 259–260
  tarts, 272
Red mullet, panfried, with orange sauce,
    117–120
Red wine
  compote of winter fruits in, 256–257
  duck with winter fruits in, 174–177
  lamb braised in, 153–154
    garlic toasts for, 154–155

lobster simmered in, 95–98
  sauce, roast pheasant with, 178–180
  and vinegar sauce, chicken in, 164–166
Relish, Provençal tomato, 74–76
Rice, saffron, 228–229
Romaine, 32
Roquefort cheese
  sauce for salads, 36–37
  with walnuts on hot toast, 236–237
Rouille, la, 28–29

Sabayon sauce, broiled orange segments
    with, 250–252
Saffron
  cream sauce, sole with mussels in, 125–
    127
  garlic mayonnaise with, 28–29
  rice, 228–229
Saint-Pierre
  blanc de, à la crème de petits légumes,
    107–110
  des pêcheurs du Suquet, 110–112
Salades
  de concombres à la crème de cerfeuil,
    41–42
  de haricots verts à la crème et aux
    noisettes, 42–44
  Mikado, 47–48
  de pamplemousse au crabe, 45–46
  de râble de lapereau aux feuilles de
    mesclun, 38–41
  de tomates, 168
Salades vertes, les, 30–37
  sauce au Roquefort, 36–37
  les vinaigrettes, 33–35
    à la crème d'ail, 35
    traditionnelle, 34–35
Salads
  cucumber with chervil and cream, 41–42
  field, 31
  grapefruit and crab meat, 45–46
  rabbit with wild lettuce, warm, 38–41
  string bean, 189
    with hazelnuts and cream, 42–44
  tomato, 168
    with avocado and mushrooms, 47–48
  See also Green salads
Salmon
  marinated raw with oil and basil, 120–
    122
  and shellfish in wine-butter sauce, 122–
    125
Salt crust, chicken baked in, 168–170
Sauces, 72–85
  anchovy, 85
    for crudités, 49–50
  bitter chocolate, 264
  butter, 79
    crayfish tails with, 86–89
    foamy white, 80–81
  champagne
    oysters with, 89–91
    shellfish in, 91–92

citrus, baked fish with bay leaves and, 112–114
fennel, 78–79
garlic and vinegar, pike with, 128–129
green herb, chicken stewed with, 161–163
mayonnaise, 77–78
  garlic and saffron, 28–29
mustard, veal kidneys in, 143–144
orange, panfried red mullet with, 117–120
paprika cream, spiny lobster with, 98–100
raisin and pepper, filet of beef with, 139–141
red wine, roast pheasant with, 178–180
red wine and vinegar, chicken in, 164–166
Roquefort, 36–37
sabayon, broiled orange segments with, 250–252
saffron cream, sole with mussels in, 125–127
shallot, 84
shallot and vinegar, rib of beef with, 137–139
sorrel, turbot with, 105–107
sweet pepper, vegetables in aspic with, 213–218
tomato
  cold fresh, 73–74
  cooked fresh, 81–82
  Provençal relish, 74–76
vinaigrette, 33–35
  with garlic and cream, 35
  traditional, 34–35
watercress, 76–78
wine, for beef, 83
wine-butter, salmon and shellfish in, 122–125
Sauternes, lobster with cream and, 93–95
Scarole, 32
Sea scallops and leeks in cream, 102–104
Shallot(s)
  choosing, 187
  sauce, 84
  and vinegar sauce, rib of beef with, 137–139
Shellfish, 86–104
  in champagne sauce, 91–92
  and salmon in wine-butter sauce, 122–125
  See also names of shellfish
Snow eggs with pralines, 260–262
Snow peas, choosing, 187
Sole with mussels in saffron cream sauce, 125–127
Sorbets de fruits frais, les, 239–247
  à l'abricot, 240
  à l'ananas, 241
  au citron, 242
  à la fraise, 243
  à la framboise, 244

  au melon, 245
  à l'orange, 246
  à la poire william, 247
Sorrel sauce, turbot with, 105–107
Soupes, les, 13–29
  crème
    antillaise, 23–24
    froide de coeurs d'artichauts, 13–14
    au lait d'amandes, 22
    de tomates fraîches, 20–21
  de fruits des isles aux fleurs, 252–254
  au pistou, 17–20
  de pois frais au curry, 15–16
  de poissons
    du Moulin, 24–26
    Parisienne, 26–28
  la rouille, 28–29
Soups, 13–29
  almond, 22
  artichoke, cold, 13–14
  fish
    with croutons, 26–28
    of the Midi, 24–26
  fresh pea, with curry, 15–16
  garlic and saffron mayonnaise for, 28–29
  Provençal vegetable, 17–20
  spinach and coconut, 23–24
  strawberry, with exotic fruits, 252–254
  tomato, cream of, 20–21
Spinach
  artichoke bottoms with ham and, 191–192
  choosing, 189
  and coconut soup, 23–24
  custards, individual, 219–220
  layered omelette with tomato, cheese and, 63–65
  veal kidney and sweetbread in cream with, 145–147
Spiny lobster
  and fish casserole, 130–134
  grilled with basil butter, 101–102
  with paprika cream sauce, 98–100
Strawberry
  ice, 243
  soup with exotic fruits, 252–254
  tarts, 271
String bean(s)
  choosing, 189
  salad, 189
  with hazelnuts and cream, 42–44
Striped bass wrapped in green lettuce leaves, 115–117
Suprême de loup au vert de laitue, 115–117
Sweet pepper(s)
  choosing, 188
  sauce, vegetables in aspic with, 213–218
Sweetbreads and veal kidney in cream with spinach, 145–147
Swiss chard
  choosing, 186
  and onion omelette, 61–63

Tapenade, 50–51
Tartines
   d'aïl doux, 154–155
   de rigottes de Condrieu au thym, 237–238
   de roquefort aux noix, 236–237
Tarts
   cherry custard, 273–274
   lemon custard, 269–270
   prune custard with Armagnac, 274–275
   raspberry, 271
   red currant, 272
   strawberry, 271
   walnut and honey, 277–278
   West Indian coconut custard, 275–277
   wild strawberry, 271
Terrines
   of beef and vegetables in aspic, 52–55
   of rabbit in aspic, 57–60
Thrush, preserved, with olives, 183–185
Thyme, melted cheese on toast with, 237–238
Toasts
   garlic, 154–155
   melted cheese on, with thyme, 237–238
   Roquefort cheese with walnuts on, 236–237
Tomato(es)
   choosing, 188
   fish baked with potatoes, onions and, 110–112
   and fresh basil omelette, 66–67
   layered omelette with cheese, spinach and, 63–65
   relish Provençal, 74–76
   salad, 168
      with avocado and mushrooms, 47–48
   sauce
      cold fresh, 73–74
      cooked fresh, 81–82
      Provençal relish, 74–76
   soup, cream of, 20–21
   stuffed with meat and herbs, 204–205
   and zucchini casserole, 210–211
Tourment d'amour, 275–277
Trévise, 32, 33
Turbot with sorrel sauce, 105–107
Turnips
   calf's liver with radishes and, 148–150
   choosing, 188

Veal
   calf's liver with radishes and turnips, 148–150
   filet of, with lemon, 141–143
   kidneys
      in mustard sauce, 143–144
      and sweetbread in cream with spinach, 145–147

Vegetable(s), 186–231
   in aspic with sweet pepper sauce, 213–218
   and beef in aspic, terrine of, 52–55
   braised young vegetables with salt pork, 211–213
   choosing, 186–189
   crudités, anchovy sauce for, 49–50
   fish cooked in cream with, 107–110
   green cabbage leaves stuffed with ham and, 196–197
   little stuffed vegetables of Provence, 190–205
   ragout Vergé, Provençal, 207–209
   soup Provençal, 17–20
   See also names of vegetables
Vidal, Raymond, 134
Vinaigrette sauce for salads, 33–35
   with garlic and cream, 35
   traditional, 34–35
Vinegar(s), 33
   and garlic sauce, pike with, 128–129
   and red wine sauce, chicken in, 164–166
   and shallot sauce, rib of beef with, 137–139
   wine, fried eggs with, 70–71

Walnut(s)
   and honey tart, 277–278
   Roquefort cheese on hot toast with, 236–237
Watercress, 31
   sauce, 76–78
West Indian coconut custard tart, 275–277
White cheese
   with fresh summer fruits, 233–235
   with herbs, 235–236
White onions stuffed with cheese and cream, 200–201
Wild lettuce, 31
   warm rabbit salad with, 38–41
Wild strawberry tarts, 271
Wine
   -butter sauce, salmon and shellfish in, 122–125
   compote of winter fruits in, 256–257
   melon and red currants in, 259–260
   sauce, for beef, 83
   See also Red wine
Wine vinegar, fried eggs with, 70–71

Zucchini
   choosing, 187
   omelette, 67–68
   stuffed with ham and mushrooms, 198–199
   and tomato casserole, 210–211